GW00362811

The Truth

The Biggest Cover-Up in History

Robert Barry

ORLA
KELLY
PUBLISHING

ISBN: 978-1-912328-09-3

The Truth

The Biggest Cover-Up in History

Dedicated To Yeshua

Preface

The Grail is the most sought after artefact in human history. For two thousand years we have searched for it. We stole, cheated, and killed for it. We started wars in pursuit of its powers. The hunt for the Grail never diminished over the ages but rather intensified. In spite of the continued quest for the Grail, when it couldn't be found, it passed into legend. However, just because something hasn't been found does not mean it does not exist. Found in the capital city of the last empire on earth, the Grail does exist. The reason why it hasn't been found until now is because we were looking in the wrong direction. The true Grail cannot be moved, it cannot be stolen and thus it cannot be the proprietorship of a single individual. The Grail was created for all who have the courage to use it, but until now, it has remained unmoved and unused for almost two thousand years. I will reveal what the true Grail is, show you where to find it and give you detailed instructions how to use it. I will also endeavour to describe to you what will happen when you do. It's time now.

About the Author

Robert Barry was born and raised in Kilkenny city, in the south-east of Ireland. He has spent over two decades working in both the engineering and legal fields. Whilst working and living in London, Robert found and used the Holy Grail, the most sought after artefact of the last two millennia. For the first time in almost two thousand years Robert's work reveals the truth about the Grail and its creator Yeshua, more commonly known as The Christ. In "The Truth", Robert recounts what is generally known about the life of Jesus Christ and in particular the week leading up to his crucifixion. He unravels the mystery surrounding Jesus's words and actions and the reason for his ultimate sacrifice. "The Truth" now returns to us that which was taken from us – our Freewill!

Contents

Preface   vii

About the Author   viii

Part 1: The Grail   xi

1. The States of the Human Existence   1

2. The Grail – The Legend   16

3. The Messenger and the Grail   43

4. Forgiveness and Repentance Vol. 1   73

5. Forgiveness and Repentance Vol. 2   99

Part 2: The Creation of the Grail   115

6. The Knowledge Based System   117

7. The Trinity: Our Creation and Fall   139

8. Entry into Jerusalem & the Belief Based System   152

9. Judgment   173

10. The Journey to Crucifixion (Vol.1)   198

11. The Journey to Crucifixion (Vol.2)   222

12. The Journey to Crucifixion (Vol.3)   239

Epilogue   260

Contents Cont.

Part 3: The Grail and the Promised Kingdom   263

13. Yeshua & Judas   265

14. The Promised Kingdom   286

15. Miracles   302

16. Summary   307

17. Final Thoughts   316

References   331

PART 1

The Grail

Chapter One

The States of the Human Existence

What is the truth? If you experienced the truth would you recognize it? If you recognized the truth would you be able to convey the truth to someone who has not experienced it? Would you even want to? Here are my thoughts.

Before I begin, let me say that this book is not meant to be in anyway religious or spiritual. I guess at this stage you will just have to take my word for it. This book is also not meant to challenge your beliefs or to replace them. If your beliefs work for you, give you support through your life, then I suggest that you may not want or need to discard them. Why discard something that works? Furthermore, this book is not aimed at challenging any established scientific theories or attempting to explain new ones.

The objective is to try and explain the different states of the human existence, the differences between them and how to go from one to the other. I believe a good starting point would be to explain that there are three different states of the human existence, which could be more aptly referred to as systems in which we reside. The three systems are, a belief based system, a knowledge based system, or the absence of both and to which I will refer as a vacuum or a void. These three systems are mutually exclusive. Furthermore, only two of these systems are

1

permanent states of existence; the belief based system and the knowledge based system. The vacuum, by its very nature, is unstable and will always seek to fill itself and thus it is a temporary state of existence.

The Vacuum

Although it is difficult to talk about any one state of existence in isolation, I will talk initially about the vacuum as there is very little to say about it and it can be dealt with quite readily.

The majority of babies will be born into neither the knowledge based system nor the belief based system and thus will reside temporarily within this vacuum. Only newborn babies can reside within a vacuum for any prolonged period of time. Eventually all babies will more than likely enter the belief based system. Let me explain how this happens. Imagine there is a six-month-old child sitting on the floor. You sit behind it so that you are not in its field of vision. You present it with a ball. The baby takes the ball in its hand. What will the child do with the ball?

It's possible that the child, after licking and biting the ball, may throw the ball. After the ball has come to rest the child may watch it for some time waiting to see what the ball will do. If the ball after coming to rest does nothing further, the child may with outstretched arms reach for the ball indicating that it wants the ball again. If you put the ball back in the child's hands it may throw the ball again. The child may repeat this procedure over and over again. This action by the child may be perplexing for any adult to watch as they don't understand the repetitive nature of the child's actions.

The reason for the repetitive nature of the child's actions is because the child does not know that the ball will do the same thing every time it is thrown. Maybe on the fifth or sixth throw, the ball will behave in a different manner. Until the child throws it for the fifth or sixth time it will not know how the ball will behave. The child stops throwing the ball because after several throws the ball has done the exact same thing every time. The child now believes that if it continues to throw the ball, the ball will do the exact same thing every time. The child of course doesn't know this to be true, how could it, but rather it believes it to be true. The child has now adopted a belief based system which will grow in complexity and strength over its lifetime. For babies, movement from a vacuum to the belief based system happens gently to limit the pain the newborn may suffer.

Many people often wish to return to this state of existence later in life. However, as adults we do not refer to it as a vacuum or void but refer to it instead as a **state of enlightenment**.

The state of enlightenment is the vacuum of which I speak. Today, it has become the new religion and it continues to grow in popularity as conventional mainstream religions fail to answer our questions and to meet our needs. Many seek enlightenment for different reasons. Some believe they will find the answers to their questions, some look for fulfillment and others hope to find peace.

Many like to say that they have achieved enlightenment because it is something to aspire to and it is believed to set you apart from and dare I say above the non-enlightened. The 'enlightened' like to tell you about the spiritual path they traveled and exactly what they did to achieve this illusive state of enlightenment. Many proudly reveal that they underwent hours, days, months, years of meditating, praying, chanting, yoga, vegetarianism, attending darshan and satsang with realized beings (whatever that means), donating money to charities, reading profusely and widely spiritual literature, purifying themselves by drinking a concoction that some Tibetan monk gave them and abstaining from life's temptations such as alcohol, drugs and sex.

The enlightened say things like the path they followed raised their vibrational frequency. However, as nobody really knows what it means to be enlightened, spiritually or otherwise, nobody can challenge the veracity of their claim. Ask the enlightened to describe what it's like and it all becomes a bit fuzzy. Ask them how they achieved enlightenment and you are in for a very long and equally unenlightening story. Seekers of enlightenment often use coined terms and buzz words such as **one truth, ultimate truth, be at one with the universe** and **no-self is true-self** which they believe is some kind of catch-all explanation.

This is how a leading expert in spiritual enlightenment, Jed McKenna[1], who himself is enlightened, tries to teach a student who is seeking enlightenment;

'Enlightenment isn't when you go there, it's when there comes here. It's not a visit to the truth, it's the awakening of truth within you. It's not a fleeting state of consciousness, it's permanent truth-realization; abiding non-dual awareness. It's not a place you visit from here, this is a place you visit from there. For instance, I myself am enlightened, right here, right now. I am free of delusion and unbound by ego, and although I have had the great fortune of experiencing mystical union on several occasions, I am not presently in that state and I have no plans to return to it.'

As this may not be very clear, he does go on to explain it. He entitles his explanation simply *Paradox* and I must admit, it's a beautiful and inspired piece of literature. Here we go;

'You will never achieve spiritual enlightenment. The you that you think of as you is not you. The you that thinks of you as you is not you. There is no you, so who wishes to become enlightened?

Who is not enlightened? Who will become enlightened? Who will be enlightened?

Enlightenment is your destiny – more certain than sunrise. You cannot fail to achieve enlightenment. Were you told otherwise? Irresistible forces compel you. The universe insists. It is not within your power to fail.

There is no path to enlightenment: it lies in all directions at all times. On the journey to enlightenment, you create and destroy your own path with every step.

No one can follow another's path. No one can step off the path. No one can lead another. No one can turn back. No one can stop.

Enlightenment is closer than your skin, more immediate than your next breath, and forever beyond your reach.

It need not be sought because it cannot be found. It cannot be found because it cannot be lost. It cannot be lost because it is not other than that which seeks.

The paradox is that there is no paradox.'

Beautiful right? And makes absolutely no sense! If you wish to be a seeker of enlightenment, I wish you the best of luck. I guess you could be doing worse things with your life. However, I can categorically say, and I feel compelled to say that this book has nothing to do with spirituality, enlightenment or spiritual enlightenment – if there is a difference between the two. This book presents to you the three different states of the human existence and how you can go from one to the other. More particularly this book concentrates on the two permanent states of existence and how you can go from one state of permanent existence to the other using a clearly defined method, which is almost two thousand years old.

Before I leave the topic of enlightenment let me describe it in relation to the different states of the human existence. Then should you wish to continue its pursuit, you will know exactly what you are pursuing, how to pursue it and when you have found it.

Enlightenment or spiritual enlightenment is not the knowledge based system of which I speak. I truly hope that this was clear, but I did feel the need to delineate this fact because the word enlightenment is often used to suggest knowledge. The best way to describe enlightenment is to imagine that the belief based system is a sphere and that you reside on one of its diameters. To the left of the sphere's center is negative belief and to its right is positive belief. Don't confuse negative with bad and positive with good. Let me give you an example. To the right of center, one might believe that ice-cream tastes good, and equidistant to the left of center, one might believe ice-cream does not taste good. All beliefs reside within the belief based system. At the center of the belief sphere is the vacuum. Enlightenment is the state of experiencing this vacuum. You will find that as you try to approach the vacuum with intent, you may overshoot it. For example, you may start on the right side believing in God, overshoot the center, and find yourself not believing in God in equal measure. Of course, the opposite can also happen. Like a pendulum you may swing from one side to the other for some time which will create a great deal of change, confusion and frustration in your life.

Meditation is often used in one's path to enlightenment. Meditation is a means of trying to extricate oneself from the belief based system. You can only ever approach this result without successfully achieving it because you cannot permanently reside within a vacuum nor reside within a vacuum for very long for obvious reasons and as I have already explained. Meditation reduces the energy invested by the meditator in the belief based system. This results in a reduced amplitude of the pendulum swing, allowing the pendulum to more closely oscillate about the center or vacuum. As the energy of the pendulum decreases and the amplitude of its swing lessens you will approach the vacuum. When as much of the energy as possible has been removed from the pendulum, it may oscillate quite slowly about the vacuum providing a certain residence time therein or the pendulum may temporarily cease to oscillate providing brief residence within the vacuum before beginning to oscillate again. During meditation you may be disturbed by internal noise, such as a thought or thoughts, or external noise, such as the sound of traffic. These noises will add energy to the pendulum, pronouncing its swing and rendering you further from the vacuum. This is the journey of the one who seeks enlightenment, and therefore each path to enlightenment will be different as there are an infinite number of diameters within the belief sphere.

The vacuum itself contains neither belief nor knowledge, nor can one reside there permanently. Those who have experienced this vacuum, claim to have achieved enlightenment. The only problem I have with this word is that it's defined by some as the state of having knowledge or understanding. This is not correct. Within the vacuum there is neither belief nor knowledge and thus the use of this word to describe this state of existence is a misnomer. The enlightened also describe the occurrence of enlightenment as a temporary state of bliss. This I wouldn't entirely disagree with to the extent that ignorance is bliss and as I have already said, residence within the vacuum is temporary. Lack of knowledge can often result in blissful happiness as it is often more comfortable not to know certain things. However, on entering the knowledge based system, I do not promise you ignorance, bliss and eternal happiness. What I promise is the truth.

Almost all people currently reside within the belief based system and thus the belief based system will be well known, though this may be the first time you have ever heard the term. The belief based system has greatest effect, control and strength when one's mind is in the past or future and can lose a lot of its strength in the present. Likewise, the vacuum is more readily achievable when ones' mind is in the present. This is because like suits like. The past is strongly subject to opinion, as is the future and the belief based system is built on opinion. The present, however, can be more accepted for what it is and thus can be less strongly subject to opinion.

The belief based system only exists when you leave the knowledge based system because outside of the knowledge based system you must have an alternative permanent residence because you cannot permanently reside within a vacuum because of its very nature. Therefore, as those who have achieved a state of enlightenment will agree but may not know why, you cannot reside in a permanent state of enlightenment. Why? Because you cannot reside within a permanent state of vacuum. A vacuum is unstable and will always seek to fill itself.

There is an underlying residual effect of being within a vacuum that cannot be fully understood because the residence time is so brief. Therefore, it can only be written about by those who have experienced it, in such vague terms that even they don't understand but rather they recognize the vacuum on a level commensurate with the time they dwelt there within. Clear? Okay, let's move on to the important stuff!

The Belief and Knowledge Based Systems

As I previously said, almost all people currently reside within the belief based system and thus the belief based system will be well known. What I mean by almost all is in fact all. Not a single person on this planet today resides within the knowledge based system. I do understand, however, that I am not the only one living today who has witnessed the knowledge based system.

The best way to describe the belief base system is to imagine your life within a room in which there is no light. There is no light because you are wearing a blindfold. You were born wearing this blindfold. As you experience the room in all the ways that you can, you develop certain views about the environment in which you live. A lot of the views you adopt in life will have been influenced to various degrees by your parents and the education and experience you receive over your lifetime. However, at the core of one's experience in the belief based system is fear. Because you reside in darkness, the overriding emotion will always be fear. When you remove your blindfold, you will leave the belief based system and enter the knowledge based system.

Before I continue let me say that trying to explain the difference between the belief based system and the knowledge based system with language skills that were created, developed, learned and thus deeply rooted within the belief based system is rather challenging. This language does not exist nor is its use appropriate within the knowledge based system.

The best way to explain the difference between the belief and knowledge based systems is to say that one cannot believe and know at the same time. Why? Because you cannot have the blindfold on and off at the same time. Therefore, within the belief based system it's impossible to impart knowledge. This statement may fly in the face of what scientists and engineers try to do in their lifetime. However, if we are completely honest we must acknowledge that as scientists and engineers, we are seekers of knowledge. The best we can hope for in the belief based system is to try to improve our understanding of the nature of our world, including our own nature and all that resides within this world. Our understanding, within the belief based system will never be complete and will constantly change and develop over time. In other words, our understanding within the belief based system, will never be faultless and thus will never reflect the truth.

Let me try to explain, by way of parable, why it's impossible to impart knowledge in the belief based system. Imagine it's a sunny summer's day with no clouds in the sky and you are out for a walk with a friend. You point to the sky and ask your friend what is the yellow circular object in the sky. Your friend replies that it is the sun. You ask your friend to describe what the sun is. Depending on your friend's level of information about our solar system that he has acquired over his lifetime his answer may include the following; the sun is a large approximately spherical ball containing hydrogen which undergoes fusion reactions which results in the emission of both heat and light. You may ask your friend how he knows this to which he may respond that he read it in a book. In this case, your friend does not know the truth about the sun. Based on the information and scientific evidence your friend has been given he believes this to be true about the sun; he doesn't know it to be true.

You are now presented with three choices. You can adopt your friend's belief about the sun, you can refuse to adopt it, or you can travel to the sun and find out the truth about the sun for yourself. Please note, that choosing not to believe is still adopting a belief, it's simply a negative and not a positive form of belief, as I have previously explained.

Imagine, for a moment that it's possible to simply fly toward the sun so that you can do your own investigations. As you exit the earth's atmosphere you note that the colour of the sun changes from yellow to green and that as you approach the sun, it becomes colder and not hotter. You collect this data and more about the sun and then return to earth. You then scrutinise your findings with the proverbial scientific microscope. Your scientific investigations reveal that when the sun's radiation hits the earth's upper atmosphere, the ozone absorbs the radiation. This absorbed radiation is subsequently re-emitted at a different frequency. The change in frequency of the radiation changes its nature from cold to hot and from green to yellow and this is why we experience the sun on the earth the way we do.

After having completed your investigations and scientific scrutiny, you discuss the findings with your friend. Your friend now has three choices. He can reject your findings and maintain his current belief about the sun. He can reject his previous belief about the sun and adopt the new one you have given him. Your scientific analysis will of course help support and strengthen his new belief about the sun. Alternatively, he can go out into the solar system and find out for himself. Until he does this he will never know the truth about the sun.

In simple words, the difference between belief (information) and the truth (knowledge) is that information comes in bits and pieces and requires evidence to support it. Knowledge comes all at once and does not require evidence to support it because evidence is knowledge and knowledge is evidence. Everything in the belief based system is subject to opinion and everyone has one. Every event or topic in this system can be viewed in an infinite number of ways. Each view or opinion is equally valid, but no singular view could ever hope to reflect the truth. An infinite number of views, all at the same time, would be required to achieve this.

Whilst one cannot reside within the belief based system and the knowledge based system at the same time as they are mutually exclusive, one can go from one system to the other and back again. Let me again use the allegory of the dark room as a way of explaining the difference between the two systems. If you continue to live your life in the dark room, you will always reside within the belief based system. You will never enter the knowledge based system to know the truth within your lifetime. Removing your blindfold will allow you to go from the belief based system to the knowledge based system. Nobody can remove your blindfold, only you can do this. This is your choice. Do you wish to reside within the belief based system or do you wish to enter the knowledge based system?

You will note that I have never tried to describe what it's like to reside within the knowledge based system other than to say the obvious; in the knowledge based system, you will know all things, nothing will be hidden from you. I do, however, feel it's important to explain why I don't describe what the knowledge based system is like.

First of all, and as I briefly explained, using a language which has been created and is deeply rooted in the belief based system to describe the knowledge based system is very difficult, even more so when the latter exhibits no reflection whatsoever to the former. But let me explain by way of parable the real reason for not trying to describe it. Imagine you are in a room. This room is full of people and all are wearing blindfolds, but nobody is aware they are wearing one; they were born this way. You know all this because you have just removed your blindfold. You have entered the knowledge based system. Everything in the room can now be seen by you, nothing remains concealed. What will you do now? Will you ignore those people in the room who are wearing blindfolds? Will you try to explain to them what the room looks like now that you have removed your blindfold? Or, will you show them how to remove their blindfolds so that they can see the room for themselves?

The blindfold can only be removed by the one wearing it. Why? Because we were given free will, the greatest gift bestowed upon us. Therefore, I have chosen to follow the third path; to show you how to remove your blindfold so that you too may witness the knowledge based system. This is the subject of my book.

How does one remove their blindfold? The blindfold can only be removed by invoking the power of the most sought-after artefact in human history, the Grail, often referred to as the Holy Grail. The Grail was created and given to us by a messenger almost two thousand years ago. Using the Grail allows you to go from the belief based system to the knowledge based system.

But the Grail is only a legend, right?

Chapter Two

The Grail – The Legend

The legend of the Holy Grail is probably one of the most enduring tales in western European literature and art. It was rumored to have immense power, the ability to heal all wounds, provide nourishment and by some accounts to bestow eternal life on its user. A brief history of the Holy Grail charts the origins of the Grail story from early Christian gospels through to western mysticism and the rise of medieval romances and Arthurian legends. The Grail then dramatically reappears once more in the story of the Crusades, during the rise and sudden fall of the Knights Templar, who it is said were the guardians of the Grail.

Various notions of the Holy Grail are currently widespread in western society, popularized through numerous medieval and modern works of both art and literature. As a result of this wide distribution, most Americans and western Europeans assume that the idea of the Grail is universally well known. This is not the case. The stories of the Grail are absent from Eastern Orthodox teachings. The notions of the Grail, its importance and prominence, are regarded as a set of ideas that are essentially linked with Christian or former Christian locales, Celtic mythology, and Anglo-French medieval storytelling. Despite the number of forms the Holy Grail has taken over the centuries, it was notoriously considered to be the chalice used at The Last Supper of Jesus Christ and his twelve disciples.

During the middle ages, four possible contenders for the location of the Holy Grail stood out from the rest. The earliest record of a chalice from the Last Supper is of a two-handled silver chalice which was in a chapel near Jerusalem. This is the only mention of the chalice situated in the Holy Land. There is also a reference, in a late thirteenth century German romance by Albrecht[2], to the Grail being in a church in Constantinople. This Grail was said to have been looted from the church during the Fourth Crusade and sent from Constantinople to Troyes, France, in 1204 AD. It was recorded to have still been there in the early seventeenth century, but it later disappeared amid the French Revolution during the late eighteenth century.

Of two Grail vessels that survive today, one, known as the Sacro Catino or the holy basin, is in the cathedral in Genoa, Italy. Traditionally said to be carved from emerald, it is in fact a dish of brilliant green Egyptian glass, about eighteen inches in diameter. It was sent to Paris after Napoleon's conquest of Italy but was returned broken, which identified the emerald as glass. According to some sources, the vessel was found in a mosque in Caesarea, a town in northern Israel in 1101 AD but its origin is still debated and uncertain. The other surviving Grail vessel is the Santo Cáliz, a cup made from agate, in the cathedral of Valencia, Spain, which, it has been told, was brought to Rome by St Peter.

The Holy Grail first appears in written text in the *Conte del Graal* (Story of the Grail) by Chrétien de Troyes around 1180 AD after which a great body of the Grail romances came into existence between the years 1180 AD and 1240 AD. Most of these romances are in French, but there are versions in German, English, Norwegian, Italian, and Portuguese. In the romances the concept of the Grail varies considerably, its nature often but vaguely indicated and in some cases left wholly unexplained. The origin of the legend itself is involved in obscurity, and scholars are divided in their views on this point.

In Chrétien's version, the Grail is a platter or dish, not a chalice. In this version of the Grail, we learn that the Grail contained a holy host, like that used in the Catholic sacrament of the Eucharist, which was capable of sustaining life and thus it was the content that was important, not the vessel itself. Even though Chrétien's account intimated that the Grail was in some way holy, he did not make an explicit connection between Jesus Christ and the Grail. Although Chrétien unfortunately died before he was able to finish his tale, many writers endeavored to complete his work by picking up where he had left off. These works became known as the Grail Continuations.

A thorough and detailed history of the Grail was also written in the *Grand St Graal,* a hefty French prose romance of the first half of the thirteenth century, where it is recounted that Jesus Christ himself presented to a pious hermit the book concerning this history.

In a German version of the Holy Grail by Wolfram von Eschenbach[3] in 1210 AD, we are presented with an entirely different concept from that of the French romances. In Wolfram's rendition, the Grail is a precious stone possessing miraculous powers which had fallen out of the sky. The Grail dates back to the time of creation itself and the angels who remained neutral during the rebellion of Lucifer were its first guardians. The essence of the stone was so pure that it was able to nourish a person and slow the aging process. It is later brought to earth and entrusted to Titurel, the first Grail King, where it is kept safe in the castle of Montsalvat. Some historians, and monks of Montserrat, have identified this castle with the real sanctuary of Montserrat in Catalonia, near the city of Barcelona, Spain. In another German romance, *Diu Krône*[4] (13th century), the Grail is first described as a crystal vessel which later becomes a golden bowl adorned with precious stones.

After the Renaissance period in Europe, generally considered to be between the fourteenth and seventeenth centuries, the Grail legend all but disappeared but was later to be rescued when the Romantic movement set in at the beginning of the nineteenth century. The most famous versions were Tennyson's *Holy Grail* in the *Idylls of the King* (1869), and Wagner's music-drama, the festival-play, *Parsifal,* produced for the first time at Bayreuth, a sizable town in northern Bavaria, Germany, in 1882. However, despite its obscure and cryptic nature, the symbol of the Grail as an object of great power and mystery has persisted into the twentieth century in the novels of Charles Williams[5], CS Lewis[6] and John Cowper Powys[7].

In purely Christian mythology, the Grail is considered to be the cup from which Jesus Christ, about whom I will talk in more detail later, drank or indeed the dish from which he ate at the Last Supper. It is told that this very same cup or dish was used by Joseph of Arimathea to catch the blood of the Christ as he hung on the cross.

Joseph of Arimathea was, according to all four canonical gospels, the man who assumed responsibility for the burial of Jesus after his crucifixion. He was a rich man, a member of the Jewish council and a secret disciple of Jesus. Joseph upon hearing of Jesus Christ's death asked Pontius Pilate, the governor of Judea at the time, could he take the body of Jesus so that he could prepare it for burial. Pilate gave him permission. Joseph immediately took the body of Jesus down from the cross and prepared it for burial, laying it in a tomb which he had previously built for himself. However, when Jesus Christ's body disappeared from the tomb days later, Joseph was accused of stealing it and was thrown into prison.

The early history of the Grail is intimately connected with the story of Joseph of Arimathea. Most of what we know of Joseph of Arimathea and his connection with the Grail comes from the Arthurian legends and in particular from the work of a French poet, Robert de Boron, entitled *Joseph d'Arimathie*, which was written around 1200 AD. Boron's source for the imprisonment of Joseph is understood to have come from the apocryphal *Gospel of Nicodemus* since there was no more information about Joseph in the four canonical gospels after the event of placing Jesus Christ's body in the tomb. Whilst Joseph was in prison, an apparition of Jesus Christ appeared to Joseph and presented him with the Grail through which he is miraculously sustained for forty-two years, until he is eventually liberated by order of the Roman Emperor Vespasian. Upon being set free, Joseph of Arimathea, his two sons, and many followers bring the Grail to Britain where it is concealed. The purely Christian legend which thus had arisen was brought into contact with traditional British lore and thus the Celtic stamp, which experts believe it undeniably bears, is accounted for.

The first Grail romances were probably written in Latin and became the basis for the work of Robert de Boron. Though Chrétien's account is the earliest and considered the most influential of all Grail texts, it was as a result of the work of Robert de Boron that the Grail truly became the Holy Grail and assumed the form most familiar to modern readers. According to Robert de Boron's account, Joseph of Arimathea brought the Grail to Glastonbury, England, a Roman outpost at the time of Christ's crucifixion, where he established the first Christian Church on the British Isles and founded a dynasty of keepers to protect the Grail. Joseph of Arimathea, his son Josephus and his son-in-law Bron were the first keepers of the Grail and upon the death of the last keeper, the Grail vanished, never to be seen again.

Although there are no connections between Joseph of Arimathea and the cup of the Last Supper in the Catholic Bible and indeed even in the apocryphal texts, those who advocate a purely Christian origin to the Grail regard the religious element in the story as fundamental, where the life giving properties of the Grail are explained by the association of the Grail with the Sacrament of the Eucharist, which believers of course hold gives spiritual nourishment to the faithful.

Following the story of Joseph of Arimathea's flight to Britain, the development of the Grail legend became interwoven into British history, becoming the object of epic quests and the subject of Arthurian legend. King Arthur, or Arthur Pendragon, was a legendary British leader who, according to medieval histories and romances, led the defence of Britain against Saxon invaders in the late fifth and early sixth centuries AD. The details of Arthur's story are mainly composed of folklore and literary invention, and his historical existence is debated and disputed by modern historians. Nevertheless, given the importance of Jesus Christ's crucifixion and the Eucharist in Christian beliefs, the search for the Grail became the principal and holiest of quests of King Arthur and his Knights of the Roundtable as it signified the pursuit of union with God. Many such quests for the Grail were undertaken by King Arthur and his Knights. Some of these tales tell of knights who succeeded, like Percival and Galahad, and others tell of knights who failed to invoke the power of the Grail because of their tragic flaws. One such quest ends with twelve knights ascending into heaven along with the Grail itself.

An important source of Arthurian legend, the *Queste del Saint Graal*[8], written in French and comprising a series of five prose volumes, tells the story of the quest for the Holy Grail and the romance of Lancelot and Guinevere. This work is considered to have been written in the early thirteenth century but scholars in this area have few definitive answers as to the authorship. The *Queste del Saint Graal* created a new hero, the knight Sir Galahad, while the quest of the Grail itself became a search for mystical union with God. It was written that only the pure of heart could touch the Grail and survive. Once touched, the Grail would divulge the divine mysteries which could not be described by human tongue. The work gained an added dimension by making Galahad the son of Lancelot, thus comparing the story of chivalry inspired by human love, Lancelot and Guinevere, with that inspired by divine love, Galahad's quest for the Grail and union with God.

Belief in the Grail, and interest in its potential whereabouts, never ceased throughout the ages. Guardianship of the Grail during the twelfth and thirteenth centuries was historically attributed to the Knights Templar. The Templars were a military religious Order of highly trained knights, founded in the Holy Land around 1111 AD. The Holy Land generally refers to a territory which includes the modern State of Israel, the Palestinian territories, western Jordan, and parts of southern Lebanon and southwestern Syria. It is considered holy by Jews, Christians, and Muslims alike.

During the twelfth and thirteenth centuries, the Knights Templar acquired extensive property both in Palestine, Syria and in Europe, especially in France. They were granted far-reaching ecclesiastical and jurisdictional privileges both by the Pope to whom they were, in their early years, immediately responsible, and by the secular monarchs in whose lands their members resided. On admission to the Order, a man was compelled to sign over all his wealth and possessions. The organisation also received in abundance from the world's rich and powerful but, as a matter of strict policy, it never gave. The organisation of the Knights Templar was among the richest and most powerful of all the western Christian military Orders and existed for almost two centuries until it was mysteriously disbanded in 1305 AD. They were so influential that the Grand Master of the Order of the Knights Templar oversaw the signing of the Magna Carta by King John in June 1215 AD.

The Knights Templar were involved in many of the early Crusades during their two-century reign. The Crusades were a series of religious wars or military campaigns sanctioned by the Catholic Church between the eleventh and sixteenth centuries. These Crusades were instigated for many reasons which included, the recapturing of Jerusalem from Islamic rule, the recapture of other Christian territories or the defence of Christians in non-Christian lands, the resolution of conflict among rival Roman Catholic groups, the attainment of political or territorial advantage, and the combat of paganism and heresy.

According to Guillaume de Tyre, a medieval prelate and chronicler, the Order of the temple initially numbered only nine knights and admitted no new recruits for nine years. It is said that these nine knights were present at the first crusade into the Holy Land in 1099 AD. However, the combined force of the crusade including non-combatants may have contained as many as 100,000 people. This army, composed mostly of French and Norman Knights besieged Antioch (an ancient Greco-Roman city on the eastern side of the Orontes River near the modern city of Antakya, Turkey), massacring the inhabitants and pillaging the city. The bulk of the crusader army held the city of Antioch and the remaining force marched south along the coast reaching Jerusalem. It is believed that during the successful siege of the city of Jerusalem a treasure which became known as the **legendary treasure of the temple of Jerusalem** was discovered by the knights who brought it back to France. Thereafter the treasure became known as the **treasure of the Templars**.

Officially endorsed by the Roman Catholic Church around 1129 AD, the Order grew rapidly in membership and power. The Templar Knights, in their distinctive white mantles with a red cross, were among the most skilled fighting units of the Crusades and the most disciplined fighting force in the world at the time. Non-combatant members of the Order managed a large economic infrastructure throughout Christendom, building fortifications across Europe and the Holy Land, and developing innovative financial techniques that were an early form of banking. In 1139 AD, a papal bull was issued by Pope Innocent II. According to this charter the Templars would owe allegiance to no secular or ecclesiastical power other than the Pope himself. This papal charter rendered the Knights independent of all kings, princes and prelates, and of all interference from religious and political authorities. They had become, in effect, a law unto themselves, an autonomous international empire.

The association between the Roman Catholic Church and the Knights Templar, however, didn't make sense to many historians as the core of the Templars, those who gave direction to the Order, were without doubt, in their minds, Gnostic mystics who gave little importance to relics or indeed to the material world itself.

The word *Gnostic* comes from the Greek word gnosis, meaning **knowledge** which is often used in Greek philosophy in a manner more consistent with the English word meaning **enlightenment**. Gnosticism is generally considered to be a term categorizing a collection of ancient religions whose adherents shunned the material world, which they viewed as created by the Demiurge, and embraced the spiritual world. Demiurge was a heavenly being, subordinate to the supreme being, considered to be the controller of the material world and antagonistic to all that is purely spiritual. The term Christian Gnostic came to represent a segment of the Early Christian community who believed that salvation lay not in faith in Jesus Christ, but by learning to free themselves from the material world. According to this tradition, the answers to spiritual questions are to be found within, not without. Although the origins of Gnostic movements are disputed, the period of activity for most of these movements flourished from approximately the time of the founding of Christianity until the fourth century when the writings and activities of groups deemed heretical or pagan were actively suppressed.

The opinion that the Templars were Christian Gnostics is of course supported by the historical evidence that there was a secret Order behind the Knights Templar, which created the Templars as its military and administrative arm. This secret Order which functioned under a range of names over the centuries was most generally known as the *Prieuré de Sion* or the Priory of Sion. Like the Knights Templar, the *Prieuré de Sion* had been directed by a succession of grand masters whose names are among the most illustrious in western history and culture. They include names like, Leonardo da Vinci, Robert Boyle, Sir Isaac Newton, Victor Hugo and Claude Debussy. It could not be said that any of these men were devoutly Christian but were more concerned with the occult, science, knowledge and the arts, which lends weight to the view that the Knights Templar were, if not a pure Gnostic organisation, were led by men who were. Given the Gnostic outlook of the Order of the Templars, to what did they owe their official papal recognition, endorsement and protection? Could it be linked to the treasure they found in Jerusalem?

If the **treasure of the Templars** taken from Jerusalem was not a cup or other such physical item, which would mean nothing to those mystics, then what was it? In the days of the Order, persecution by Roman Catholic Church inquisitors was widespread and non-traditional groups of Christians had to hide their practice and find secret codes to communicate. The Templars were such a group. Despite this, the Church offered them protection rather than torture and execution. What **treasure** could be so important that would warrant or indeed force the issuance of a papal bull giving the Templars such broad ranging powers especially considering their non-traditional Christian beliefs? Given the numerous secret codes by which the Templars operated, if a chalice stood for something else, what could it be? As a cup would mean nothing to these mystics, many historians and seekers of the Grail believe that the idea the Grail was the cup that Jesus Christ used in the last supper was simply employed by the Templars as a ruse to protect the true Grail. If this was their objective, it worked well.

The first record of the Holy Grail surfacing was shortly after the founding of the Templar Order. The nine founding Gnostic Knights, almost immediately started digging around Solomon's Temple where they were headquartered during the first crusade. When they had found what they were looking for, they made their way to Rome where they exacted the huge concessions from the pontiff that guaranteed the successful growth of their new Order. Of course, there has been great speculation as to what it was they found that they could persuade the Pope in this way.

Solomon's Temple, also known as the First Temple, was the Holy Temple in ancient Jerusalem which was destroyed by Nebuchadnezzar II (605 BC – c. 562 BC), a Chaldean King of ancient Babylon, after he lay Siege to Jerusalem during 587 BC. It was said that the Temple of Solomon had contained the legendary Ark of the Covenant. The Ark of the Covenant also known as the Ark of the Testimony, was a gold-covered wooden chest described in the Book of Exodus as containing, among other things, the two stone tablets of the Ten Commandments given by God to Moses, leader of the Jews at that time. The Book of Exodus is the second book of the Torah, the Hebrew Bible; a collection of religious writings by ancient Israelites. The biblical account relates that, approximately one year after the Israelites' exodus from Egypt, the Ark was created and given to Moses by God when the Israelites were encamped at the foot of Mount Sinai. However, the likelihood that the Ark still existed after all those centuries would be unlikely as the temple had been destroyed and rebuilt many times. Nevertheless, even if it had been the Ark the Templars had found, its possession would not have given them such a powerful bargaining position with the Pope. So, what did they find?

Many historians believe what the Templars had found were *Gnostic Gospels* and among these were one written by Jesus Christ himself. It is accepted by many that after Jesus Christ had risen from the dead that he passed eleven years in discourse with his disciples, instructing them. What became known as the Gnostic Gospels tells us that Jesus Christ gave secret instruction to the select few who could understand. His teachings became known as Gnosticism. Although it is unclear to how many of his disciples Jesus Christ imparted these secret teachings, what survives today as the Gnostic Gospels were found in a cave in Egypt in 1947 and became known as the Nag Hammadi Library.

The Nag Hammadi Library is a collection of thirteen ancient books (called codices) containing over fifty texts. This immensely important discovery includes a large number of primary Gnostic Gospels, including scriptures such as the Gospel of Mary Magdalene, the Gospel of Thomas, the Gospel of Philip, and the Gospel of Truth. The emergence of the Nag Hammadi Library in 1945 and its translation into English and other modern languages has had a significant influence upon modern western culture. The Gospel written by Jesus Christ, however, was never found. Did such a document ever exist? Was this the Templars Holy Grail – a Gospel written by Jesus Christ himself?!

Among the Gnostic Gospels found in Egypt, there is one called the *Dialogue of the Savior*, but it is unclear who the author is. Nevertheless, if there was a Gospel by Jesus Christ, would it not have been hallmarked and proclaimed to all? Many argue that his Gnostic Gospel included lessons and guidance intended for the select few, and that he gave specific instructions that it should not be propagated among those outside the selected minority. They believe that Jesus Christ meant his secret teachings only for those who were ready, and to the rest he spoke in parables. Such a document, if it existed, would have validated Gnosticism as Jesus Christ's true teachings. This would have rendered a blow to the power of the Roman Catholic Church, one from which they may never have recovered. It is maintained by many experts on the Holy Grail that select copies were made and disseminated by the Templars among other Gnostic groups such as the Cathars who were an Gnostic revival movement that flourished in some areas of Southern Europe between the twelfth and fourteenth centuries, but are now mainly remembered for a prolonged period of persecution by the Catholic Church which did not recognize their belief as truly Christian. Legend has it that when the Cathar castle of Montsegur in the Languedoc region of France fell to the Pope's army in March of 1244 AD, that a handful of Cathars took the Holy Grail with them before the castle fell.

When the Holy Land was lost to the Muslims, support for the Templar Order faded. Rumors about the Templars' secret initiation ceremony created distrust and they were accused of heresy. King Philip IV of France, deeply in debt to the Order, took advantage of the situation. In 1307 AD he had many of the Order's members in France arrested, tortured into giving false confessions, and burned at the stake. They were accused of ritually denying Christ and of repudiating, trampling and spitting on the cross. In France, at least, the fate of the arrested Templars was sealed. Philippe pursued the Order relentlessly, torturing, burning and imprisoning his quarry. He also harassed and bullied Pope Clement V, demanding that ever more stringent measures against the Order should be taken. After resisting for a while, the Pope relented, and the Knights were officially disbanded in 1312 AD without any conclusive verdict of guilt being pronounced. This did not quell Philippe's pursuit of the French Templars however, which he assiduously continued, conducting trials, inquiries and investigations culminating in the trial of the Grand Master of the Order in 1314 AD, Jacques de Molay, who was summarily convicted and roasted to death over a slow fire. After the death of the Grand Master, the Templars ostensibly vanished. However, given the number of Knights who escaped, remained at large, or who were acquitted, they did not cease to exist.

The Knights were well aware that the tide was turning against them, especially in France. It is rumored that with this foresight, the Order moved their tremendous collection of treasures, including documents and records to a secret location. Did this collection of treasures include the Grail? Did they secrete the Grail in a location in France or somewhere outside Philippe's domain to ensure its safety?

Philippe did not stop pursuing the Knights. In fact, he tried to influence his fellow monarchs, hoping to ensure that all Templars anywhere in Christendom would be eradicated. It's not clear why Philippe would be so intent on exterminating all Templars especially outside France. Their rumored religious infringements would doubtless be of no concern to Philippe who himself had arranged for the deaths of two popes. Did Philippe simply fear reprisals from the Order if they remained intact outside France, or was there something else involved?

In any case, his attempts to erase Templars outside France were not entirely fruitful. In England, Edward II initially rallied to the Order's defence. However, after pressure from both the Pope and the French King, Edward yielded to their demands but not with any great enthusiasm. In Germany, the Templars openly defied their judges, displaying a show of force. Cowed, the judges found them innocent. However, when the Order was officially dissolved, the Templars often rebranded their Order or found refuge in other Orders such as the Teutonic Knights. In Spain, the Templars also defied their persecutors and found refuge in other Orders. In Portugal the Templars were found innocent and upon dissolution simply modified its name becoming the Knights of Christ. Elsewhere, culling of the Templars met with even greater difficulty. Nowhere was this more evidenced than in Scotland. At this time, Scotland was at war with England and as such, the papal bulls dissolving the Order were not proclaimed and thus the Order was never technically dissolved in Scotland. In fact, a sizable contingent of French Templars were said to have fought at the side of Robert the Bruce at the battle of Bannockburn in 1314 AD defeating the English and winning freedom for Scotland.

Many historians believe that the literature on King Arthur and his Knights was loosely based on the Knights Templar whose existence unlike the former is not considered legend. However, if King Arthur and his Knights of the Round Table had engendered a plethora of romantic legend, the mystification surrounding the Templars was even greater. At their Zenith, they were the most powerful and influential organisation in the whole of Christendom, with the single possible exception of the papacy. At the end of their two-century long career these white garbed champions of Christ were accused of denying and repudiating Christ and of trampling and spitting on the cross.

Although the Knights Templar were effectively destroyed and dissolved, the *Prieuré de Sion* remained untouched and continued to function through the centuries, acting covertly and orchestrating many of the critical events in western history that has shaped our world today. However, the abrupt reduction in power of a significant group in European society gave rise to speculation, legend, and legacy through the ages.

Pursuit of the Grail, however, did not stop with the demise of the Templars but continued throughout the ages to the present time. It is reported that Hitler became interested in the legend of the Grail and ordered many fruitless excavations especially in France, during Germany's occupation from 1940-1945. The Knights Templar were of course heavily populated in France before they were disbanded, and Hitler mainly concentrated on sites which had previously been excavated by the Knights themselves.

To date, the fate of the Grail appears to be unknown and conspiracy theories abound on the nature of the Grail and its final location. The top ten current and most popular possible resting places of this mysterious object include;

1. **Accokeek, Maryland, USA.** The locals of the Accokeek area claim that a Jesuit priest stowed away onboard a ship which sailed up the Potomac

River around the beginning of the seventeenth century. It is said that this priest had ties with the Knights Templar who by then were disbanded two centuries. The legend states that he was guardian of the Grail and purposively fled to a part of the world where few people would care about it. However, its location in the Accokeek area is unknown.

2. **Oak Island, Nova Scotia, Canada.** The location, a pit, was discovered by three teenage boys playing on the island in 1795 AD and over the centuries, six people have died attempting to excavate the mysterious treasure everyone is sure is down there. The more failed attempts to excavate, the wilder imaginations ran as to what was buried there. The pit is now no longer thought to hold merely chests of gold doubloons, but the Holy Grail itself, which is believed, was hidden there by the Knights Templar in the early to mid-fourteenth century. The most compelling evidence to the existence of the Grail is the ingenious design of the pit, which was fitted with a water channel booby trap and because whatever is down there lies at exactly one hundred feet.

3. **Rosslyn Chapel, Roslin, Scotland.** Building of the Chapel began in 1456 AD at the behest of its founder, William Sinclair, a nobleman and knight. He was rumored to have been the descendant of a Templar Knight. This legend was

made famous by Dan Brown in *The Da Vinci Code*. The legend centers on secret stone chambers and channels under the chapel and there is a plethora of extremely strange carvings in and around the chapel that add ominous weight to the legend. A substantial undertaking, the chapel's carvings took almost forty years to complete. One of the most notable and unique architectural features of the Chapel is the Apprentice Pillar. The legend states that the Grail could reside inside the Apprentice Pillar or in the family crypt which is sealed shut. The Sinclair's still own the chapel and refuse to authorize any digs as this would necessitate tearing down the chapel, the resting place of their ancestors.

4. **Glastonbury Tor, Glastonbury, England.** *Tor* is a Celtic word meaning conical hill, and that is what Glastonbury Tor is. Legend has it as the resting place of King Arthur and the Lady Guinevere. Although there is no evidence to support this, the hill did serve as a fort since about 600 AD. Many of the Arthurian and Templar legends are entwined, and the story goes that the Templars, having returned from the First Crusade, brought with them numerous holy relics, including those from Jerusalem, and hid them throughout the British Isles. It is believed that the Grail was buried somewhere on Glastonbury Tor. Some historians maintain that it was buried between Arthur and Guinevere.

5. **The Dome of the Rock, Jerusalem, Israel.**
   Many believe that the Holy Grail is not the
   chalice at the Last Supper but rather the cup,
   bowl, or plate which happened to be near the
   Cross and caught the blood of Jesus Christ as
   he died. His Crucifixion site is believed to have
   been a cleft between two rocks, one of which
   has since been completely eroded. The other
   sits at the top of a hill on which the Dome
   of the Rock, an Islamic shrine, now sits. It is
   sacred to all three major monotheistic religions,
   Judaism, Christianity and Islam. Judaism holds
   that Abraham, at God's behest, almost slew
   his son Isaac on this rock. The Islamic faithful
   believe that their prophet Mohammed sprang to
   Heaven on a horse from this rock and of course
   Christianity maintains that Jesus Christ's cross
   was planted between this rock and another. The
   cup which caught Jesus Christ's blood at his
   crucifixion was then buried with him by Joseph
   of Arimathea. The location of his burial tomb is
   not known but is described in the Catholic Bible
   as nearby and thus possibly somewhere close-at-
   hand.

6. **The Cathedral of St Lawrence, Genoa, Italy.** In
   this Cathedral there is a bowl formed of green
   glass which was originally believed to be emerald
   until it was broken during Napoleon's reign.
   Its origin is uncertain, but it is believed to have
   first appeared in a mosque in Caesarea, Israel, in

1101 AD. Very little is known about the artefact and it has not yet been carbon dated.

7. **Cathedral de Santa Maria de Valencia, Spain.** This is a chalice made of dark red agate, set in a gold stem, with an upturned bowl of chalcedony as its base. Agnostics claim that should the legend of the Grail be legitimate; the Valencia Chalice is the front contender. The chalice was carbon dated in 1960 to a date of somewhere between 300 BC and 100 AD and its origin has been traced to the Middle East. Should this chalice not be the Grail, its age nevertheless makes it extremely valuable.

8. **Santa Maria de Montserrat, Catalonia, Spain.** Santa Maria de Montserrat is a Benedictine abbey located on the mountain of Montserrat, in Catalonia, Spain. The monastery was founded in the tenth century AD and still functions to this day as a monastery with over one hundred and fifty Benedictine monks. The monastery is thirty miles west of Barcelona and is Catalonia's most important religious retreat where groups of young people from all over Catalonia make overnight hikes to watch the sunrise from the heights of Montserrat. The Grail is said to be hidden somewhere under the church grounds. Others say that it has been concealed elsewhere on the mountain. If this is true, the Grail may never be found as the mountain is very large

and its terrain is very rugged. The mountain's peak, at 4,055 feet, is called Sant Jeroni (Saint Jerome) who features prominently in several Grail legends.

9. **The Sewers of Jerusalem.** In this version of the legend, the Knights Templar of the First Crusade never found the Grail. It is said that Jesus Christ's disciples buried the Grail with the Ark of the Covenant in the sewers below the city. Today, excavation within the city is expressly forbidden by the state except for professional archaeologists intent on uncovering sites of antiquity. Relic hunting is specifically banned as random and excessive digging would undermine the structural integrity of the cities buildings.

10. **The US Gold Depository, Fort Knox, Kentucky, USA.** This legend grew on the basis that the Depository is probably the most protected, defended and secure place on the planet. Not even the President is allowed on the property. The security consists of electrified fences, alarms, cameras, armed guards, motion-activated mini-gun turrets, landmines, snipers and 30,000 active troops who train every day with Apache helicopter gunships and tanks. The vast majority of the internal security measures of course are unknown. I understand that the Americans are very protective of their money but surely this is overkill unless they are also protecting something else.

Numerous times over the past century, newspaper headlines have declared the quest for the Holy Grail over. In the early twentieth century, it was supposedly discovered near England's Glastonbury Abbey. A few years later, a battered silver goblet with elaborate ornamentation unearthed in the ancient city of Antioch was put forward as the Holy Grail. The Antioch Chalice, now in the collection of New York's Metropolitan Museum of Art, toured museums all over the world including the Louvre in Paris and even went on display at the World's Fair in Chicago in 1934 before it was dated to the early sixth century and thus discounted.

The hunt for the Grail has endured for the last two thousand years to the present day. In 2014 it was reported that two Spanish researchers, Margarita Torres and José Ortega del Rio discovered the Holy Grail, the cup Jesus Christ drank from at the Last Supper. In their book, 'The Kings of the Grail'[9], charting three years of scientific research, medieval history lecturer Margarita Torres and art historian José Miguel Ortega del Rio claim the Holy Grail rests inside the Basilica of San Isidoro in the northern Spanish city of León. The historians say that a three-year investigation led them to conclude that the hallowed cup that Jesus Christ allegedly drank from at the Last Supper is a jewel-encrusted goblet that has long been known as the chalice of the *Infanta Doña Urraca* – in honor of the daughter of King Ferdinand I, ruler of León from 1037 AD to 1065 AD.

Prior to their discovery, the researchers had been investigating Islamic remains in the Basílica of San

Isidoro, León, when they came across a medieval Egyptian parchment which revealed that this particular chalice had been taken from Jerusalem to Cairo. It was subsequently given to an Amir (an Arabic term for one of noble birth or high office), who ruled an Islamic kingdom on Spain's Mediterranean coast, in return for the help he gave to Egypt whose people were suffering a famine. Later, the Amir gifted the chalice as a peace offering to the Christian King Ferdinand. From their research, the co-authors were led to believe that the chalice of Christ made a journey from Jerusalem to Cairo and then from Cairo to León as this chalice had done. Carbon dating also placed the origin of the cup between 200 BC and 100 AD which meant that this chalice was a strong contender to be the Holy Grail. The chalice has been in the basilica's possession since the eleventh century and in the church's basement museum since the 1950s for all to see. Since the publication of their book, the basilica has been inundated with visitors.

The myths surrounding the Grail have been more powerful than the facts and its allure has attracted the attention of modern writers and artists in search of an ancient symbol of purity and power. The psychologist Carl Jung, composer Richard Wagner, poets William Blake, and T. S. Eliot and the Pre-Raphaelite painters have all been seduced by the legend. Today the Grail quest can be found in films such as Lord of the Rings, Star Wars, Indiana Jones, and Excalibur, as well as Dan Brown's, The Da Vinci Code.

I believe that most myths are not created to encourage us to find the truth but rather to distract us from it; to have us embark on endless fruitless quests for something that just doesn't exist while the truth remains undiscovered, unknown, dormant. The greater the legend the greater the truth that it is hoped to conceal. The legend of the Grail is probably one of the greatest examples of this. For millennia we have sought the Grail as a physical item of power. We started wars over it. We killed, raped and stole in a perpetual, ceaseless and ultimately futile attempt to acquire its secrets and power. So, what is the truth? Does the Grail exist or is it simply a myth? The truth of course is that either nobody knows, or nobody told us.

Chapter Three

The Messenger and the Grail

What is the Grail? Before I reveal what the Grail is, who created it and how to use it, let us first consider the etymology of the word Grail. Etymology is a linguistic discipline. It is the study of the origin of words and their historical development. More particularly, it's a study of the birth of the word and how it developed, including its change in meaning throughout history and from language to language. Throughout the centuries, many etymologists, lacking historical records as well as the scientific methods to analyse them, based their explanations on allegory and guesswork. Unfortunately, therefore, etymology is not an exact science but rather can be used sometimes as a useful yard stick which can occasionally give unexpected and interesting results.

If you study the accepted etymology of the word Grail you may begin with the English Oxford dictionary if your mother tongue is English. The dictionary initially describes it as Holy Grail, being its full term, rather than simply Grail. The dictionary goes on to ascribe two meanings to this term. The first is that it describes the cup or platter used by the Christ in his very last supper prior to his crucifixion. The second is that the term can be used simply to describe any object of a quest.

If you dig a bit deeper you will learn that the term *Grail* comes from the Latin word *gradale*, which meant a dish brought to the table during different courses of a meal. This now widely accepted meaning of the word Grail was given by the Cistercian chronicler Helinandus in about 1230 AD. Others derive origin from the Latin word *garalis* meaning a mixing bowl. You may find that most studies of the origin of the word Grail will lead you to discover this meaning. Therefore, we are led to believe that the Grail is a vessel of some sort, such as a cup, a dish or a bowl. Although it is unclear, it appears that it was only after the cycle of Grail romances were well established, bestowing the cup of the Last Supper with great power, that late medieval writers came up with this etymology for the word Grail.

Other and more recent etymologists have derived the word from old French rather than directly from Latin. This to me seems more reasonable as many English words would have come either directly from the French language or at least would have been heavily influenced by the French language rather than having come directly from Latin, Greek or Hebrew. In old French, *san grial* means Holy Grail. Due to the now well-established connection between the word Grail and the elusive cup used by Jesus Christ at the Last Supper, many modern-day authors, story tellers and conspirators manipulate the words *san grial* to read *sang rial* which means royal blood. They use this manipulation to create the theory that Jesus Christ may not have died on the cross, but lived to marry Mary Magdalene and father children, whose Merovingian bloodline (royal blood) continues to this day. The best book I have read in this field of endeavor is one called

Holy Blood, Holy Grail by Michael Baigent, Richard Leigh and Henry Lincoln. It is well written, incredibly well researched and a thoroughly enjoyable read.

Nevertheless, after having conducted a brief study of the word Grail, here is what I found regarding the origins of the word. It stems from the old French word *greille* later more commonly written as *graille*. Both forms of the word have origins in the ninth through to the thirteenth centuries. This word later developed into the modern form of the French word we find today, *grille*, which means gate. The French today often use this word to describe the bars on a prison cell window; *Les fenêtres des prisons ont des grilles*. During my study of the word Grail, I also found that the word has roots in the Latin word *gradatus* which means step-by-step or step-after-step. The importance of this study will only become apparent when you understand what the Grail is and how to use it.

So, what now? At this stage it may be appropriate to introduce the messenger who created this Gate and showed us how to use it. The messenger's name was Yeshua, the protagonist in the New Testament of the Roman Catholic Bible. Yeshua was a Jew and during his time, Jews normally had only one name. However, where greater specificity was required, it was common practice to add the father's name or the place of birth. Thus, Yeshua is referred to by many names such as Jesus (the Greek expression of the Hebrew name Yeshua), Jesus son of Joseph, Jesus of Nazareth, Jesus the Nazarene, the Nazarene, Jesus of Galilee, Jesus Christ or simply, the Christ.

I know I promised that this book would not be religious or spiritual. It's not. To understand, you'll just have to keep reading. The truth of the matter is that Yeshua himself was not religious and thus he was not bound by the restrictions a religious belief imposes. Furthermore, he continuously challenged the established religious dogma which existed at the time, Judaism, and to which he was indoctrinated. You may also find it a surprise to hear that Yeshua himself did not believe in God. The believers among you will refuse to accept this and hot-headed believers would crucify me for this revelation! Those of you who are agnostic may simply be puzzled.

Before I reveal who and what Yeshua was and the true mystery behind the Grail, let me first describe what is generally known about him. I understand for some, in particular for Christians and Roman Catholics, who were indoctrinated from birth with the stories of this man, that this description will be somewhat inadequate and wholly unnecessary. However, this book is not meant to reveal the enigma of the Grail to a specific group or groups of people, but to all. It is important, therefore, that all are aware of what is commonly known about him. Please understand, however, that what is known about this man is sparse at best. There is no exhaustive account of his life and many of the accounts are contradictory. Most written documents simply cover his birth, his early years, and his ministry to the people which we are informed began when he was about thirty years of age. The rest of his life, more than two decades of it, is predominantly un-documented. Yeshua's life, including his birth and death is the subject of a whole area of study. The volumes written about this man would take a lifetime or more to study in any detail. Therefore, it is not my objective to review this area in any depth but rather to give some background and context.

It is widely accepted that Yeshua was born between 6 BC and 4 BC in the town of Bethlehem which is now a Palestinian city located in the central West Bank, about seven miles south of Jerusalem, the capital city of the state of Israel, in the Middle East. At this time, the Middle East was part of the Roman Empire, but that area generally represented by the now state of Israel and Palestine was ruled by Rome's client (puppet) king, Herod the Great. This area was strategically important because it lay between Syria and Egypt, two of Rome's most-valuable possessions. Due to their importance, Rome had many legions in both countries but not in Israel-Palestine. Roman imperial policy at the time required that Israel-Palestine be loyal and peaceful so that it did not undermine Rome's larger interests, but Rome had no interest in spending valuable resources trying to govern the area. This was achieved for a long time by permitting Herod to remain King of Judea (37 – 4 BC) and allowing him a free hand in governing his kingdom, as long as the requirements of stability and loyalty were met.

Herod not only ruled Judea which includes the mountainous southern part of the present-day state of Israel, which was predominantly Jewish at the time, but also some of the neighbouring Gentile areas as well. Galilee and Judea, the principal Jewish areas were surrounded by Gentile territories such as Caesarea, Dora and Ptolemais on the Mediterranean coast. There were also two inland Gentile cities on the west side of the Jordan River near Galilee; Scythopolis and Sebaste. The proximity of Gentile and Jewish areas meant that there was some interchange between them, including trade and exchange of populations. As such, Jewish merchants most likely spoke some Greek, but the primary language of Jews at this time was Aramaic, a Semitic language closely related to Hebrew.

Jewish-Gentile relations in the land were often uneasy because the Jews considered the land to be theirs. Owing to this constant state of uneasiness, Herod found it prudent to treat the Jewish and the Gentile parts of his kingdom differently, fostering Greco-Roman culture in Gentile sectors but introducing only very minor aspects of it in Jewish areas. The Roman emperor, Augustus, also permitted Jews to keep their own customs, even when they were antithetical to Greco-Roman culture. Furthermore, and in respect for Jewish observance of the Sabbath, Rome exempted Jews from conscription in Rome's armies.

Yeshua's life is generally documented in terms of his birth, baptism, ministry, crucifixion and resurrection. Accounts of his life have been recorded in what are known as gospels. The most widely known gospels are the four canonical gospels of Matthew, Mark, Luke, and John which are included in the New Testament of the Roman Catholic Bible. Matthew and John were two of Yeshua's twelve Apostles. Mark was a follower of Peter another of Yeshua's twelve and Luke was a doctor and friend of Saint Paul who is generally considered one of the most important figures of his age. During 30-50 AD, Paul founded several churches and took advantage of his status as both a Jew and a Roman citizen to minister to both Jewish and Gentile audiences alike.

All four canonical gospels, the only gospels accepted by the Catholic Church as genuine, are generally considered to have been written between 60-100 AD. Christianity places a high value on all four canonical gospels, which it considers to be revelations from God and central to its belief system. Christianity traditionally teaches that all four canonical gospels are an accurate and authoritative representation of the life of Yeshua, but many scholars and historians, as well as some liberal Christians, believe that much of what is contained in the gospels is not historically reliable. Yeshua's life is also recorded in the Qur'an, the central religious text of the faith of Islam. Indeed, he is mentioned more times in the Qur'an than Muhammad himself, the cardinal figure of Islam.

Yeshua's entire life is shrouded in mystery and his birth, and more particularly his conception, are no exception. Although born in Bethlehem, Yeshua was a Galilean from Nazareth which today is the largest city in the northern district of Israel. He was born to Joseph and Mary shortly before the death of Herod the Great.

The accounts of Yeshua's birth, report that Mary was a virgin when Yeshua was conceived. It is recounted that God sent the Angel Gabriel to Mary to inform her that she would conceive a male child, not by normal intercourse, but through the power of the Holy Spirit. In Christian lore, this is known as the Annunciation which came to pass while Mary still lived with her parents and during her betrothal to Joseph, the first stage of a Jewish marriage. Before coming together as husband and wife, Joseph found her already pregnant and decided to divorce Mary quietly so as not to bring her any shame. However, an angel appeared to Joseph in a dream and told him not to be afraid to take Mary as his wife. The angel told Joseph that Mary conceived of the Holy Spirit and that she would bear a son who would set his people free from their sins. Obeying the angel, Joseph and Mary formally completed the wedding rites and became man and wife.

At this time the Roman Caesar Augustus issued a decree that a census, the first of its kind, should be taken of the entire Roman Empire. The main purpose of the census was to ensure that everyone in the Empire was paying their taxes correctly. Unlike the rest of the empire, for Jews this meant that families had to register in their historical tribal town rather than where they resided. Joseph and the now very pregnant Mary would have had to travel from Nazareth to Bethlehem, a distance of seventy miles, as this was the town Joseph's family originally came from.

As many people traveled to Bethlehem for the census, by the time Joseph and Mary arrived, all the guest houses were full. Eventually they found refuge in an enclosure which housed animals. Whilst there, Joseph and Mary were visited by three wise men, or magi; considered of noble birth, educated, learned, wealthy and influential. Driven by their understanding of the messianic prophecies of the Old Testament and guided by a star which heralded the Messiah's birth, the three magi came to pay homage to Yeshua. The Old Testament is the first section of the Christian Bible, based primarily upon the Hebrew Bible (Tanakh), a collection of religious writings by ancient Israelites believed by most Christians and religious Jews to be the sacred Word of God. The prophecies identified Yeshua as the Messiah who would be King of the Jews.

Herod, on hearing the news, bade the three magi to send word of the Messiah's location so that he too could pay homage to the new king. Of course, King Herod had no intention of paying tribute to a usurper. He intended to slay this pretender to the throne. Mary, Joseph and the three magi were warned in a dream of King Herod's intention to slay Yeshua. The three magi avoided Jerusalem on their return home, and Joseph and Mary fled to Egypt. When no word came from the magi, Herod realized he had been outwitted and it is reported that he gave orders to kill all boys of the age of two and under in Bethlehem and its vicinity. Herod died soon after, around 4 BC. Upon hearing of his death, Mary and Joseph returned to Israel. According to some Islamic sources, Yeshua and his parents had remained in Egypt for twelve years. Upon their return to Israel and avoiding Bethlehem out of fear of Herod's successor, his son Herod Archelaus, they settled in Nazareth, Galilee, in the north. For now, Yeshua, the Messiah, the one who would be King of the Jews, had evaded Herod and his progeny.

The concept of the Messiah is important both in Christianity and Judaism. It was widely understood among the Jews at this time that several prophecies in the Old Testament promised a Messiah descended from King David who would deliver Israel from her enemies and usher in a new kingdom.

King David is regarded as one of the most important figures in Jewish history and most of what is known of him comes from biblical literature. He was born around 1040 BC in the town of Bethlehem and died at the age of seventy. It is told that he reigned as King of Israel for forty years and he was loved by his people. He is depicted as a great ruler and a valorous warrior of great renown. It is told that his piety was so great that his prayers could bring down things from heaven. Legend also has it that when war broke out between Israel and the Philistines, the Philistine ruler challenged the Israelites to single combat, the result of which would determine who was victorious. This was common practice at the time and was often employed to prevent widespread bloodshed. David, without armour, met the Philistine giant, Goliath, on the battlefield and killed him with a single shot from his sling. The Roman Catholic Church celebrates his feast day on 29th December.

The Psalms, writings in the third section of the Tanakh, record a promise from God to establish the seed of King David on his throne forever and the Jewish prophets Isaiah and Jeremiah speak of the future reign of a righteous king of the house of King David. The New Testament, the second major part of the Christian Bible, provides two accounts of the genealogy of Yeshua, one in the Gospel of Matthew and another in the Gospel of Luke. Matthew's account follows the lineage of Joseph and Luke's follows the lineage of Mary, both of which are shown to come from the Davidic royal line. In tracing Yeshua's lineage, the Gospels of Matthew and Luke hoped to demonstrate that Yeshua is indeed descendant from King David and that the messianic prophecies are thus fulfilled in him.

Those who believe Yeshua was not the prophesied Messiah, argue that Jewish law does not accept maternal ancestry in relation to lineage claims and thus Yeshua's ancestry must be established through his Father only. However, as Joseph is not the biological father, his lineage does not apply to Yeshua and there is no provision available within Jewish law for this to be altered. The faith of Islam which is not fettered by the restrictive view imposed by Jewish law, also considers David to be one of the major prophets sent by God to guide the Israelites, upholds the virgin birth of Yeshua and considers his genealogy only through Mary (Maryam), without mentioning his father Joseph.

Unfortunately, very little is known about Yeshua's childhood. After the age of twelve he was brought up in Galilee by both parents, where he was taught the craft of carpentry by his father Joseph. From all accounts, Yeshua was a precocious child. However, we are given very little information about this time of Yeshua's life from the canonical gospels. Only Luke (2:41-48) records a single event from when Yeshua was about twelve. Every year, both Joseph and Mary would go to Jerusalem to celebrate the feast of the Passover. This was customary according to Jewish religious beliefs and as Yeshua was now of age, he accompanied his parents to Jerusalem. However, on their return journey to Nazareth his parents realized he was missing so they returned to Jerusalem looking for him. *'After three days, they found him in the temple, sitting among the teachers, listening to them and asking questions. And all the people were amazed at his understanding and his answers.'* (Luke 2:46-47) When Joseph and Mary found him in the temple they were beside themselves with worry and chided the young Yeshua. He simply responded by saying; *'Why did you seek me? Did you not know that I must be about My Father's business?'* (Luke 2:49)

Similar to the canonical gospels of the New Testament, the Qur'an mentions Yeshua to have healed the blind and the lepers; *'I also heal the blind and the leper,'* and to have power over death *'and I bring to life the dead, by the permission of God.'* (Q 3.49) However, the Qur'an gives us further information regarding Yeshua's childhood. It records the miracle that Yeshua was able to speak from the cradle at only a few days old and is reported to have often done so to defend his mother from accusations of adultery. When Mary was approached about the miraculous virgin birth, it is reported that she merely pointed to the infant Yeshua, and he miraculously spoke, just as God had promised her upon Annunciation; *'He shall speak to people while still in the cradle, and in manhood, and he shall be from the righteous.'* (Q 3.46) Indeed, Yeshua is reported as having said to his mother as an infant; *'I am Yeshua, the Son of God, the Logos, whom thou hast brought forth, as the Angel Gabriel announced to thee; and my Father has sent me for the salvation of the world.'* It is reported that he further spoke to the people saying; *'I am indeed a servant of God. He has given me revelation and made me a Prophet... so peace is on me the day I was born, the day that I die, and on the day that I shall be raised up to life (again).'* (Q 19.30-33)

During Yeshua's time in Egypt, many more miracles were chronicled including raising the dead. Although no mention of these miracles is recorded in the four canonical gospels, accounts can be found not only in the Qur'an but in the many non-canonical gospels, some of which were dedicated to recording events during Yeshua's infancy and which became known as the non-canonical infancy gospels. Many of these non-canonical gospels were discovered near Nag Hammadi, Egypt, in December 1945, among a group of books known as the Nag Hammadi Library. For example, the Qur'an mentions a miracle which resonates with how God Himself created Adam; *'I create for you out of clay the likeness of a bird, then I breathe into it and it becomes a bird with God's permission.'* (Q 3.49) This miracle is also found in the non-canonical Infancy Gospel of Thomas; *'Yeshua when he was five years old was playing at the ford of a brook. Having made soft clay, he fashioned thereof twelve sparrows. And it was the Sabbath when he made them. And when a certain Jew saw what Yeshua did, playing upon the Sabbath day, departed straightway and told his father Joseph: Lo, thy child is at the brook, and he hath taken clay and fashioned twelve little birds, and hath polluted the Sabbath day. And Joseph came to the place and saw. He cried out to him, saying: Wherefore doest thou these things on the Sabbath, which it is not lawful to do? But Yeshua clapped his hands together and cried out to the sparrows and said to them: Go! And the sparrows took their flight and went away chirping. And when the Jews saw it they were amazed, and departed and told their chief men that which they had seen Yeshua do.'*

Al-Tabari (839–923 AD), a prominent and influential Persian scholar, historian and exegete of the Qur'an recounts that when Yeshua was about nine or ten years old, his mother Mary sent him to a Jewish religious school. But whenever the teacher tried to teach him anything, he found that Yeshua already knew it. Al-Tabari further relates that when Yeshua was in his youth, his mother committed him to the priests to study the Torah. While Yeshua played with the youths of his village, he used to tell them what their parents were doing, eating and what food they have kept for them when they return home. He would say, "Go home, for your parents have kept for you such and such food and they are now eating such and such food." As parents became annoyed by this, they forbade their children to play with Yeshua, saying, "Do not play with that magician."

Based upon several Hadith narrations of Muhammad, a physical description of Yeshua as a young man can be gleaned. A Hadith is one of various reports describing the words, actions, or habits of the Islamic prophet Muhammad. Hadith are second only to the

Qur'an in developing Islamic jurisprudence, and regarded as important tools for understanding the Qur'an and commentaries written on it. According to these sources, Yeshua grew to be a well-built man of average height and with a broad chest. He had lank, slightly curly, long hair that fell between his shoulders and was of fair complexion of finest brown. It is generally agreed that he spoke Aramaic, the common language of Judea and the region at large in the first century AD.

As a young adult, Yeshua went to be baptized by the prophet John the Baptist near the river Jordan and shortly thereafter became an itinerant preacher and healer - (Mark 1:2–28). Luke (3:23) also intimates that Yeshua was about thirty years of age at the beginning of his ministry. A chronology of his life typically estimates the beginning of his ministry at around 27-29 AD. The Gospel of John refers to three Passovers, suggesting that Yeshua's ministry lasted approximately three years but some believe it was much shorter than this. In any case, the New Testament presents John the Baptist, whom Luke intimates is a cousin of Yeshua, as the precursor to Yeshua and the Baptism of Yeshua as marking the beginning of Yeshua's ministry. During his ministry, the tetrarch ruling over Galilee and Perea was Herod Antipas, who obtained the position upon the division of his father's kingdom, Herod the Great, into four parts, after his death in 4 BC.

It is generally understood that Yeshua began preaching near Galilee where he grew up. During this time, he recruited his first disciples who traveled with him and who eventually formed the core of the early Church. Yeshua eventually recruited twelve disciples in total. According to Christianity, the names of the twelve disciples were Peter, Andrew, James, John, Philip, Bartholomew, Thomas, Matthew, James, Jude, Simon and Judas.

The four canonical gospels are probably the greatest source of the teachings of Yeshua. From these gospels we learn that Yeshua spoke of the love God has for all of his people. He told us that we should love one another, to be our brother's keeper, and that we should treat our neighbour as we would wish to be treated. He spoke of the coming of the Kingdom of God and how we should prepare ourselves for its coming. Yeshua often spoke to the people in parables in order to explain his message and the four canonical gospels contain many of these parables which indeed form a large portion of his recorded teachings. During his ministry, he journeyed across Judea and Galilee, traveling from town to town, preaching in the synagogues, in people's houses and on the country hillsides, spreading his moral teachings.

Yeshua also performed many miracles during his ministry, including healing lepers, curing the blind, the crippled and the deaf. It's also documented that he demonstrated control over the elements of nature, and the gospels record miracles such as Yeshua walking on water and calming storms. Yeshua's teachings, parables and miracles attracted considerable attention not only among the people to whom he preached and who were growing in number every day, but also among the Jewish religious elite, the tetrarch Herod Antipas and the governing Roman prefect who was ultimately responsible for keeping the peace in the region.

The Jews of the first century, living in the shadow of Herod and under the heel of the Roman Empire, longed for the promised messianic kingdom. The first century Jewish historian Josephus and the Roman historian Tacitus, both attest to the fervour of Jewish messianic anticipation during this time. It was in this charged atmosphere of occupation and anticipation that Yeshua claimed that he was sent to free his people and that the Kingdom of God was at hand. The Jews anticipated this glorious messianic reign where the promised Messiah would rule all nations *'with a rod of iron'*. The people were constantly told by their Rabbis, Jewish spiritual teachers, how the Messiah would overthrow the enemies of Israel, and all the peoples of the world would know that the God of Israel was the true God. Maybe, just maybe, this miracle-working carpenter from Nazareth really was the great warrior King promised. If Yeshua was the Messiah, then their deliverance was near.

In Matthew (11:2-6), two messengers from John the Baptist arrive to ask Yeshua if he is indeed the expected Messiah or *'should we wait for another?'* Yeshua does not confirm that he is the Messiah but rather replies; *'Go back and report to John what you hear and see: the blind see, the lame walk and the lepers are made clean.'*

Then Yeshua did the impossible. During his ministry Yeshua received a message that his friend Lazarus was sick and was in need of healing. Lazarus was from Bethany about two miles from Jerusalem and lived with his sisters Mary and Martha. When Yeshua heard the news, rather than going immediately to Bethany he stayed where he was for another two days. Only then did he journey to Bethany. When he arrived, Yeshua found that Lazarus was already dead and had been in the tomb for four days. Upon his arrival, Martha said to him; *'Lord, if you had been here, my brother would not have died. But I know that whatever you ask from God, God will give you.'* (John 11:21-22) Yeshua goes to the tomb and requests that the stone be taken away. He then lifts his eyes skyward and says; *'Father, I thank you for you have heard me. I know that you hear me always; but my prayer was for the sake of these people, that they may believe that you sent me.'* (John 11:41-42) Yeshua then cried in a loud voice; *'Lazarus, come out!'* The dead man came out, his hands and feet bound with linen strips and his face wrapped in a cloth. So Yeshua said to them; *'Untie him and let him go.'* (John 11:43-44)

As Bethany was so close to Jerusalem, many had come to offer consolation to Lazarus's family. Crowds of people had now witnessed firsthand a truly great miracle and word of it spread quickly to Jerusalem and the surrounding area. Yeshua became known to his many followers as Jesus Christ or the Christ, the term Christ being derived from the Greek word Christos which means 'the anointed one' (as in a king) or 'meshiah' (Messiah) in Hebrew. This title given to Yeshua reveals that his followers now believed him to be the Messiah, descendant from the line of King David, whom many expected would liberate them from Roman rule and restore Israel to greatness.

Yeshua's final ministry ends in Jerusalem where he enters the city to a rapturous crowd. Thousands of believers lined the road to Jerusalem cheering that the Son of David, the King of Israel, had finally arrived. The Jewish religious leaders were appalled. They asked Yeshua to tell the crowds to stop this nonsense. He refused. Instead he antagonised them by preaching in the temple and criticizing their hypocrisy. This is followed by the cleansing of the temple where Yeshua expels, by force, the money changers and those selling their wares, accusing them of turning the temple into a den of thieves through their commercial activities.

The Jewish religious elite had enough and decided to get rid of this would-be Messiah. They hatched their plans behind closed doors as they were afraid of the multitude of followers which always surrounded Yeshua. They decided to wait until after the Passover when most of his followers would leave Jerusalem and return to their homes. What the Jewish leaders were unaware of was that they were to be presented with a gilt-edged opportunity to have Yeshua arrested, tried, convicted and put to death by crucifixion. This opportunity was to be given to them by Judas Iscariot, one of Yeshua's twelve Apostles. This part of Yeshua's ministry is often referred to as The Passion Week. Indeed, the four canonical gospels devote about one-third of their text to this seven-day period of his life.

Before his arrest, Yeshua had a final meal with his friends and apostles, known appropriately as The Last Supper. At this meal, Yeshua gave final instructions to his friends. He confirmed to them that he would be betrayed by one of them and put to death, but that he would rise again. This caused great confusion and upset among his disciples. When the meal was finished, Yeshua, together with three of his apostles went to the Garden of Gethsemane which is just outside the city of Jerusalem. There he prayed. Night had fallen. While he was there, Judas went to the Jewish elders and informed them that Yeshua was now alone and that he would lead them to him. In return for this service the elders agreed to pay him thirty pieces of silver. Judas led a contingent of the Jewish Temple guard and located Yeshua in the garden. Judas identified Yeshua with a kiss. They bound Yeshua's hands and led him away. Again, behind closed doors, Yeshua was tried by the Sanhedrin, the highest court or tribunal of the Jews, and convicted of heresy.

However, the Sanhedrin knew that they were not allowed by law to put a man to death and that this type of punishment was only permitted by Roman law. Yeshua was therefore brought before the prelate and Roman governor, Pontius Pilate, and accused of stirring up the people and causing great unrest by claiming to be the King of the Jews. This charge could not go unpunished as it was a direct challenge to Caesar himself. Yeshua did not defend himself against any of the charges brought against him. He was convicted, beaten severely, made carry his cross through the streets of Jerusalem where he was constantly beaten, humiliated and ultimately nailed to the cross where he died in agonizing pain.

Instead of throwing his dead body into a nearby pit with all the other dead who had been crucified, Yeshua was placed in a private tomb. It was reported that sometime later, approximately a day and a half after his death, he rose from the dead. His eleven disciples became convinced that he still lived and indeed claimed he had appeared to them on more than one occasion. They spread the belief that Yeshua was alive, that he had risen from the dead, that he had conquered death. Armed with their beliefs, they converted others to belief in him. This belief took root and spread rapidly. This belief eventually led to the birth of a new religion, Christianity, one of the world's major religions.

Although there is a plethora of sources dedicated to the question of whether Yeshua existed at all, most modern historians agree that Yeshua existed and consider his baptism and crucifixion historical events, the timing of which can be closely estimated. However, they do not agree about the beliefs and teachings of Yeshua as well as the accuracy of the details of his life that have been described in the four canonical gospels which are generally considered by historians to be written as theological rather than historical documents. Therefore, for one reason or another, the authenticity and reliability of these sources have always been questioned and few events mentioned in the gospels are universally accepted. In particular, elements whose historical authenticity are disputed include the accounts of the nativity of Yeshua, certain details about the crucifixion, and many of the miraculous events including turning water into wine, walking on water and the resurrection.

If this is the view of most historians, what do the world's major religions think of this trouble maker? Most Christians consider Yeshua to be the Christ, the long awaited Messiah, as well as the one and only Son of God. Christians in general believe that the four canonical gospels recount actual historical events and that Yeshua's miraculous works were an important part of his life, attesting to his divinity and hypostatic union. Hypostatic union is a technical term in Christian theology to describe the union of Yeshua's humanity and divinity in a single individual existence. In other words, Christians think that Yeshua is God or as they would say, the Son of God. They believe that while Yeshua's experiences of hunger, weariness and death were evidences of his humanity, the miracles were evidences of his deity.

Christianity takes this idea even further and advocates the doctrine of the Trinity which holds that God is three consubstantial persons – the Father, the Son (Yeshua), and the Holy Spirit – one God in three Divine Persons. According to this central mystery of Christianity, there is one God in three persons: while distinct from one another in their relations of origin and in their relations with one another, they are stated to be one in all else, co-equal, co-eternal and consubstantial, and each is God, whole and entire. It is believed that Yeshua rose from the dead, ascended into heaven to sit at the right hand of God, and that he will return to earth again (The Second Coming) for the Last Judgment and to establish the Kingdom of God here on earth.

In Islam, Yeshua (Isa) is considered one of God's greatest and most-beloved prophets, the penultimate prophet and messenger of Allah (God) and the precursor to the prophet Muhammad, the greatest prophet in the Islamic faith. Yeshua is considered a Muslim who by definition is anyone who submits to the will of God. Islam does not consider Yeshua to be divine and they reject the Christian doctrine of the trinity of gods. Islam traditionally regards all prophets, including Yeshua, to be mortal without any share in divinity. They believe in one God only. (Q 4.171)

According to Islamic scriptures, the belief that Yeshua is God or the Son of God is shirk; the practicing of idolatry or polytheism. Islam recognizes Yeshua's miracles and his virgin birth which they consider demonstrates the power of God rather than the divinity of Yeshua. Muslim tradition believes that Yeshua was sent by God with a new revelation or gospel. Many, however, hold the view that Yeshua's original message was lost or altered and that the Christian New Testament does not accurately relate God's original message to mankind. It is also believed that Yeshua was neither killed nor crucified, but that God made it appear so to his enemies, and that he ascended bodily into heaven and is alive. Muslim tradition also believes that Yeshua will return to earth near the day of judgment to restore justice, champion the cause of Islam and to defeat the **al-Masih ad-Dajjal** or the **false Messiah**, also known as the **Antichrist**.

Apart from Yeshua's own disciples and followers, the Jews of his time, and indeed today, generally reject him as the Messiah. Furthermore, Judaism's idea of the Messiah differs substantially from the Christian view. The Jewish faith advocates that the coming of the Messiah will be associated with a specific series of events which will usher in an age of peace and understanding during which 'the knowledge of God' will fill the earth. Jews believe Yeshua died without completing these tasks and although references to him and his execution exist in the Talmud (a central religious work of the Jewish people), they aim to discredit his actions rather than deny his existence.

Judaism has never accepted any of the claimed fulfillments of prophecy that Christianity attributes to Yeshua. In fact, among followers of Judaism, Yeshua is viewed as having been the most influential, and consequently the most damaging, of all false Messiahs. As the central belief of Judaism is in the absolute unity and singularity of God, the idea of Yeshua being God, the Son of God or a person of a trinity of gods is heretical and the worship of a person is a form of idolatry. The *Mishneh Torah*, an authoritative work of Jewish law, states that Yeshua is a stumbling block who makes the majority of the world err to serve a divinity besides God. They believe the first one to have adopted this plan was Yeshua, and Jewish leaders of the time, having become aware of his plans before his reputation spread, meted out fitting punishment to him.

The Bahá'í Faith consider Yeshua as a bridge between a perfect and transcendent God on the one hand and humanity and the physical world on the other. Although their explanation is somewhat complicated, their faith basically views Yeshua as a divine messenger rather than a God. In Scientology, the teachings of Yeshua are considered to be earlier forms of belief systems and Yeshua is classified as below the level of Operating Thetan, but as a shade above the Scientology state of Clear. In Raëlism, Yeshua and several other religious figures are considered prophets sent by an extra-terrestrial race called the Elohim. Followers of Religious Science consider Yeshua to be a teacher of the Science of Mind principles, but reject he is the only son of God, arguing that every person is equally divine. Other world religions such as Buddhism, having but a minor intersection with Christianity, have no particular view on Yeshua. However, some scholars have noted similarities between the life and teachings of Gautama Buddha and Yeshua.

Irrespective of both religious and non-religious perspectives on Yeshua, all of which can vary quite substantially, Yeshua's teachings and the retelling of his life story have significantly influenced the course of human history, and have directly or indirectly affected the lives of billions of people including non-Christians. He is considered by many to be the most influential person to have ever lived.

Of course, none of this is important, not even Yeshua. What is important is what he did. You must understand, the opinion held by the Jewish faith that Yeshua is a stumbling block to their beliefs is indeed correct. What they failed to understand, however, is that Yeshua is not only a stumbling block to their beliefs but to all forms of belief. Yeshua's task was to destroy belief in its totality and in its place to establish the knowledge based system, which he referred to as the Kingdom of God. *'The days will come when there shall not be left one stone upon another of all that you now admire; all will be torn down.'* (Luke 21:6)

It was Yeshua's plan to achieve this by undertaking two ministries. The first was the creation of the Grail allowing us to open our eyes to the truth and re-enter the knowledge based system. This was his message of good news and this is how he was going to set his people free; free from imprisonment within the belief based system.

He achieved this by creating the Grail, the gate through which we can pass from the belief based system into the knowledge based system, the Kingdom of God, our home. This is what Yeshua meant when he said; *'I am the gate. Whoever enters through me will be saved.'* (John 10:9) His second ministry was a teaching on how to live and love each other; *'Now I give you a new commandment: love one another just as I have loved you.'* (John 13:34 & 15:12) The purpose of the secondary ministry was to keep us alive, as a species, long enough that one day we would come to recognize the Grail and not only understand how to use it but to have the courage to do so.

Before I explain how to use the Grail, and to fully understand why it was necessary to create it in the first place, one must first be aware of how we were created.

In the beginning we knew the truth. We knew who and what we are, the guardians and custodians of all creation. We knew we were made equal and in the image of the Source, the Creator, Our Father. Later, we were offered a choice; we could accept the truth we were given, or we could believe whatever we wanted to believe. We were told that choosing to believe whatever we wanted to believe would set us free. It would open our eyes and allow us to create the world in our image. We were deceived.

Instead of opening our eyes, it closed them, plunging us into darkness: after all, one cannot truly choose to believe what they want to believe unless they are in complete darkness. *'Because our eyes were closed we could no longer see the truth; we have eyes that don't see.'* (Mark 8:18) We no longer knew the Father. This sin has been handed down from generation to generation.

Please understand that this is a complex issue which I am trying to describe using words that are deeply rooted in the belief based system. This story is not meant in any way to support the idea of creationism over evolution. If it helps, think of it like this; we have not been created but rather we are being created. After all, ultimately the only real significant difference between these two points of view is time.

Choosing the belief based system over the knowledge based system was our first sin; the original sin. To live in the belief based system is to live without knowledge of the Source, the Source from which all life springs. Do not give ear to those who claim to know what sin is and then when they are asked, they give you endless examples rather than a clear definition. These are not sins but rather are simply actions perpetrated by one who is leading a sinful life, i.e. one who has closed their eyes to the truth, the Source. Sin is not an action or inaction; it is a state of being. To live in the belief based system is the definition of sin. According to this definition of sin we now know who among us are living sinfully (all of us) and who among us are living without sin (none of us). I guess we can all stop pointing fingers now! Nevertheless, the day will come when we will be given an opportunity to atone for this original sin, reversing its affect by opening our eyes and allowing us to make the choice of accepting the truth and returning to the knowledge based system.

We will not be expected to make this choice until we again see the truth. We were shown how to open our eyes again allowing us the opportunity to make this choice. We can open our eyes by invoking the power of the Grail. Showing us how to do this was the primary mission of the Christ. When you have invoked the power of the Grail you will see the truth allowing you to make the choice of accepting the truth or again to close your eyes to the truth and choose to believe whatever you want to believe. This is your choice. Please let me be clear. You cannot choose to believe and know at the same time; this is impossible. One's eyes cannot be open and closed at the same time.

One of the greatest barriers to entering the knowledge based system will be your current belief based system, whatever that may be. If you choose the truth you must accept it completely. This means you must accept that this life is a mirage. Please let me be clear. I do not promise you eternal happiness, I only promise you the truth. You may hold certain things in this life very dearly and passionately, but these will need to be relinquished if you wish to enter the knowledge based system.

So how is the power of the Grail invoked? What do we have to do to earn passage through the gate? The instructions of how to invoke the Grail's power were put in a prayer. This prayer was given to us by Yeshua, the creator of the Grail. For those of you who don't know the prayer, here it is:

Our Father, who art in heaven,

Hallowed be Thy Name;

Thy kingdom come,

Thy will be done,

on earth as it is in heaven.

Give us this day our daily bread,

and ***forgive us our trespasses,***

as(because) we forgive those who trespass against us;

and lead us not into temptation,

but deliver us from evil. Amen.

I have put the message of how to invoke the power of the Grail in bold italics. This is where the message has been hidden, in clear view, unmoved and unused for the last two-thousand years. Surprised? So was I. Please understand, the Grail (the gate) requires two steps which must be undertaken step-by-step. First you must forgive and then you must be forgiven. The first step is a mirror image of the second step; '*And when you stand to pray, forgive whatever you may hold against anyone, so that your divine Father may also forgive your sins.*' (Mark 11:25) When you have completed both steps in the correct order, your eyes will be opened, allowing you to pass through the gate and enter the knowledge based system. As this point is of paramount importance, let me re-state it. You must complete the steps in this order; '*For if you forgive men their trespasses, your Heavenly Father will also forgive you. But if you do not forgive men their trespasses, neither will your Father forgive yours.*' (Matthew 6:15)

Chapter Four

Forgiveness and Repentance Vol. 1

Some say that forgiveness is different for everyone. Some say that forgiveness is about moral development. Some say that the examination of forgiveness should be left to the clergy. The truth is that everyone has their own idea of what it means to forgive, but they can't all be right, can they? Of course not, otherwise the act of forgiveness would be indeterminate, confusing and vague at best. So, what is forgiveness and how do I forgive?

I have found that the biggest hurdle to successful communication in the belief based system is the misunderstanding that one has in fact communicated. To help avoid this happening, I believe that all parties should first define the critical words they use during communication. If we fail to do this, one party may have, in their mind, defined a crucial word in one way and a second party may have defined the same word in another way. In this case, if both parties end up in agreement, it would be by mere chance only. To obviate this possibility, the critical words in the question, "What is forgiveness and how do I forgive?" must be defined in some way. The critical words of course are forgiveness and forgive. Let us define the former word as the process of forgiving and thus, we only need to define what is meant by the word forgive.

Both the need and desire to forgive are widely recognized, but people are, more often than not, at a loss as to how to accomplish the act of forgiveness. For thousands of years, religion, in all its forms, has been the main proponent of forgiveness. In fact, one might even go as far as to say that they monopolised the whole process. In years gone by, if you wanted to know how to forgive, your only option was to go to a priest or other form of religious leader, and history has shown us that you would be left in no doubt as to how one should forgive. As such, it would be natural to consider them experts in the field and thus an ideal place to begin to understand what the word forgive means. Therefore, let us consider how the major religions of the world define the word and understand the process.

In Judaism, a person who has harmed another must go to the victim, sincerely apologise and try to rectify the wrong he has done in order to be entitled to forgiveness. In this case, the wronged individual is encouraged to forgive; *'It is forbidden to be obdurate and not allow yourself to be appeased. On the contrary, one should be easily pacified and find it difficult to become angry. When asked by an offender for forgiveness, one should forgive with a sincere mind and a willing spirit.'* (Mishneh Torah, Teshuvah 2:10)

The doctrine of forgiveness is considered central to Judaism, and Rabbinic Jewish literature contains extensive discussions on the subject where it is often considered necessary for the attainment of salvation. Due to its critical nature, Jews observe a Day of Atonement known as Yom Kippur which is probably the most important holiday of the Jewish year. Prior to this day, Jews will ask forgiveness of those they have wronged during the preceding year, if they have not already done so. This is important because their faith teaches them that a person cannot obtain forgiveness from God for wrongs the person has done to other people; only the person who has been wronged can forgive. The corollary is also true; God can only forgive those sins which are committed against him.

During Yom Kippur, Jews fast and also pray for God's forgiveness for the transgressions they have made against God in the previous year. According to Leviticus 23:27 (third book of the Old Testament), sincere repentance is required; '*In the seventh month, on the tenth day of the month, you shall afflict your souls, and you shall not do any work... For on that day he shall provide atonement for you to cleanse you from all your sins before the LORD.*' Sincere repentance is manifested when temptation to commit the same sin, under the same conditions, is ever after resolutely resisted. In essence, Yom Kippur is a day set aside to 'afflict the soul' to atone for the sins of the past year. The day is understood to be one's last appeal, one's last chance to change God's judgment against them for their sins of the past year, and to demonstrate repentance and make amends which are believed to be a prerequisite of atonement.

According to the Torah, offenses against man require, in addition to confession and sacrifice, restitution in full of whatever has been wrongfully obtained or withheld from one's fellow man, with one-fifth of its value added thereto.

(Lev 5:20-26) The idea of restitution by the wrong-doer is essential in the forgiveness process. If the wronged man has died, restitution must be made to his heir. If he has no heir, some form of offering must be given to the priest who officiates at the sacrifice made for the remission of the sin. (Num 5:7-9)

Islam teaches us that Allah is *Al-Ghāfir,* The Forgiver, and is the source of all forgiveness. Islam advocates forgiveness because Allah values forgiveness and there are numerous verses in the Qur'an and the Hadiths which recommend forgiveness. However, although the entire chapter nine of the Qur'an (At-Tauba) is dedicated to the topic of repentance, the process is not clear. Furthermore, the teaching on forgiveness can sometimes be somewhat vague and duplicitous at times. For example, the Qur'an teaches us that the *'recompense for an injury is an injury equal thereto: but if a person forgives and makes reconciliation, his reward is due from Allah.'* (Q 42.40) The Qur'an also associates restitution with repentance. (Q 3.89) Therefore, it would appear that Islam teaches us that both restitution and a sincere attempt at reconciliation are required in the forgiveness process.

The word *tawbah* (repentance) is also mentioned in the Qur'an. In an Islamic context, it refers to the act of leaving behind what Allah has prohibited and to taking up again that which he has commanded. The act of repentance can redeem sins and give the opportunity to go to heaven; *'O you who have believed, repent to Allah with sincere repentance. Perhaps your Lord will remove from you your misdeeds and admit you into gardens beneath which rivers flow [on] the Day when Allah will not disgrace the Prophet and those who believed with him. Their light will proceed before them and on their right; they will say, Our Lord, perfect for us our light and forgive us. Indeed, You are over all things.'* (Q 66.8)

It appears, however, that the Qur'an does not advocate forgiveness in all circumstances. Whilst it is encouraged that Muslims should treat other Muslims with forbearance, tolerance and forgiveness, the dispensation of forgiveness is not necessarily required in the relationship between Muslims and non-Muslims. For example, forgiveness is not recommended against infidels, apostates, and blasphemous people. (Q 9.5-8) There are even situations where Allah himself will refuse to grant forgiveness. For example, where one continues to reject their faith in Islam (Q 4.137) or where one commits the act of shirk, which is the sin of practicing idolatry or polytheism, i.e. the worship of anyone or anything other than the singular God, Allah; *'Indeed, Allah does not forgive association with Him, but He forgives what is less than that for whom He wills. And he who associates others with Allah has certainly fabricated a tremendous sin.'* (Q 4.48)

In Buddhism, forgiveness is viewed in a more practical way. Buddhism recognizes that negative feelings such as anger, hate, shame and regret can have a harmful effect on our peace of mind and our physical wellbeing. Forgiveness is practiced to remove such harmful thoughts and feelings, and to encourage the cultivation of positive thoughts that produce positive feelings which have a wholesome and nourishing effect on both body and mind. The forgiveness process, as practiced by Buddhists, centers on release from suffering through meditation. Buddhism also questions the reality of the passions that make forgiveness necessary as well as the reality of the objects of those passions[10]. *'If we haven't forgiven, we keep creating an identity around our pain, and that is what is reborn. That is what suffers.'* [11] Buddhism places much emphasis on the concepts of *Mettā* (loving kindness), *karuna* (compassion), *mudita* (sympathetic joy), and *upekkhā* (equanimity), as a means of avoiding negative feelings in the first place. These conceptual reflections are used to understand the context of suffering in the world, both our own and the suffering of others.

The theological basis for forgiveness in Hinduism is similar to what motivates the Buddhist. The Hindu believes that a person who does not forgive will carry a heavy load of negative feelings and unresolved detrimental emotions that will adversely affect the person's present and future wellbeing. Forgiveness in Hinduism does not necessarily require that one reconcile with the offender, but rather it is about being compassionate, kind and the letting go of the hurt caused by the offender. Hindu philosophy regards forgiveness as essential to free oneself from negative thoughts so that a happy, moral and ethical life can be had. In Hinduism, one is encouraged not only to forgive others, but also to seek forgiveness from anyone that they may have wronged. Forgiveness is to be sought from the wronged individual as well as society at large, by acts of charity, purification, fasting, rituals and meditative introspection. *Holi*, which is a Hindu festival also known as the *festival of colours*, is celebrated in spring. Both young and old celebrate by dancing, laughing and smearing each other with coloured powder. Traditionally, this is also a day to mark forgiveness and to mend broken relationships.

As with other religions, the concept of forgiveness is oftentimes inconsistent in Hindu philosophy and in some Hindu texts[12] certain sins, for example murder, rape and intentional acts are debated as naturally unforgivable. It is argued whether blanket forgiveness is morally justifiable in every circumstance, and whether forgiveness encourages crime, disrespect and social disorder. The concept of forgiveness is further complicated in Hinduism by its expression in the feminine form through Lakshmi (the Hindu Goddess of wealth, called Goddess Sri in some parts of India) and the masculine form through her husband Vishnu. The feminine form expresses forgiveness even when the one who does wrong does not repent, but the masculine form, on the other hand, forgives only when the wrong-doer repents. In Hinduism, the feminine form of forgiveness granted without repentance is considered superior and nobler than the masculine forgiveness granted only after there is repentance. Nevertheless, forgiveness is considered one of the five cardinal virtues in Hinduism, together with temperance, prudence, courage and justice. It is interesting to note, however, that both forgiveness and justice, which are often seen as incompatible in the secular world, are both viewed in equally high regard by the Hindu religion.

In the Bahá'í Faith, the following explanation is given of how to be forgiving toward others;

> '*Love the creatures for the sake of God and not for themselves. You will never become angry or impatient if you love them for the sake of God. Humanity is not perfect. There are imperfections in every human being, and you will always become unhappy if you look toward the people themselves. But if you look toward God, you will love them and be kind to them, for the world of God is the world of perfection and complete mercy. Therefore, do not look at the shortcomings of anybody; see with the sight of forgiveness.*'[13]

In Jainism, forgiveness is viewed as an essential virtue and one which needs to be cultivated. One appeals for forgiveness by uttering the phrase, *micchāmi dukkadam*, which is a Prakrit language phrase meaning '*may all the evil that has been done be fruitless.*' As a matter of ritual, people of this faith personally greet their friends and relatives with the words *micchāmi dukkadam*. In their daily prayers and samayika (Jain meditation), Jains recite *Iryavahi Sutra* (Jain Mantra) seeking forgiveness from all creatures.

The Christian faith also says that forgiveness is a good thing to do. But good for whom and what makes it a good thing to do? Forgive because God asks you to do so. Who is this God I have never met and do not know and why would he ask me to forgive? Forgive because it's morally right. What does that even mean and who cares?

When the disciple Peter asked Yeshua; '*Lord, how many times must I forgive the offenses of my brother? Up to seven times? Yeshua replied, No, not seven times, but seventy times seven.'* (Matthew 18:21-22) Yeshua's entire message was one of forgiveness, to forgive without limits, and thus forgiveness is central to the Christian faith and is a frequent topic in sermons and theological works.

It is not uncommon to hear in these somewhat vague sermons that we are saved by grace through the redeeming sacrifice of Jesus Christ. When one sins, one must repent and confess the sin and believe by faith that they are forgiven. Therefore, it is considered the duty of all Christians to forgive even when forgiveness is not deserved. One might even say that forgiveness is not an option to a Christian but rather one must forgive to be a Christian. The process of forgiveness however is not unexpectedly obscure. Whilst the Christian Bible, and commentaries there on, are quite vocal on the why of this topic they are rather ambiguous regarding the how. It is often referred to by proponents of this faith as 'the mystery of forgiveness.'

In general, if you are a religious person, you may yearn for God's forgiveness. Indeed, this may be the case even if you do not subscribe to any religion. However, how will you know if, or when, God has forgiven you? If we are simply to believe that our sins are forgiven once we have confessed and repented, it appears that blind faith or belief is also an essential step in the process of forgiveness as defined by religious doctrine. Otherwise, how can one tell when they are forgiven? Furthermore, and equally as important, when can one tell when they themselves have truly forgiven?

Okay, let us consider what the academics in this area have to say.

Academic sources often endeavor to define what is meant by the word forgiveness which I believe is of paramount importance before one embarks on the process itself. The American Psychological Association describes forgiveness as the intentional and voluntary process by which a victim undergoes a change in feelings and attitude regarding an offense, lets go of negative emotions such as vengefulness, with an increased ability to wish the offender well[14]. Psychologists generally define forgiveness as a conscious, deliberate decision to release feelings of resentment or vengeance toward a person or group who has harmed you, regardless of whether they actually deserve your forgiveness[15].

When you delve further and ask the question, "What is forgiveness?" it is not unusual that you will be answered in the negative, i.e. you will be told what it isn't. You may be told that forgiveness does not mean denying the seriousness of the offense, condoning the offense, or indeed justifying the offense, pretending that the offense never happened or indeed forgetting that it ever happened in the first place. You may also be told that forgiveness does not necessarily require reconciliation and in some cases where the offender continues to offend, any attempt at reconciliation may be strictly advised against. Instead, forgiveness is described as the healing of ourselves by replacing negative feelings, thoughts and behaviors associated with the perpetrator and their act with their positive equivalent. For example, when we forgive someone, we replace the thoughts of revenge with goodwill toward, or at least acceptance of, the offender.

If you care to look, you will find a plethora of sources, including courses, lectures, books and academic papers about the process of forgiveness, many of which propose challenging your perspective and expound the practice of empathy, compassion, meditation, prayer and mindfulness. What all these sources have in common is a desire to help the victim let go of, or cope with, negative thoughts and emotions associated with abuse or a wrong they suffered at the hands of another.

A book I found of particular interest was *Forgiveness Is A Choice*[16] by Dr Robert D Enright. Dr Enright is a licensed psychologist, professor of educational psychology at the University of Wisconsin, Madison, USA, and founder of the International Forgiveness Institute.

Much of Enright's research has focused on people who forgive the seemingly unforgivable. He gives many examples of people who have forgiven, and the book follows their journeys through the forgiveness process. When Dr Enright first got interested in forgiveness, his colleagues thought he'd lost his mind. "How can a scientist study something so fluffy?" he recalls them saying. Although this is a cutting indictment of our understanding of the forgiveness process, it is not, I'm sure you will agree, entirely unfair. Nevertheless, after decades of study and research in this area which he considers to be a subset of moral development, Enright developed a model for the forgiveness process which he sees as a journey through four phases.

1. Uncovering your anger

During this phase, one faces the pain that they have experienced, pain which may have been repressed for many years. They finally face the true emotional stress they have suffered and how this has affected their life.

2. Deciding to Forgive

Here, one is forced to face the immutable fact that what they have previously being doing to cope with their pain has not worked. The nature of forgiveness is discussed, the victim commits to the decision to forgive and to embark on the forgiveness process rather than continuing to focus exclusively on his/her suffering.

3. Working on Forgiveness

One is encouraged to accept, but not condone, the pain he has suffered, no matter how undeserved. An effort is made to work toward empathy and compassion and the focus of the process is shifted from the victim to the perpetrator in an effort to gain insight and understanding. It is hoped at the end of this phase, that the victim will have evolved emotionally to the point where they could consider giving the offender a gift as part of their healing process. Enright does admit, however, that such beneficence may take a long time to achieve.

4. **Discovery and Release from Emotional Prison**

The victim moves toward resolution, becoming aware that he or she is not alone, and finds meaning, purpose and healing in the forgiveness process. At this stage, the victim will no longer feel controlled by their pain.

Within these four phases Enright has further identified twenty guideposts which are flexible and do not necessarily have to be addressed in a specific order. Indeed, some of the guide posts may not apply to everyone as he admits that "the forgiveness process is not rigidly fixed" because we do not all forgive in the same way. He also says that "because each person's experience is uniquely individual, each person's forgiveness process will also be uniquely individual", and therefore, the forgiveness process is largely different for everyone.

Enright teaches that the forgiveness process is a gradual change rather than a onetime event and he recommends keeping a journal of your progress to which he gives ten principles which would be helpful in keeping the journal. He says that a person may forgive at one level and then months or even years later get angry all over again, therefore suggesting that the forgiveness process can take some time, is not a quick fix and indeed, that there are levels of forgiveness.

Enright, although very thorough, does confess that the forgiveness model is not carved in stone but rather is the product of his observation of what works. He sees forgiveness not only as a practical matter but as a moral imperative. "The decision to forgive touches you to your very core, to who you are as a human being", he says. "It involves your sense of self-esteem, your personal worth, the worth of the person who has hurt you and your relationship with that person and the larger world."

Enright believes that the motivation to begin the forgiveness process is down to self-preservation, the person's need for their own pain to stop, the desire to heal and move on. He believes that, "forgiving someone is interpersonal as we reach out to the one who hurt us", and he claims that the forgiveness process is inherently paradoxical, "As we reach out to the one who hurt us, we are the ones who heal." He advocates that we should choose a companion for our forgiveness journey, who should not be the one who hurt us. He beseeches us not to do it alone as *'anger and resentment can trap us in a cycle of negative thinking, self-justification, shame, and guilt. Another person, one who is sensitive and who has experienced forgiveness, can help sort things out. Without that other voice, we can just go round and round, telling ourselves the same lies over and over again, because we don't know they are lies.'*

Another expert in the field I found interesting was Dr Fred Luskin who holds a PhD in counselling and health psychology from Stanford University, where he is the cofounder and director of the Stanford Forgiveness Project. Luskin is also the author of *Forgive For Good*[17]. Like Enright, Luskin believes that forgiveness is a choice and a trainable skill that everyone can learn and that the capacity for forgiveness is an intrinsic part of human nature. The problem he admits is most of us don't know how to do it. In his *Nine Steps to Forgiveness* program, which involves a mixture of cognitive and meditative strategies, from articulating your grievance to shifting your expectations of life, to revising the way you look at your past, Luskin emphasizes that forgiveness is best seen as something that will bring you peace, closure, and reduce your suffering. Like Enright, he explains that forgiveness is a process, not an event, and that true forgiveness doesn't happen instantaneously but instead, it takes time and energy to achieve and might not come easily.

It is understandable that the forgiveness process as conceived by the academics is about solving a perceived problem. You do not want negative emotions to control your life. This is your problem; now how do you solve it? This is essentially what you are doing. If you wish to resolve anger in your life and to experience powerful emotional healing, the processes as taught by the academics are ideal.

If you are having difficulty forgiving someone and it is impacting your life in a negative way, you may also be encouraged to seek professional help from a counsellor or therapist. There are many different therapists who practice an array of different forgiveness techniques from cognitive behavioral therapy, to spiritual counselling and the power of prayer. Therapies intended to promote forgiveness can be successful in helping people overcome past hurts and achieve peace and resolution.

Other ways that one may be encouraged to forgive is by listening to, or reading about, other peoples' horror stories. A good example of this is the story of Richard Moore which is recounted in his book *Can I Give Him My Eyes?*[18]. His story recounts that he '*was about ten feet away when a soldier fired the rubber bullet that struck me on the bridge of my nose. I didn't hear the bang of the discharge. All I remember is that everything went blank. And that was the moment my life changed forever.*' Richard Moore was ten years old when he was shot by a British soldier on his journey past an army base on his way home from school. "Can I Give Him My Eyes?" was the question Richard's father asked the doctors when they broke the news that they could not save his sight. The book shares his remarkable story, from his early years growing up on the Catholic working-class Creggan Estate in Derry, Ireland, the second youngest of a family of twelve children. In it he describes the moment of grace that accompanied the realization that he would never see again, where he accepted his fate instantly and without bitterness, and tells of wonderful childhood escapades, including 'endless cycles down Malin Gardens' guided by the voices of his friends. Years later, in an extraordinary turn of events, Richard then met and befriended the man who shot him.

In 1996 Richard gave up a successful business career to found Children in Crossfire and dedicated himself to improving the lives of the many children in the world suffering from destitution. Children in Crossfire has become a highly respected international development organisation working in partnership with local organisations to deliver programmes which protect and promote the rights of young children, through the provision of healthcare, education services and advocacy initiatives. He was given the Lifetime Achievement award in recognition of his tireless campaigning and work across the globe. *Can I Give Him My Eyes?* is an inspiring life story of a man whom the Dali Lama describes as "not only my friend but my hero."

Another publication I found which may be of interest to those who wish to pursue this path of healing is a book written by the Nobel Peace Laureate Archbishop Desmond Tutu together with his daughter Revd Mpho Tutu. *The Book of Forgiving*[19] offers a deeply personal testament and guide to the process of forgiveness. Not uncommonly, the book admits that the path to forgiveness is not easy, and the process is unclear. It asks the difficult and pertinent questions to which we all look for answers. How do we let go of resentment when we have been harmed, at times irreparably? How do we forgive and still pursue justice? How do we heal our hearts? How do we heal the harm we have caused others? And how do we forgive ourselves?

Drawing on his memories of reconciliation in post-apartheid South Africa, Archbishop Desmond Tutu, together with his daughter, Revd Mpho Tutu, herself an experienced teacher and preacher, offer four concrete steps along the path to forgiving and being forgiven.

1. Admitting the wrong and acknowledging the harm.

2. Telling one's story and witnessing the anguish.

3. Asking for forgiveness and granting forgiveness.

4. Renewing or releasing the relationship.

Each chapter contains reflections and personal stories, as well as exercises for practicing each step of the path. *The Book of Forgiving* can be a welcome tool for anyone seeking to understand the process of resolving psychological pain and an inspiring guide to healing yourself.

Academics and researchers are now also using functional magnetic resonance imaging to see if the answer to the forgiveness process lies within the brain. A team at the University of Pisa in Italy asked people to imagine forgiving someone and then observed changes in cerebral blood flow, which signalled the parts of the brain that became more active. They found that several regions lit up, especially areas that regulate emotional responses, moral judgments, perceptions of physical pain, and decision making. By creating a kind of neural map, researchers hope to learn more about how forgiveness works on both a physical and a psychological level.

The benefits of forgiveness have of course been explored in religious thought and the correlation between forgiveness and physical health is a concept that has gained significant traction in academic research. Forgiveness is advocated to improve existing and future relationships, your self-esteem, your physical, mental, emotional and spiritual wellbeing, alleviate the symptoms of depression and help us reach positive psychological adjustment.

Not forgiving, however, may impair the immune system because of the stress it puts on the individual. As such, we are told that when we hold on to resentment, the only person we hurt is ourselves, not our transgressor. We are encouraged to try and let go of our negative thinking, emotions and behaviors; to let go of the pain we feel about the injustice and the perpetrator as you will suffer if you don't. If you cannot let go of the negative feelings caused by the abuse you suffered, you might find yourself swallowed up by your own bitterness and sense of injustice. Thus, we are encouraged to talk about it, write about it, attend appropriate group talks, and to see a therapist if necessary. We are told that whilst not excusing the wrong that was done, you can refuse to be consumed with anger.

Of course, such academic research studies have been refuted by some critics who claim that there is no direct correlation between forgiveness and physical health. Forgiveness, due to the reduction of directed anger, contributes to mental health and mental health contributes to physical health, but they claim that there is no evidence that forgiveness directly improves physical health. These critics claim that most of the studies on forgiveness cannot isolate it as an independent variable in an individual's wellbeing, so it is difficult to prove causation[20]. I think, however, that we can all agree that the forgiveness process as advocated by the academics can and does heal the emotional state of the victim and thus would have a beneficial knock-on effect on the person's existing and future relationships, their self-esteem, physical and mental wellbeing.

So, what does it mean to forgive? The English Oxford dictionary defines the word forgive as follows: cease to feel angry or resentful toward a person, remit or let off a debt. The English Oxford thesaurus uses the following synonyms: pardon, excuse, exonerate, absolve, acquit, let someone off the hook, bear no malice, harbour no grudge.

Enright asserts that forgiveness is essentially, the *'foregoing of resentment or revenge'* when the wrong-doer's actions deserve it and instead giving the offender gifts of *'mercy, generosity and love'* when the wrong-doer does not deserve them. In other words, when people forgive, they essentially give up the anger to which they are entitled and give to their offender a gift to which he or she is not entitled. Depending on the seriousness of the offense and the length of time the person offended has lived with and perhaps denied the harm caused by the offense, Enright claims that forgiving may be a long, difficult and painful process.

Enright, not unsurprisingly, also defines forgiveness by way of what it is not. For example, genuine forgiveness does not mean forgetting that the offense occurred, condoning or excusing the offense, renouncing efforts to obtain restitution or legal justice, or suppressing or no longer feeling anger about what happened. In addition, genuine forgiveness does not require offenders to first admit their offenses, ask for forgiveness, make appropriate restitution, or be willing and able to change their offensive ways. While it may be easier to forgive an offender who responds in these ways, one who has been offended need not remain trapped in unforgiveness due to the offender's inability or unwillingness to do so.

Many different definitions of forgiveness can also be found in modern philosophy. The philosopher Joanna North gave the following definition; '*When unjustly hurt by another, we forgive when we overcome resentment toward the offender, not by denying our right to the resentment, but instead by trying to offer the wrong-doer compassion, benevolence, and love; as we give these, we as forgivers realize that the offender does not necessarily have a right to such gifts*' [21]. While there is some debate over whether true forgiveness requires positive feelings toward the offender, all the experts in this area do agree that forgiveness at least involves letting go of deeply held negative feelings, bringing the forgiver peace of mind and freeing him or her from corrosive anger. In this way, it empowers you to recognize the pain you suffered without letting that pain define you, enabling you to heal and move on with your life.

Most people will confess that they struggle with the theme of forgiveness. The majority of people who believe they have forgiven in their lives will admit that they had no idea how to begin the process of forgiving or what to expect once they had. Many will admit that they didn't have any guideposts and that they stumbled along, some with the help of a therapist. They assert that when they said, "I forgive you" that this was merely a first step and in many ways no more than an intention to begin the process of forgiveness. We are told that the process of forgiveness will take time and for most of us, the work of forgiveness is ongoing.

Scholars in this area admit that although there are no guarantees, there is genuine hope that forgiveness will make a change in your life. They consider what forgiveness is and what it is not and what it is more than. Some believe that forgiveness includes the offer of compassion, benevolence and love toward the one that hurt you. Some believe that the healing process of forgiveness takes time and they compare the emotional healing of forgiveness with a physical injury such as a broken leg which does not heal instantaneously but takes time.

After having reviewed what many of the experts, both religious and academic, have to say on this topic, I believe that the meaning of forgiveness, although still open to interpretation, could generally be defined as a decision to let go of resentment and thoughts of revenge. The act that hurt or offended you might always remain a part of your life, but forgiveness can lessen its grip on you and help you focus on other, more positive parts of your life. Forgiveness can even, in some cases, lead to feelings of understanding, empathy and compassion for the one who hurt you. An alternative definition of forgiveness could be an intention, a desire, or wish to resolve negative feelings which drain your energy, adversely affect your mood, pulling you down into a whirlpool of resentment and self-pity, which overtime, if not resolved, can lead to severe health problems.

In our pursuit of self-healing, we are told that we may also need to learn how to seek forgiveness through

The Truth

repentance or if this is not possible, to forgive ourselves. Self-forgiveness is required in situations where an individual has done something that they perceive to be wrong and the process is the overcoming of negative emotions that the wrong-doer associates with the wrongful action. Negative emotions associated with the wrongful action can include, for example, guilt, regret, remorse, shame, self-hatred and self-contempt.

Studies suggest that the capacity to honestly forgive oneself is significantly beneficial to an individual's emotional as well as mental well-being[21]. The research indicates that the ability to forgive one-self for past offenses can decrease feelings of negative emotions such as shame and guilt, and can develop more positive practices such as self-kindness and self-compassion. However, and not unexpectedly, the research has indicated that it is possible for the process of self-forgiveness to be misinterpreted and therefore not successfully completed.

I have found that the process of seeking forgiveness is not given as much attention by the academics as the process of rendering forgiveness. This is probably due to the fact that what you may have done to someone else may not be causing you as much emotional turmoil as what was done to you! I guess some negative feelings are simply stronger than others and need to be attended to first. Nevertheless, I did find the following therapeutic model[21] which will indicate what is generally understood by the process of self-forgiveness. The model that has been proposed has four key elements. These elements include

responsibility, remorse, restoration and **renewal** and are explained as follows:

1. Assuming **responsibility** for one's actions is the first step toward genuine self-forgiveness. In order to absolve negative emotions such as overwhelming guilt or regret, the offender must first recognize that they have hurt another individual, and accept responsibility for their actions.

2. Once the offender has accepted the fact that they have indeed caused offense to another, it is natural for them to experience feelings of **remorse** or guilt. However, these feelings must be confronted and exposed before they can be genuinely expressed, processed and resolved.

3. The processing and resolution of these negative emotions is helped by acts of **restoration** toward the individual they have hurt, allowing the offending individual to make amends.

4. The ultimate step in this model of self-forgiveness is **renewal**. The offending individual is now in a position to be genuinely able to forgive themselves for their past transgressions, affording them the freedom to engage in more positive and meaningful behaviors such as self-compassion and self-kindness.

From the above model, it appears that the practice of repentance or seeking forgiveness not only plays an important role in religious doctrine, where it is often considered necessary for the attainment of salvation, but also plays an important part in self-healing as advocated by academics. Whether the other person will forgive us or not is something outside of our control. They may forgive us, and we can move on. If not, I guess we can still use the above model to forgive ourselves and I don't believe that there is anything selfish about this type of healing process as it not only benefits the user but everyone around them.

According to the English Oxford dictionary, the word repent means to feel deep sorrow or regret about one's actions. The English Oxford thesaurus gives the following synonyms; regret, feel remorse for, be sorry, be regretful, be ashamed, feel guilt, see the error of one's ways, see the light.

The doctrine of repentance as taught by the world's religions is a call to make a radical turn from one way of life to another. It is a change of mind that involves a conscious turning away from wrong actions, attitudes and thoughts that conflict with a Godly lifestyle and biblical commands, and an intentional turning toward doing that which the Bible says pleases God. In religious contexts it often involves an act of confession to God or to a spiritual elder such as a monk or priest.

Is the process of forgiveness as described by the academics or any of the religions clear to you? Do you know what you have to do to forgive others and to be forgiven in return? As a rule of thumb, I have found that if a person can't explain a topic in the clearest and simplest of terms, then that person simply does not understand the topic. This is not an indictment but simply a method of separating the wheat from the chaff.

The forgiveness process as taught by both religious doctrine and academic research can generally be accepted to include both steps of rendering forgiveness to an offender and requesting forgiveness from a victim or self-forgiveness where this is not possible. We are encouraged to undertake the forgiveness process because it will help manage our pain, improve our health and help mend our relationship with the offender and improve our relationships with others generally because we will be less angry as a person. However, it is my opinion that if you undertake a process for a specific reason, then the reason is the label you should use and no other. For example, if you claim to have forgiven because you wanted to manage your anger, then the process you undertook was anger management.

There is a myriad of sources, both from an academic and religious point of view, on the topic of forgiveness. I have purposively not gone into much detail here as it is not the subject of this book. This book is not about pain management. If you wish to manage or resolve your pain, in whatever form it manifests itself (fear, anger, hurt, regret, shame etc.), I would recommend the plethora of religious and academic teachings on the subject of forgiveness and in particular, the academic sources I have mentioned. However, if you wish to unlock the power of the Grail, then you must complete the dual act of forgiveness as revealed to us by Yeshua.

Chapter Five

Forgiveness and Repentance Vol. 2

Over the centuries the teaching of the acts of forgiveness has been corrupted for obvious reasons. The powerful within the belief based system can only retain their power if we all choose to remain within the belief based system. As soon as you step from the belief based system into the knowledge based system, the belief based system for you evaporates along with the power the belief based system has over you.

You will find the teaching of the act of forgiveness described in many books as the act of pardoning an offender. What does this mean? How do you get to the stage where you would even want to pardon an offender? By saying that you have pardoned an offender, have you truly forgiven? If you take no reprisals against your offender does that not prove you have forgiven? If you had truly forgiven would you feel the need to prove it? If you say that you have forgiven an offender and you prove it by taking no action against them should you still feel angry toward the offender if you have truly forgiven?

In the Bible, the Greek word for **forgiveness** literally means **to let go**. But which comes first, letting go or forgiving? Is letting go a step among many required to forgive or is letting go the only step required? When we let go, what do we let go of? Do we let go of our memory of the act of the offender or is it our feelings associated with the act we let go of, or possibly both? Do we let go of our need to take revenge or indeed to seek justice? How does one let go of bad feelings such as, hate and anger associated with being wronged?

Teachings on forgiveness to date are vague at best and keep us floundering in the dark which only compounds our anger through frustration. We want to get on with our lives but our inability to let go keeps us rooted in the past. This is through no fault of our own. The act of forgiveness has specific steps and unless you have been shown these steps how could you possibly know. For example, if you had an object in your hand and I asked you to let it go, you may ask me how to do this, to which I would respond that you have to move your fingers in an outwardly direction from your palm. When you complete the act of letting go, the object will fall from your grip and you will be free of it. If only we had such specific instructions on how to forgive.

Not forgiving is now socially acceptable but only because we don't know what it is. We are taught as children that wrongs should be punished and good should be rewarded. In fact, our whole legal system is based on this premise. Therefore, as adults the desire for justice, although natural, will always act as a stumbling block to forgiveness.

Showing us how to forgive and to be forgiven in turn was the mission of the Christ, Yeshua. Please don't think you know how to forgive because you have heard the word spoken a thousand times. If you have not witnessed the truth, then you have not yet completed the dual act of forgiveness. This is almost certainly through a lack of understanding how to complete the acts of forgiveness or maybe you are not yet ready. In any case, here are the steps required to complete the first act of forgiveness which is to forgive:

Step 1: Choice

Step 2: Pain

Step 3: Reason

Step 4: Belief

The first step may seem somewhat redundant, but it is in fact the most important, not because it expresses a desire to forgive but because it is an expression of the freewill we have been given. Freewill is the greatest gift that has been bestowed upon us. Because of this great gift, you cannot be prevented from or indeed coerced into making this decision. This is your choice.

To take the second step, one must have been wronged and experience pain due to this wrong. Pain can come in many forms and I use it as an umbrella term to include all forms of disturbing negative emotional experiences such as hurt, hate, anger, rage, humiliation, fear, anguish, sorrow, grief, shame, guilt and remorse. This list is not conclusive or exhaustive in any way but is given by way of example only.

Pain acts as a motive force for movement from the belief based system to the knowledge based system. If you have no pain, you will not be able to forgive. Having said that, if you do not feel pain, you probably have not been wronged and thus have nothing to forgive! Nevertheless, I think you will agree when I say that it's impossible to pass through this life without having wronged and being wronged in return. The pain you felt at the time of the wrong being perpetrated, if not expressed at the time, will reside inside you waiting for its release. The body will remind you from time to time that the pain still resides inside you waiting for this release and it may do this through the manifestation of an illness, for example.

To complete the second step, you must recognize that you are in pain; you must feel this pain. When you recall the injustice, which you will do in the first step, the pain associated with it should return to you. This pain is the motive force which will fuel the process of the first act of forgiveness. This may be the hardest step for some. For example, it is not uncommon for people in their eighties to live with anger over injustices they endured as children. Whilst they are still suffering from the emotional pain, they have over time coped with it by dissociating themselves from the pain. As a result, they no longer feel the pain and thus don't recognize that they are angry. While this pain resides within, waiting for its release, it may change form and become less and less familiar. The pain may also disassociate itself from the reason of its own creation. This is not good because the act of forgiveness must be reasoned. Therefore, it is best if you can forgive earlier rather than later. However, having said that, it is never too late to forgive.

The third step in the first act of forgiveness is reason. Forgiveness must be reasoned. As a child I had always wondered why Yeshua used the words; *'Father, forgive them for (because) they do not know what they do.'* (Luke 23:24) Why not just say, Father, forgive them or I forgive you? Please don't believe that Yeshua's words here were superfluous. Throughout his teachings, he chose his words very carefully. This was no exception. This is how the Grail was created, through reason, and you will not be able to invoke the power of the Grail unless you reason your forgiveness. Let me be clear, the third step must be conducted as follows: "I forgive you because…"

The fourth and final step of the first act of forgiveness is belief. It is imperative that you must truly accept your reason or reasoning for forgiving. The reason or reasoning you apply here does not have to be factually correct or accurate, but you must believe it completely. If you cannot accept or believe your own reasoning, then you will not be able to complete the first act of forgiveness.

There is a certain justice here. In the beginning we resided in the knowledge based system and thus we knew the truth. However, we chose to close our eyes to the truth so that we could reside within the belief based system allowing us to believe whatever we wanted to believe. Now we have been given the opportunity to open our eyes again to the truth allowing us to reside within the knowledge based system. However, to take advantage of this opportunity, given to us by Yeshua, we must **believe** our reasoning. In the beginning we knew but we wanted to believe. Now to know again, we must truly believe!

The second act of forgiveness is to be forgiven. Here are the steps required to complete the second act of forgiveness:

Step 1: Choice

Step 2: Pain

Step 3: Reason

Step 4: Belief

There is not much to explain here as the second act of forgiveness is a mirror image of the first act. When you take the first step of seeking forgiveness for yourself you will automatically recall the injustice you committed. With this recollection, the second step will immediately follow with the return of the pain associated with that injustice, which in this case could be sorrow, grief, shame, guilt or remorse, or a combination of these and other feelings. Following this, you can then take the third step which is to provide a reason why you should be forgiven. As with the first act of forgiveness, it is crucial that you must truly accept your reason or reasoning. Again, the reason or reasoning you apply here does not have to be factually correct or accurate, but you must believe it completely. If you cannot accept or believe your own reasoning, then you will not be able to complete the second act of forgiveness.

This bears repeating as it is most important. To unlock the power of the Grail requires two acts of forgiveness which must be undertaken in order; step-by-step. First you must forgive and then you must be forgiven. The second act is a mirror image of the first act; *'And when you stand to pray, forgive whatever you may hold against anyone, so that your divine Father may also forgive your sins.'* (Mark 11:25)

Going forward, I will use the word **repentance** as an umbrella term to mean the dual act or step-by-step action of forgiveness given to us by Yeshua. Therefore, it is repentance which invokes the power of the Grail. Let me be clear, living your life according to Yeshua's ministry without repentance will not save you.

You may wonder why seeking forgiveness is the second act and not the first act of forgiveness. Apart from the fact that free will dictates that you must make the first move, some negative feelings are stronger than others and must be dealt with first. Forgiving clears the emotional anger you were feeling toward the offender because of what they did to you, allowing you to feel lesser forms of pain such as guilt or shame which you may then realize you feel because of how you reacted to the injustice, for example, the hate you held in your heart toward the offender for so many years or indeed the part you played in the whole situation.

When you have completed both acts in order, your eyes will be opened, allowing you to pass through the gate and enter the knowledge based system. Due to the critical nature of these instructions, Yeshua put them in a prayer for us, which we call the **Our Father**. In the prayer is the line, '*forgive us our trespasses as(because) we forgive those who trespass against us.*' Yes, Yeshua put the message of how to unlock the Grail's power in a prayer. This prayer is probably the most widely and repetitively spoken prayer in the world over the last two-thousand years. Yeshua put the instructions of the Grail in plain view of the world and we missed them!

Don't confuse the dual act of forgiveness with the desire to heal yourself. Most forgiveness processes are associated with not holding onto destructive feelings such as anger, hurt or regret et cetera. This is not forgiveness but born of a desire to save yourself from the potentially destructive nature of such negative feelings. These forgiveness programs will teach you how to expunge these negative feelings from your life, or if this is not possible, how to manage them so that they don't control you, allowing you to look forward to a brighter future. This type of forgiveness process is in fact a process of emotional healing. This is the core objective of these programs which we are told can take months or even years to successfully complete. However, this is not part of the forgiveness process of which I speak. The process I speak of does not seek to resolve negative emotions. Instead, it uses the negative emotions to propel the process. You will find that when you have completed the dual act of forgiveness, the energy from the negative emotions has become depleted. This is a side effect only and not the core purpose of the process. The purpose of the dual act of forgiveness is to open your eyes so that you can see the knowledge based system for yourself.

Forgiveness does not mean reconciliation. Reconciliation requires a renewal of trust between the offender and offended which is not required in the dual forgiveness process. Robert D Enright emphasizes that *'forgiveness is something we give to those who have hurt us.'* This may be the case for the healing process he advocates but it simply is not the case in the dual act of forgiveness as taught by Yeshua. The dual act of forgiveness may open the door to reconciliation, but the dual act is so powerful that it can occur where there was no trust to begin with.

If the forgiver lets the offender know the extent of the injury, the offender has the opportunity to change. If you wish to extend this privilege to the offender, this is your prerogative, but it's not necessary to complete the acts of forgiveness. If you wish to maintain a relationship with the offender, it may be necessary for you to make clear to the offender that what was done should not have been done and will not be tolerated in the future. This, however, is part of the process of reconciliation and relationship building and not part of the forgiveness process of which I speak.

Making amends to the one you have offended is also not necessary to complete the acts of forgiveness. The acts of forgiveness do not require the input of a third party in any way and thus they are truly private and personal. It does, however, require you to reach out to the Source in the second act of forgiveness, but believe me when I say that the Source is waiting for you to reach out as he wants so much to forgive you; he wants the cycle of pain to end for you, he wants you to return home.

Are some people unforgivable? No. Suppose one faces an unrepentant abuser. This person sees nothing wrong with verbally abusing you and telling you that the abuse they gave you was deserved. Can one forgive under these circumstances? Yes. But only if one does not confuse the first act of forgiveness with the act of rendering compassion to the offender. The forgiveness process is for you, not the offender. The offender has absolutely no active part to play in either act of forgiveness. In this way, it's possible to even forgive the dead!

Is it possible to forgive yourself? No. Saying, "I made a mistake, I'm human and I'll do better next time" is not self-forgiveness, it's self-compassion. What is happening here is simply a recognition that you are human, and humans make mistakes. This process is not forgiveness but rather it's a way of resolving negative feelings which are having an adverse impact on your life. The process of self-compassion stops you from ruminating on the past over which you have no control and which over time will deplete your energy. This process usually follows strong feelings which were created because of what you did, feelings such as shame, disappointment and guilt. When you are unable to resolve these feelings, you turn to accepting them after which they begin to lose power over you. You now feel more in control as you look forward to the future. This process is not forgiveness, but it is an effective coping mechanism.

We are often told that knowing the person who injured us did not intend to hurt us can actually complicate the process of forgiveness. A specific example of this is given in Enright's book[16]. He recounts that not only do we feel angry and resentful because we have been hurt but we also feel guilty for being angry and resentful toward an innocent person. This is a clear lack of understanding of the forgiveness process and in particular the dual nature of the process. This is of course an ideal opportunity to complete both acts of forgiveness; to forgive the offender for the hurt caused you and to ask for forgiveness for the anger you held in your heart toward an innocent person.

Many believe that forgiveness is only possible when the offender repents and asks for forgiveness. This belief renders you powerless as the offender is required to make the first move. The corollary is also true. If wishing for forgiveness from a third party requires you to wait until that party is willing to forgive, this process could take a long time. But none of this is true. What makes the acts of forgiveness truly powerful is that all that is required is you and the Source, and the Source is willing, waiting and ready to forgive you as soon as you have forgiven.

We are told that forgiveness is for those who are caught in an endless cycle of anger, resentment or guilt. We are told that forgiveness will help you find freedom from such feelings and the self-destructive behavior patterns that accompany them. If it doesn't work, you will be told that the forgiveness does not work for everyone! Now you know that this is also not true.

Some believe that we lack self-respect if we forgive unconditionally. I don't know about this, but as true forgiveness needs to be reasoned, it's not given unconditionally. The forgiveness process of which I speak is very personal and requires absolutely no input from the offender; it's between you and the Source. In this way, the offender has absolutely no power over you. This makes the dual act of forgiveness very powerful indeed.

Some believe that forgiveness is a sign of weakness. This simply can't be true because completing the acts of forgiveness requires no outwardly sign at all! Some believe that forgiveness is a paradox and that the process is full of paradoxes. Although these concerns are understandable they are not justified because they are a misunderstanding of what true forgiveness is.

If you believe that the process of forgiveness as described and exemplified by the academics I have mentioned, or by those I have not, who have done and continue to do great work in their field of endeavor, is extremely difficult, then we would both agree. However, the true dual act of forgiveness as given to us by Yeshua is even more difficult to accomplish. The best way that I can describe its difficulty is by way of analogy. Imagine you are standing on your feet, with your hands clasped behind your back. With knees unbent you fall forward unto your face without putting your hands out to save yourself. '*Whoever tries to save his life will lose it, but whoever gives his life will be born again.*' (Luke 17:33) You must approach the dual act of forgiveness with complete abandon, submission and above all, honesty. If you fail to complete the dual act of forgiveness, you will never unlock the power of the Grail and you will be forever trapped in the belief based system in which you will ultimately perish.

The forgiveness process and its progress, as described by the academics, seems to be evaluated based on changing feelings; are you less angry, less tired, less depressed, how do you feel toward the offender, etc. Enright suggests, "Hoping that the offender's life is going well whether or not you are a part of that life is an indicator that forgiveness is occurring." Forgiveness seems to have a scale, are you now more forgiving than you were at the beginning of the process or are you less forgiving or have you stayed the same. Enright advocates that the forgiveness process must be done for each and every hurt but that each time you do it, it becomes easier. Not unexpectedly, the process is still unclear, and people ask the question, "How do I know when I have forgiven?" They look for a concrete sign that forgiveness is complete. They are uneasy until they know that they have completed the journey. Enright answers by saying, "Being open to further developments in forgiving might become the goal."

Let me be clear. If you can achieve true feelings of compassion toward the offender, I am sure that this will help reduce your anger, but it will not unlock the power of the Grail. There are no levels of forgiveness here; you complete the acts of forgiveness unlocking the Grail or you do not. This renders the question, "How do I know when I have forgiven?" redundant. You will know you have successfully completed the acts of forgiveness when you have unlocked the power of the Grail which will open your eyes to the truth.

The academics and religious leaders advocate that forgiveness is about learning to cope with your pain but as you can now understand, pain is required to complete the dual act of forgiveness as taught by Yeshua. Don't learn how to cope with the pain, learn how to use it! If you follow the forgiveness process as recommended by the academics or endeavor to follow the process as loosely described by religious doctrine, you may eventually experience some peace, peace from the torment the memories have caused you. However, if you complete the forgiveness process as given to us by Yeshua, I guarantee you, you will not feel peace, you will become peace. 'I *give you my peace. Not as the world gives peace do I give it to you.*' (John 14:27) Pain has no place in the knowledge based system.

Many academics promote exercises in mindfulness to facilitate the forgiveness process. Mindfulness helps you focus on the positive rather than the negative emotions instilled in you because of the wrong you were done. This takes control from the negative emotions and instead gives it to the positive emotions. Whilst this has a more positive affect in your life, you are simply trading one master for another. This type of forgiveness process, I have no doubt, will heal you emotionally and may even help the one forgiven by healing the relationship. What it will not do is to unlock the power of the Grail allowing you to enter the knowledge based system.

The victim who wishes to forgive will naturally be in a vulnerable state because of the pain they are in. Many forgiveness programs will advocate that the forgiveness process will not happen overnight but rather is a life long journey. Some people say things like this to exercise control over you, after all, if you completed the steps of forgiveness as recommended by your chosen guide, you would no longer need the guide. Therefore, it is in the interest of some guides to misguide! They may say things like, "when you have completed the forgiveness process, you will find that it's a beginning and not an end." Don't be fooled. When you are ready, the dual act of forgiveness can be completed in less than sixty seconds. When you have truly invoked the power of the Grail using the dual forgiveness process, you will no longer be controlled by these people. You will no longer need them, you will no longer need me!

Therefore, I am not here to guide you through the process of the dual act of forgiveness. Think of what I'm giving you as a map. I cannot make this map any clearer than I have. Therefore, you do not need me anymore. Now it's down to you and only you. Will you use the map or not?

I am also not here to impugn anybody's work. If you wish to believe that your idea of forgiveness is correct and what I propose is something entirely different, that's okay. Call my proposal what you like, after all, it's just a word. By completing the dual act of forgiveness, I don't promise you bliss and eternal life, I only promise you the truth. You will enter the knowledge based system where you will know all things. You will know all things because you are connected to all things and through this connection you can communicate with all things. You can then decide if you wish to remain in the knowledge based system or to return to the belief based system. This is your choice.

PART 2

The Creation of the Grail

Chapter Six

The Knowledge Based System

There are many myths surrounding Yeshua's life, his work, and the reason for his ultimate sacrifice. What do people generally believe?

Some say Yeshua sacrificed his life to atone for the sins of the entire world. Yeshua's death on the cross secured the salvation of countless millions and provided the only way God could forgive sin without compromising his holiness and perfect righteousness. Yeshua's death was God's perfect plan for the eternal redemption of his people. Yeshua bore God's judgment for sin as a substitutionary sacrifice for the sins of the world. On the cross God piled our sins on Yeshua, and he bore the punishment due us. God put Yeshua to death for our sins so that we could live without sin.

Some people believe that Yeshua's task was to destroy the works of the deceiver and to free all those who were oppressed by him. Others believe Yeshua's death was a victory for the deceiver. Others indeed believe that God Himself, the omnipotent Creator of the Universe, came to earth, became incarnate in man in order that we could be saved. Yes, some believe that Yeshua was God and that he allowed himself to be killed to wipe away our sins. General belief also suggests that all I must do is believe in God or Yeshua, or God and Yeshua and not only are my sins forgiven, but I will receive eternal life.

We are told that Yeshua had to sacrifice his life because he never sinned and thus he was the only one who could pay this price. He was the sacrificial lamb who took upon himself the sins of the world. He was nailed on the cross to wash away our sins. We were saved from sin through his sacrifice.

We are led to believe that our salvation comes only through the grace of God toward man, and that we can only receive it by faith; '*For God so loved the world that He gave His only begotten Son, that whoever believes in Him should not perish but have everlasting life.*' (John 3:16) We are told, to be saved we must believe in Yeshua. This belief is a heartfelt conviction that transforms an unbelieving sinner into a child of God. This belief changes one's everlasting destiny and enjoins him to God giving everlasting life. God has given us the grace to receive this salvation and all we must do is open the door by faith.

I find the above language to be imprecise and misleading at best, and a downright mystery at worst. When we ask questions, we are told that this truth is beyond the capacity of even the born-again believer to explain or fully understand. Instead of answering our questions, we are told to receive God's gift of salvation we must believe in Yeshua and Yeshua alone. We must trust in Yeshua's death on the cross as payment for our sins. This of course raises the obvious question, "What does it mean to **believe** in Yeshua?" It is widely held among the Christian community that this means Yeshua himself must be worshiped, obeyed and emulated. We are told that we should do this because he died for our sins.

Yeshua died for our sins. What does that mean? Did his death atone for past, present or future sins or all sins whether past, present or future? Who forgave and continues to forgive these sins, God or Yeshua or both? Was Yeshua God? Was this a pact between God and himself (Yeshua)? Did God say to himself (Yeshua) that he would forgive all sins if he (Yeshua) allowed himself to be killed?

None of these possibilities make even the slightest bit of sense. Indeed, the belief based system has never made any sense to me, and to continually accept something that does not make sense is senseless. Furthermore, has this method ever worked for anyone in the last two-thousand years? Has your belief saved you? If we are honest, the answer is no. Not a single person has ever been saved through belief. Therefore, the evidence is stacked heavily against this theory of salvation.

Believers claim that Yeshua died so that we could be free from sin. I have found that all believers have at least one thing in common. None of them can give you a universal and clear definition of sin, which renders their theories on the abolition of sin, at best, very vague. Of course, whilst believers can't give a definition of sin, they can give endless examples of it.

Are you free from sin? I'm not, or at least I'm sure I wouldn't be if I knew what the believers' definition of sin was! Therefore, if the task of the Christ was to save us all from sin and at least one of us is not thus saved (namely me) then one would have to conclude that he failed in his task. In truth and if we are honest, no sin has been taken away by Yeshua's death. As such, there are only two possibilities. Either Yeshua failed in his task to take away sin and his promise of eternal life was hollow or we misunderstood his task and his task was not to take away sin but something else entirely. Is it possible we misunderstood? Surely not.

People ask questions such as, "What is more important, the death of Christ or His resurrection?" This question is very popular, but it is a cold indictment of our misunderstanding of Yeshua, his task and the reason for his ultimate sacrifice. People who say the former are those who believe that without Yeshua's death, we would still live in sin. The truth is we still do live in sin. Those who believe his resurrection is more important, advocate that if Christ did not physically rise from the dead, then we ourselves have no hope of resurrection. The logic of such beliefs, as is normally the case, is poor to say the least. Apart from Yeshua, have you ever witnessed or heard of a bodily resurrection in the last two-thousand years? My guess is you haven't.

Others argue that his death and resurrection are both equally important. It is said if Yeshua had not died and been raised from the dead, he would have failed to complete the prophecies about him and that he simply would have been another false prophet to be ignored. Scripture links the death and resurrection of Yeshua. Thus, we are told we must maintain that link, to believe in one without the other is to believe in a false gospel that cannot save. In order for Yeshua to have truly risen from the dead, we are told he must have truly died and in order for his death to have a true meaning for us, we are told he must have had a true resurrection. Therefore, we cannot have one without the other. Nonsense!

There was a time when I was conflicted because of what Yeshua did. I simply didn't understand what he did or why he did it. I was told by priests within the Catholic religion that he died to save me. This caused me further guilt and confusion. Was I saved? What was I saved from? Was I saved from sin? What was sin?

I felt guilty because he died in such a horrific manner for me, I was not saved, and I was apparently still living in sin. This led me to two conflicting conclusions. If Christ was sent here to save me from sin and I was still living in sin, then he had failed in his mission. Was the Christ unsuccessful? Alternatively, if I was not saved and I was still living in sin maybe the mission of the Christ was something else entirely. If this is the case, what could his mission really have been? It made me ask the question, "What is it about Yeshua's death that benefits me?"

Yeshua's task in life and the reason for his ultimate sacrifice is the biggest cover up in history. It is said, remove the impossible, whatever remains, no matter how improbable, must be the truth. Therefore, Yeshua did not come here to save us. That was not his task. Why? To say that was his task is to say that he failed because we are not saved no matter how broadly you wish to define the word 'saved'.

So what was his task? It is now my understanding that his task was not to save us but to show us how to save ourselves. There will be those among you who think that I'm splitting hairs. This of course is your prerogative but the difference between the two is choice, free will.

Consider this. If Yeshua's resurrection was as important as his death, why did he not make a public demonstration of both? Why just make a public demonstration of his death? The truth is that the public demonstration was not of his death but of how to forgive. He gave his life to show us how to forgive; 'Forgive them for they know not what they do'. Believing in Yeshua, whatever that actually means, will not save you. It will not allow you to exit the belief based system and enter the knowledge based system. Nothing will allow you to do this but the dual act of forgiveness.

Yeshua told his disciples; "You know **the way** to where I am going." In response, Thomas, one of my favorite disciples, not so much 'the doubter' as the guy who's willing to admit his lack of understanding, blurts out that he has absolutely no idea what Yeshua is talking about; *'Lord, we don't know where you are going; how can we know the way?'*. (John 14:5)

Since Thomas, very few people ask such direct and probing questions. I was brought up to believe, and I'm sure I'm not the only one, that to question our faith was somehow wrong and that those who blindly accepted the faith were pious and should be held up as shining examples for us all to emulate. The ones who questioned their faith were ridiculed and labeled a 'Doubting Thomas'. As a result, Christians to this day hold the view that if you do not **believe** in Yeshua without question, you cannot come to know God. I ask you, has your belief in Yeshua ever allowed you to **know** God?

The knowledge based system is the eternal life of which Yeshua spoke; '*For this is eternal life; to **know** you the only true God* '. (John 17:3) To know God you must engage the power of the Grail and this is done through repentance, i.e. by completing the acts of forgiveness.

The only one who can save you is you, and your beliefs, whatever they may be, will stop you from trying and keep you waiting for a savior that quite frankly is not coming. We were sent a savior and we killed him. One person, one task; we will not be sent another. Save yourself. You have been clearly shown how to do this; the rest is up to you.

What will you do with this knowledge? Will you follow Yeshua, save yourself, or continue to wait for a savior like countless have done before you. This may anger some of you, but then you'll remember, you don't believe in any of this. This is your choice. It is also your choice to enter the knowledge based system or to remain in the belief based system. Only you can make this choice. The Source itself cannot and will not make this choice for you.

Making the choice to complete the acts of forgiveness will set you free, but remember, where there is no forgiveness there will always be death. (Luke 13:3-5)

Furthermore, you cannot help another human being until you open your eyes and enter the knowledge based system. If you try, it will be like the blind helping the blind; *'Can a blind man lead another blind man? Surely both will fall into a ditch.'* (Luke 6:39) If you truly wish to help mankind, open your own eyes first; *'First remove the log from your own eye and then you will see clearly enough to remove the speck from your brother's eye.'* (Luke 6:42)

It is very difficult to describe what the knowledge based system is like which is why Yeshua dedicated his life to show us how to witness this system for ourselves. It was his mission in life to show us the way back to the knowledge based system; *'I am the way, the truth, and the life. No one comes to the Source except through me.'* (John 14:6) The Source does not reside in the darkness – the belief based system, but only in the light – the knowledge based system, because the Source is the light.

People believe, to this day, that we can only enter the knowledge based system through allegiance to Yeshua and obedience to his commandments. This is not true. Yeshua showed us how to enter the knowledge based system in a very clear and precise manner, so that we could do it by ourselves. No allegiance to him is required, just understanding. In fact, only allegiance to the Source is natural, all other fealties are forced and perverse.

Others believe that you can enter the knowledge based system through good deeds. This is not true. In the belief based system, good and bad are subjective terms and can be better understood by considering them simply as opposite sides of the same coin. Therefore, good men can sometimes seemingly do bad things and bad men can seemingly do good things. It doesn't make a good man bad or a bad man good. Furthermore, and as you have no doubt experienced in the belief based system, in which we all reside, bad things can be born from good beginnings. The opposite is also true. Therefore, I have found the best that one can do in the belief based system is to do what you think is right and hope for the best!

It is commonly accepted that the Source made Yeshua the cornerstone of salvation for all who believe. This is incorrect. The truth is the Source made Yeshua the cornerstone of salvation for all who understand; '*The stone which the builders (of this belief based system) rejected has become the keystone (of the knowledge based system).*' (Matthew 21:42) Your current beliefs, whatever they may be, blind you to the truth and keep you from understanding.

The deception here is insidious. We are educated from an early age to acknowledge belief and faith as attributes to be cherished and aspired to and that those with strong faith are to be admired. Many of us grew up to believe that to be true followers of Yeshua we must abide in him and bear much fruit by continuing in a daily, personal relationship with God. This relationship is characterized and nurtured by adhering to Yeshua's words and by obeying his commandments, particularly the one to love one another. We are told that those who remain in Yeshua have confidence in prayer and know that God will hear and answer their requests because they desire what Yeshua desires and pray accordingly, in keeping with his will. (John 15:7) A bit vague, right?

We are told that as believers in Yeshua we should try to achieve sanctification. We are told this is a lifelong process where believers progressively grow in holiness and purity in their thoughts, words and actions. This is the path of the righteous who believe that they are virtuous, morally upright and without sin and guilt. The path of the righteous is an endless and fruitless journey. The righteous believe that they are continuing the mission of Yeshua until his return. What they fail to understand is that the mission of the Christ, his task and his alone, was completed by the Christ. Their beliefs and dedication to this lifelong process will keep them busy and distract them from their true purpose which is to do the will of the Source, i.e. to complete their own tasks.

Belief, its propagation and maintenance is big business, probably the biggest and most long-standing business in man's history. We have been misled by those in power within the belief based system. Please do not confuse the powerful with the rich and famous, after all, money itself is merely a concept, it does not really exist, and like all things without substance it can only reside within the belief based system. In order to keep the belief based system strong, Yeshua's life, message and purpose must be embraced and smothered by keeping it vague. Most importantly, the way to the knowledge based system must be concealed. This is the constant task of those who wish to perpetuate the belief based system and thus hold onto the power they have over others. They have done their job well.

It is not in the interest of the powerful in this belief based system that the way back to the knowledge based system become known. The belief based system can only exist if we all choose to participate or are successfully forced or otherwise duped into participating. As soon as we open our eyes, the belief based system for us evaporates and we will again reside within the knowledge based system. Those in power within the belief based system know that Yeshua is their number one enemy. He is the destroyer of the belief based system. This was his task in life. Believers, of course, would argue that Yeshua brought belief into the world. The truth is that belief was already in the world long before Yeshua arrived. Yeshua came to destroy all belief and to replace it with knowledge. Yeshua was the first knower and heralded the end of the belief based system.

Unlike us, Yeshua was not born into the belief based system but rather was born into the knowledge based system as a single or pure energy signature. (Q 19.19 & 3.36) You may recall from chapter three that Yeshua became separated from his parents during a visit to Jerusalem to celebrate the Passover. After seeking him for three days, they found him in the temple, sitting amid the teachers, listening to them and asking them questions. (Luke 2:46) It wasn't long before they were asking Yeshua questions, and they were astonished at his understanding and his answers. (Luke 2:46-47) Yeshua was already an astounding teacher at twelve years of age, whose understanding of the Scriptures amazed Israel's finest scholars. When Mary found Yeshua she said to him, "Son, why have you done this to us? Look, your father and I have sought you anxiously." Yeshua simply answered her saying; *Did you not know that I must be about my Father's business?* (Luke 2:49) As Yeshua was born into the knowledge based system, he was able to be about the will of the Source from an early age. Yeshua was here, not to do his own will, but to do the will of the One who sent Him. The task given to Yeshua by the Source was to show us how to return to the knowledge based system, our home.

Every religion in the world is based on man's desire to reach God. The majority of religions teach that man must do righteous deeds and perform religious service to become good enough for salvation. We have practiced one sort of religion or another for thousands of years; has this approach ever worked? This is the deceiver exercising his control over us due to our lack of knowledge and understanding. At the core of this deception is a desire to distract you from the truth, to keep you occupied trying to decipher the teaching of your religious beliefs and thus from what you should be doing, the will of the Source.

The religion built up around the teachings of Yeshua, Christianity, has thus far failed to reveal the purpose of his life. I'm not sure whether this has been done through ignorance or design. Like all religions, Christianity is full of rules and rituals which bear no relevance to the truth which Yeshua was to bear witness to. Yeshua himself was not religious and held little credence in religious rituals. Religious rituals serve only to distract us from the truth which leads me to believe that there is deception here at some level. In truth, religion and its many rituals keep us so busy fighting for the scraps that fall from the table that we have missed our God-given right to sit at the table.

I will admit, at this juncture, that my thoughts seem somewhat religious in nature which would violate entirely my promise at the beginning of our journey. I guess the best way to dissuade you of any thoughts that this book is trying to establish a new religious dogma or reinvent an old one is to highlight that religious dogma can only survive in the belief based system. Think about it. All religious dogmata are based in belief which finds rich soil in which to grow if you live in the belief based system. The problem that exists when trying to talk about the truth is that the belief based system, and in particular religion, has insidiously intertwined itself with the truth, like weeds trying to strangle a flower. Religion is the biggest weed.

Religious belief is, and always has been big business. I'm told the heart of this business is to save your soul. When one adopts a religion, the knowledge that one's soul is in peril is big news. Prior to adopting a religion, some may not have even realized they had a soul and after having been initiated into their new religion still don't understand the concept. This is understandable as the religious definition of the soul is somewhat obscure and advice on how to experience it is rare and vague at best.

The core of religious belief has not changed since it was invented. At the center of all religions is the belief in a higher power which created us lesser beings. Most mainstream religions refer to this higher power as God. Each religion believes that its God is the true God, but the truth is that each person, regardless of religion, has their own concept of who and what God is, and nobody is right. You didn't actually think that the God you believed in was the true God, did you? What about the God your neighbour believes in? Is that the true God as well? What about your neighbour's neighbour? There are over seven billion people living on this earth and they all believe in a different God. Can all of them be right? Can any of them be right?

As enlightened believers we disapprove of adoring false gods. The truth of the matter is of course that each and every believer has their own concept of who and what God is and worship this concept. All believers will find it a challenge to verbally express their concept of God and they find themselves using vague terms to do so and justifying their inability to describe God by saying that we could never explain the divine; it is simply beyond our understanding. However, if each and everyone's concept of God is different, and it is, then how can the God you worship not be a false idol? For those who reside in the belief based system, which is all of us, the only way that your worship could not be of a false idol is if your concept of God is a real and true reflection of who and what God is, in which case, you are the only one. The only other way that your worship of God could not be of a false idol is if you reside in the knowledge based system, in which case, you are the only one. Are you the only one?

If one employs laws of probability, the odds of any one of the many concepts of God being a true reflection of who and what God is would be significantly less than the chance of one kicking a rugby ball and hoping to land it on the head of a pin which is traveling at high speed in random directions. Of course, I could have just said that it's impossible that anyone's concept of God is correct, but you just never know! In any case, as believers we still worship false idols like we did when religion was first invented. The only difference may be that years ago, believers put more effort into creating physical representations of their concept of God than we do today. In short, as believers, we worship false gods because we believe but do not know – 'You Samaritans worship without knowledge...' (John 4:22) How could your God not be a false idol if you do not know who and what you are worshipping? One can only know God if one resides in the knowledge based system.

To live without knowledge of the Source is the definition of sin. Therefore, to live within a vacuum or the belief based system is sinful. Sin is not a feeling, a thought or the absence thereof, it's not an action or inaction; it's a state of existence. This world (we who reside within the belief based system) does not **know** the Source. This is sinful. Therefore, don't be afraid to think, to feel or to act in the belief based system. Don't be paralysed by such things because you think certain thoughts, feelings and actions may be sinful. They are not. Don't allow such things to exercise control over you. Instead be their master. In the belief based system, it's important that you be the master of your beliefs, not the other way around. When you are blind, use a guide dog; do not let the guide dog use you. Make such things work in your favor and not against you as you will need all the help you can get to complete the task given to you by the Source.

If Yeshua had not spoken to us, we would have been unaware that we were guilty of living in sin; '*If I had not come to tell them, they would have no sin, but now they have no excuse for their sin.*' (John 15:22) Now we have no excuse for our sin because he has shown us how to leave the belief based system, which we chose to enter, and how to return to the knowledge based system. We are now aware of our sin and how to expunge it.

I trust that the definition of sin is now clear. This definition of sin makes it very obvious who is living in sin, all of us, and who is not, none of us. I guess we can all stop pointing the finger now! It's also now unequivocal, that any act, including acts of charity and righteousness, performed in the belief based system and thus without knowledge of the Source are hollow acts perpetrated in sin. This is why such acts are corruptible because they stem from the actions of the corrupted. Regardless of what you do within the belief based system, you are leading a sinful life. This may be very hard to take and fly in the face of all that you previously held to be true, but at least you now have a very clear definition of sin. This is important because it makes clear to all how to leave a sinful life behind. It can only be done by entering the knowledge based system.

Yeshua was born into the knowledge based system. This is why he could say; '*I know the Father and the Father knows me.*' (John 10:15) This is why it was told that Yeshua lived without sin because he resided in the knowledge based system and not the belief based system. As such, he did not **believe** in the Source, he **knew** the Source. Let me repeat this because it's critical. Yeshua didn't believe in God. Yeshua knew God. To believe in God is sinful. If you wish to live without sin, you must know God, you must reside in the knowledge based system.

It was the task of the Christ to create a way for us to return to the knowledge based system. The Grail or gate is the way he created, and he included instructions how to operate this gate in the prayer he gave us. Repentance invokes the power of the Grail allowing you passage from the belief based system into the knowledge based system. This of course made him very unpopular with those in power at the time because if we all decided to leave the belief based system and to reside within the knowledge based system, those in power within the belief based system would suddenly become powerless. This was and still is a very scary prospect and a continuing threat for those who hold power in the belief based system. At the center of this power structure is the deceiver. The belief based system is his domain.

Yeshua didn't come specifically to bear the burden of sin but to create the Grail allowing us to return home. However, in doing so, he had to bear the burden of sin, as the Grail had to be created from this side, the belief based system.

The idea that the Holy Grail was a physical item was a story created by those in power and was created to misdirect people so that, not only would they not devote themselves to considering and deciphering the message in the prayer given to us by Yeshua but would be completely distracted by a fruitless quest to find an Unholy Grail created by them. They wanted to make people look in the wrong direction, to distract them from the truth. This seed of misdirection sown by those in power was watered by our belief and grew so strong that those in power were eventually able to start wars over it encouraging those with strong beliefs to kill each other so that they could profit. To ensure their power, they needed to keep the knowledge based system and the way to enter it a secret.

Yeshua put the message of the Grail in a prayer in the hope that if we said it enough times it would hopefully enter our psyche and finally be understood. Those in power ensured that the prayer itself (the Our Father), wherein the path to the true Grail lay, was never hidden whilst at the same time creating and spreading rumors about a false Grail that was hidden. Why? The best place to hide something you do not want found is in clear view of all to see because you will not seek that which is not hidden. This was damage limitation by the deceiver which demonstrates that he knows human nature very well. The hypocrisy here runs very deep indeed. People committed all sorts of atrocities in the hunt for a false Grail – war, torture, theft, rape, murder, and the path to the true Grail was a message of forgiveness! The deceiver did and continues to do his job well.

Nevertheless, when you invoke the power of the Grail by completing the acts of forgiveness, you will see the truth allowing you to make the choice of accepting the truth or again to close your eyes to the truth and choose to believe whatever you want to believe. This is your choice.

You must understand, you cannot choose to believe and know at the same time, this is impossible. One's eyes cannot be open and closed at the same time. One of the greatest barriers to entering the knowledge based system will be your current belief based system, whatever that may be. I did say at the beginning of our journey that this book is not meant to challenge your beliefs or to replace them and that if your beliefs work for you giving you support through your life, then I suggest that you may not want or need to discard them. However, this advice only applies when you reside within the belief based system. The best way to explain this is to compare your beliefs to a cane. A blind man needs a cane to help him navigate in the darkness – the belief based system of which I speak. In the knowledge based system where your eyes are open, the cane (your beliefs) become redundant. Why would you need a cane when you can see all things?

When you are ready to choose the truth, you must accept it completely. This means you must accept that this life, the belief based system, is a mirage. You may hold certain things in this life very dearly and compassionately, but these will need to be relinquished, all of them. If you do not completely relinquish your beliefs and all that you hold dear within the belief based system, whatever or whomever that may be, you cannot permanently reside within the knowledge based system.

What a person holds dear in the belief based system is irrelevant. It could be your money, property, achievements, religion, wife, husband, father, mother, child, body, intellect or spirituality. It's not what you hold dear that is important, but your relationship with it. What you hold dear can become like the roots of a tree. The deeper the roots, the more anchored you will become in the belief based system and the more difficult it will be to pass into the knowledge based system. It could even be something as seemingly insignificant as a coat or other item or idea you hold dear for whatever reason. If you do not completely relinquish all that you hold dear within the belief based system, you cannot permanently reside within the knowledge based system. The reason for this is because what you hold dear in the belief based system does not belong in the knowledge based system. This may sound very cold to some of you, but it is exactly that compassion that will blind you from the truth. Yes, the deception is very subtle indeed!

One must also understand that nothing within the belief based system bears an authentic reflection of its true nature, giving you false representations, which constantly corrupts one's understanding of reality, i.e. the knowledge based system. For example, we continually fail to grasp the concept and passage of time because we reside in the belief based system and everything within the belief based system is subject to belief/opinion including time itself. Depending on your beliefs which constantly fluctuate, your concept of time will vary. By way of exemplification, when you believe that you are having a good time, time itself can feel shorter than it is. When you are having a bad time, which can happen at any moment, even when you are having a good time, time can seem longer than it is. This demonstrates that the belief based system can be so strong that it can even warp one's perception of time. The truth of course is that the passage of time is constant and not in any way subject to your feelings!

When you use the Grail, you will enter the knowledge based system and realize who and what you are. You are the pinnacle of creation, you are its guardian, its custodian. You will no longer be interested in things which can only be important in the belief based system.

As guardians and custodians, this world and everything in it is ours, yours and mine equally. It's ours by birth right. We have a responsibility to it and to each other. The idea that you can have another person convince you, for whatever reason, that you should now fight and kill each other over a small part of it when the truth is it's all yours, is ridiculous! You also have the right to roam this earth without restriction and words like foreigner and immigrant were created to restrict you from doing this. This deception can only occur in the belief based system and it can create conflict and war. War of course, next to religion, is the second biggest business in the world. War, conflict and religion are intrinsically intertwined. Religions can create wars and wars can create religions.

On entering the knowledge based system all your questions will be answered even ones you never asked. You will know who and what you are. You will know all things because you are connected to all things. Through this connection you will be able to feel and communicate with all things. You will be able to be what you were created to be – the guardian and custodian of all creation. You will be able to take your rightful place at the table of creation itself. This is your inheritance, claim it!

Chapter Seven

The Trinity: Our Creation, and Fall

Why are we not born into the knowledge based system like Yeshua? The best way to explain this is to use the parable of the *Garden of Eden,* a euphemism for our fall from grace.

The story of our creation and the Garden of Eden told in the opening chapter of the Catholic Bible (Genesis), is one of the earliest descriptions of paradise. Accounts of the Garden of Eden are also written about in the Talmud, the Jewish Kabbalah and the Qur'an. Although the Garden of Eden is considered by many to be mythological, let us consider the story in general terms and as described in Genesis.

According to the narrative, God created Adam and Eve, the first man and woman. God placed them in the Garden of Eden where they lived with God. Man and woman were in a perfect environment, with all their needs taken care of. The Garden of Eden was the symbolic space of perfect harmony, the place in which absolute happiness reigned. It was nothing less than what was speculated to have been heaven.

God told Adam and Eve that they could eat the fruit from any of the trees in the garden except for the tree of knowledge of good and evil. God warned them that if they ate from this tree they would die. They were also warned of the deceiver who lived in the garden.

One day the deceiver came disguised as a snake and spoke to Eve, tempting her to eat the fruit from the tree of knowledge. Eve told the serpent that God said they should not eat its fruit and they would die if they did. The deceiver told her that this was a lie and instead she would become like God if she consumed the fruit. Eve believed the lie and took a bite of the fruit. She then gave some to Adam for him to eat. Breaking God's commandment not to eat from the tree of knowledge is considered to be man's original sin.

The story recounts that after having eaten the fruit from the tree of knowledge, their eyes were opened, and they became aware of their nakedness and hid from God. When God became aware that they had disobeyed him and eaten from the tree of knowledge, he expelled them from the garden to prevent them from eating from the tree of life and becoming immortal.

Like most religious texts, the Genesis story is somewhat obscure and ambiguous. Eating from the tree of knowledge is a clear transgression of God's command, but it also appears to transform Adam and Eve into something more than they were before. The deceiver told them that consuming the forbidden fruit would make them *'like gods, knowing good and evil'* (Genesis 3:5), and God later expels them from the garden precisely because they have *'become like one of us, knowing good and evil.'* (Genesis 3:22) It's also clear that they did not die from consuming the forbidden fruit like God said they would. It appears therefore that the deceiver told the truth, but God lied.

In fact, many Gnostics believe that the snake should be thanked for bringing knowledge to Adam and Eve, and thereby freeing them from the Demiurge's control. They believe that Demiurge, a supreme being responsible for the fashioning and maintenance of the physical universe, banished Adam and Eve from the garden, because man was now a threat.

The best way to hide the truth is not by concealing it but by corrupting it – turning it on its head. The truth is that we were created to be placed above all creation, to be its custodian and guardian. We were born into the Garden of Eden, the knowledge based system. Like Yeshua, we were born as a single or pure energy signature. Our downfall was not that we ate from the tree of knowledge but that we consumed from the seed of belief. This seed was planted in the garden by the deceiver. He told us that we could accept the truth we were given, or we could consume the fruit from the seed of belief and believe whatever we wanted to believe. We were told that choosing to believe whatever we wanted to believe would set us free. It would open our eyes and allow us to create the world in our image. We were deceived.

Instead of opening our eyes, it closed them, plunging us into darkness. After all, one cannot truly choose to believe what they want to believe unless they are in complete darkness. Because our eyes were closed we could no longer see the truth; *we have eyes but we cannot see.* (Mark 8:18) We no longer knew the Source. Choosing the belief based system over the knowledge based system was our first sin – the original sin. To live in the belief based system is to live without knowledge of the Source, the Source from which all life springs. The garden was the Garden of Knowledge, but we banished ourselves from it by closing our eyes to it.

After consuming the fruit from the seed of belief we became impure, a mixture of two energy signatures. The second energy signature based in belief, blinded us from the truth. We were cut off from the Source, isolated and alone. Despite our actions, the Source never disowned us, and he never will. Instead of condemning us he sent us the Helper. The Helper can see where we cannot. This is when we became a trinity of energy signatures.

The teaching of the trinity has been corrupted over the centuries. The trinity was never, God, the Son and Holy Spirit. Think about it. Is the Son of God and the Holy Spirit equal with God? Did the Christ ever call himself God and who is this Holy Spirit? The Christian doctrine of the trinity defines God as three consubstantial persons (whatever that means!), the Father, the Son (Yeshua), and the Holy Spirit, *one God in three persons*. The three persons are distinct but one.

According to the contemporary teaching of the trinity, there is one God in three persons. While distinct from one another in their relations of origin (*'it is the Father who generates, the Son who is begotten, and the Holy Spirit who proceeds'*) and in their relations with one another, they are stated to be one, co-equal, co-eternal and consubstantial, and *'each is God, whole and entire'*. In as simple terms as I can muster to explain the trinity as I was taught growing up under the Christian doctrine, God exists as a unity of three distinct persons – Father, Son, and Holy Spirit. Each of the persons is distinct from the other, yet identical in essence. In other words, each is fully divine in nature, but each is not the totality of the trinity. Each has an independent will. The Father is not the same person as the Son, who is not the same person as the Holy Spirit. Each is individual and divine, yet there are not three gods but one God.

Wow how confusing is that? The trinity as it is taught today is often referred to as the *'mystery'* of the trinity, a title which I completely endorse. I was educated not to question the teaching of the trinity and I was made to feel that I couldn't understand it because I was in some way cognitively lacking. However, I have found if someone cannot explain a topic in the simplest of terms, that can be understood by all, then that person does not really understand the topic. Let's be honest, the above explanation of the trinity is confusing at best.

The teaching of the trinity was either misunderstood or intentionally perverted. In any case, here is the truth about the trinity. During Yeshua's ministry on earth, he was often asked if a person led a good life would they enter heaven when they died. He replied saying that nobody could enter heaven without changing their very nature and that this nature could only be changed by completing the acts of forgiveness. Yeshua explained that each person, in the belief based system, was an amalgamation of three different energy signatures which occupy the one space. Each of these energy signatures has its own independent consciousness but together they are one.

To be clear – yes, it's you. You are the trinity. You are an embodiment thereof. Is it so hard to believe? Consider sunlight. Sunlight (or white light) is invisible to the naked eye but we know that it exists because of its effect. We can see things in its presence but not in its absence. We consider sunlight to be a single independent energy signature and it is. It has its own well-defined characteristics such as wavelength, frequency and speed and will always behave in the same way under the same circumstances.

However, we know today that sunlight is made up of seven individual and independent energy signatures that are visible to the naked eye. Sunlight also includes many more individual and independent energy signatures which are not visible to the naked eye, for example, infrared and ultra violet radiation. The seven visible energy signatures we call red, orange, yellow, green, blue, indigo and violet. When they appear together in nature we call the display a rainbow. This is where the rain drops split the sunlight into its component parts and although I know exactly what it is and how to reproduce it in a laboratory, I still find the display to be very beautiful and I always stop to admire nature's exhibit.

If light is an amalgamation of more than seven singular and separate energy signatures which come together to give white light, a single energy signature, then why can you not be a single energy signature formed by the combination of three? *'Truly, I say to you, we speak of what we know and we tell about the things we have seen, but you don't accept our testimony. If you don't believe when I tell you earthly things, what then, when I tell you heavenly things?'* (John 3:11-12) When the seven individual energy signatures (red, orange, yellow, green, blue, indigo and violet) come together, they form a single energy signature which we call white light. We are formed in a similar way. When our three individual energy signatures come together, they form a single energy signature which we call a human being.

Can each of your individual energy signatures recognize each other? Yes, they can to one degree or another. Think about it. Have you ever felt conflicted? A single energy signature cannot experience conflict and be divided against itself; *'If a house is divided against itself, that house will not be able to stand.'* (Mark 3:25) It takes at least two individual energy signatures, which recognize each other as such, with their own consciousness and attributes to create conflict. However, where conflict prevails, unity will not, for Satan himself could not stand divided against himself; *'If Satan has risen up against himself and is divided, he cannot stand, but he is finished!'* (Mark 3:26)

What else should I reveal about the trinity? Everything you do in this life is being observed and recorded. By whom? By you! Everything you do, say, think and feel is being recorded in precise detail. The ability to record and retain these details is an attribute of one of the three. Therefore, the belief that one can hide their true intentions from the world is a falsehood; you are the true observer.

One of the energy signatures does not, and cannot, reside within the knowledge based system and this is why your very nature must change before you can enter. One of the three will also take part in your day of judgment. Sounds scary? Don't worry because the person who will bear witness against you or for you, will be you, i.e. one of the three. I guess that this is only fair as this person knows all things about you and has always been with you. I guess I should finish on this topic by at least giving some practical advice that will be useful in the belief based system in which we reside. Do not practice judgment of others in this life, as the more you practice, the better you will get. In the end, as you will judge yourself, you do not want to be too good at it; *'Your own words will be used to judge you – to declare you either innocent or guilty.'* (Matthew 12:37)

Why did the deceiver show us how to close our eyes to the truth? What was his motivation? The best way I can describe this to you is to attempt to invoke within you, empathy for an easily conceivable situation in your youth. Imagine you are a child at school and you have misbehaved. You are singled out by the teacher for reprimand and your punishment is expulsion from the school. How do you feel? Most likely, you feel frightened, lonely and humiliated in front of the class. You may also feel hurt and angry that you are being singled out. If you have strict parents, your fear may even run deeper at the thought that the teacher will inform them of your poor behavior and punishment. Your fear may run so deep that you argue and refuse to admit that you are culpable of or singularly responsible for the act you are being accused of. If you have a clear understanding of how you felt or may have felt in this moment, I want you to rate your feelings out of ten. Ten being the most scared (and/or hurt, angry, lonely, humiliated or any other bad feeling et cetera) you have ever felt and zero being no fear or bad feelings at all.

Now imagine that instead of just you, the teacher has singled out you and another. Does the number you had given your bad feelings, whatever they may have been, decrease? What happens to your feelings if the number of people the teacher reprimands continues to increase? Does the number you had given your bad feelings continue to decrease? Now imagine that the teacher has singled out the whole human race for expulsion. Now how do you feel? My bet is that your feelings of pain at being expelled are at the very least substantially reduced and thus easier to cope with if not completely dispensed with and possibly replaced with more positive feelings such as joy or at least a euphoria which comes with a successful rebellion. This is why he did it – to manage his pain.

Although the deceiver was instrumental in our fall, he has no power over us, over and above what we give him. However, let me explain by way of parable how far we have fallen. Imagine you come across the most beautiful being you have ever seen. This beautiful and amazing being has been charged by the Source as custodian and guardian of all creation. This being is so special that the universe itself created a coat to shelter it from the elements and to help it in its position as custodian. The custodian is connected both to the Source and to the entire universe. Through this connection he knows all things and can communicate with all things. He has power beyond measure.

As you approach this being you see that it has a blindfold on. This blindfold prevents the being from knowing who and what it is and what it is supposed to be doing. The blindfold severs the connection between itself and the Source. This severed connection will ultimately result in his demise; *'I am the vine and you are the branches. As long as you remain in me and I in you, you will bear much fruit, but apart from me you can do nothing. Whoever does not remain in me is like a branch that is thrown away and withers; and the withered branches are thrown into the fire and burned.'* (John 15:5-6) You cannot remove this blindfold for him, only he can do that. However, he thinks the blindfold is part of him because he was born wearing the blindfold.

The being is on its knees and is scratching at the ground. You approach and ask him what he is doing. He replies that he is looking for gold. You ask why. He replies that he believes that gold is very precious and that its acquisition will make him wealthy and powerful. You ask who told him this. He becomes suspicious of your presence and questioning, and covetous of his quarry and asks you to leave. How does this make you feel – sad, puzzled, incredulous, angry or maybe a combination of all these? This being thinks very little of itself if it believes that it needs gold to make it important.

Don't get hung up on the details of the parable but rather consider, for example, that gold can represent anything that distracts you from the will of the Source. It could represent your career, your family, your spouse, your children, your material wealth or indeed your own body.

Although custodians of creation, we destroy that which we were charged to protect. We do this because we are no longer aware of who and what we are. We are blind to the truth. We chose to close our eyes. Closing our eyes however does not change who and what we are. You are the guardian and custodian of all creation. Yeshua explained this to his disciples and this explanation was recorded by Matthew (21:18-22) and Mark (11:12-14).

Matthew (21:18-22) and Mark (11:12-14) are famously known as *'the cursing of the fig tree'* . Matthew writes that one day, early in the morning, as Yeshua was on his way back to Jerusalem from Bethany, he was hungry. Seeing a fig tree by the road, he went up to it but found nothing on it except leaves. Then he said to it, "May you never bear fruit again!" Immediately the tree withered. When the disciples saw this, they were amazed. "How did the fig tree dry up at once!" they asked. Yeshua replied, "Truly I tell you, if you have faith and do not doubt (who and what you are), not only could you do what I have done with the fig tree, but you could even say to that mountain, 'Get up and throw yourself into the sea!' and it would be done."

Many of us believe today that this was a symbolic act by Yeshua. A fruitful fig tree is considered to be a symbol of blessing and prosperity whereas the absence or death of a fig tree symbolizes poverty and death. Symbolically, the fig tree was considered to represent the spiritual deadness of Israel, who while very religious outwardly with all the sacrifices and ceremonies, were spiritually barren. By cursing the fig tree, causing it to wither and die, it was considered that Yeshua was pronouncing his coming judgment of Israel and demonstrating his power to carry it out. Even after all this time, some think Yeshua came to bring judgment when it was quite clear that it was not judgment he brought but a message of forgiveness; *'God did not send the Son into the world to condemn the world; instead through Him the world is to be saved.'* (John 3:17)

The parable of the fig tree is also considered, by others, to teach that religious observance is not enough to guarantee salvation, unless that person bears spiritual fruit, whatever that means! Some even argue that as the fig tree was destroyed by Yeshua that he is guilty of destroying property that did not belong to him. They believe this demonstrates that Yeshua made mistakes just like everyone else. Some also say it wasn't fair of Yeshua to condemn a fig tree for not bearing fruit out of season; *'for it was not the season for figs.'* (Mark 11:13)

Of course, none of this is the truth. I understand that it is very difficult to comprehend Yeshua's words and actions regarding the fig tree. This lack of understanding stems from the fact that you do not yet understand who and what you are. What Yeshua meant is that creation itself will obey your every command as you are its guardian and custodian. You are the pinnacle of all creation and everyone knows this but you. The deceiver keeps this knowledge from you and he is so far doing a very good job of it. If you knew who and what you are you would realize that the *'cursing of the fig tree'* was not a symbolic act by Yeshua but rather he was simply telling us what we are capable of.

Historians, of course, consider this event to be either a fabrication or an exaggeration because such an act would be impossible. We accept such rational thoughts and reasoning because we are unaware of who and what we are. However, the Source has restored all of these things to us by sending a Savior, a Messiah, who provided for our deliverance from the bondage of sin, the belief based system.

Thus, the day will come when we will be given an opportunity to atone for our original sin, reversing its effect by opening our eyes and allowing us to make the choice of accepting the truth and returning to the Source. We will not be expected to make this choice until we again see the truth. We were shown how to open our eyes again allowing us the opportunity to make this choice. We can open our eyes through the acts of forgiveness. When you have completed the acts of forgiveness, you will see the truth allowing you to make the choice of accepting the truth or again to close your eyes to the truth and choose to believe whatever you want to believe. This is your choice. Now you have choice...now you have power!

Chapter Eight

Entry into Jerusalem & the Belief Based System

Don't feel sorry for Yeshua and his final moments on earth. Don't feel sorry that he was scourged and nailed to a cross where he ultimately died. He was able to predict his ultimate demise not because he was able to predict the future but because he planned it. Unless Yeshua planned the event of his death we could never be sure he lay down his life willingly. If the truth was he could simply tell the future and the future foretold his death, then his willingness could be construed simply as resignation that such events could not be changed. This is not the truth.

Yeshua planned the event of his death and he used those around him to make it happen. This is why he was able to say; *'I give my life for the sheep... No one takes it from me, but I lay it down freely.'* (John 10:15-18) Why did he feel the need to do this?

When Yeshua spoke to the general population preaching forgiveness and explaining how to complete the acts of forgiveness he was berated by those who felt that the wrong they had suffered was unforgivable. These people challenged him saying that it was easy for him to preach forgiveness when he had never been wronged in the way that they had. They said he could never understand the anger and hurt they felt and under such circumstances it was impossible to forgive.

The Truth

This event in Yeshua's life told him what he needed to do. All that remained were the details of how it would be done. It was from this point that Yeshua planned his final moments on earth. If you do not trust what I say, think of the alternative. If Yeshua did not plan his final moments on earth the alternative is they happened by pure accident or by divine intervention as believers like to think. If this was the case, then all that he suffered would not have been done willingly. If this was the case, then Yeshua may simply have resigned himself to the fact that his life was forfeit and thus met his end meekly by making no intervention to save it. Yeshua was no fool and he was not meek. He was a lion among sheep. He planned his final moments on earth and thus his willingness to lay down his life to show us how to forgive is explicit in both his actions and forethought.

I think, however, it is important to point out that a willingness to die to the point of planning the circumstances around one's own death, to demonstrate to the world the act of forgiveness, is not the same thing as wanting to die. Yeshua loved life and he demonstrated this in the way that he lived.

Yeshua knew a public demonstration of how to forgive was necessary. He knew that he needed to reach as large an audience as possible so that many would bear witness to his actions. He also knew he needed to demonstrate forgiveness for an act perpetrated on his person that would universally be considered unforgivable – his murder.

He knew he had to pay this ultimate price. If it had been anything else, such as false imprisonment, a beating, rape or other type of injustice, there would have been endless debate, argument and comparisons made that the injustice perpetrated on him wasn't as bad as some other injustices. For example, one may argue that rape is worse than a beating which is not as bad as false imprisonment and thus some injustices are forgivable or more forgivable than others. Of course, taking someone's life, especially in the horrific way that occurred to Yeshua was the worst injustice that can be perpetrated on a person, especially an innocent. Yeshua's act of laying down his life trumped all other injustices that can be perpetrated on a person. This eliminates any possibility of arguing that some acts can be forgiven but not others.

Yeshua knew his reputation was growing among the people and that he was feared and hated by many among the Jewish Sanhedrin. He was winning the support and approval of the people while exposing the failure and hypocrisy of the ruling Jewish leadership. He knew the Jewish authorities, for their part, would not and did not take this lying down and they were perpetually trying to figure out a way to have him arrested. He also knew his popularity and ability to draw crowds was being watched closely by the occupying force of the time, the Roman army.

The Sanhedrin was fully aware of the strong and ever-growing support Yeshua enjoyed. At the Passover in Jerusalem, there was a palpable anticipation of the pilgrims from Galilee, whose lives had greatly benefited from Yeshua's extensive healing ministry, together with the Judeans for whom the Lazarus incident had greatly increased Yeshua's credibility and status. All this would have proven to his many followers that he was indeed the Messiah who was prophesized would set his people free.

The Passover held every year in Jerusalem was a huge event and attracted crowds from all over. Yeshua knew, due to his growing reputation, that his presence in the city that weekend would draw even bigger crowds than usual. After all, hadn't the Messiah just raised a man from the dead! The weekend of the Passover would thus provide the largest crowd possible to witness the act of forgiveness. Truly, this would be the greatest Passover in Jewish history.

Those in the Jewish Sanhedrin who hated Yeshua would need very little provocation to have him killed should the opportunity arise. They knew of course it was unlawful for them to take this matter openly into their own hands. Yeshua would not only provide them with the opportunity they so desperately sought but would also provide them with encouragement to ensure they helped him to complete his task.

How did Yeshua encourage them? Here are just some of the things he did.

Entry to Jerusalem

Yeshua instructed his disciples to bring a donkey on which he would sit for his entrance into Jerusalem. Yeshua knew the prophecy of Zachariah 9:9, that Israel's future king would come riding on a foal of a donkey, copying Solomon's entrance into Jerusalem when he was declared king. However, Yeshua had no intention of becoming King. He was mocking the prophecy and the Jewish leaders in turn. He hoped his actions would infuriate the Jewish Sanhedrin and he did this to intentionally provoke them. Of course, the majority of his followers would have seen this as a symbolic action by Yeshua, communicating his kingship to the expectant crowds. Yeshua at the very least would not have discouraged this interpretation because he wanted his public demonstration to get back to the leaders within the Sanhedrin.

The crowds responded by laying robes and leafy palm branches in his pathway to create a royal carpet and by claiming him their Davidic King. The crowds openly acclaimed Yeshua as King instead of Caesar! This would have not only infuriated the Sanhedrin but it was an important act by Yeshua because he knew the Sanhedrin would not have the power to take his life but that they would need action to be taken by the local authority, Pontius Pilate. By allowing himself to be claimed king, together with the public unrest his presence in this city caused, he gave sufficient reason for the local authority to reprimand him at the very least if not to take more robust action.

The whole of Jerusalem was in turmoil over the presence of Yeshua and his entrance into the city. The crowd spread the word to all in Jerusalem who had not yet heard of Yeshua. Due to the unrest created by Yeshua in the city, some Pharisees requested of Yeshua to rebuke the crowds for their messianic exuberance, but he refused to correct or curtail the excitement of the crowd caused by his entrance into the city. Yeshua's behavior in exciting the crowds to near frenzy had crossed the point of no return. His actions prepared the ground to complete the task he was given by forcing the situation to come to a head. If the local government officials wished to keep the peace and the current Jewish religious establishment hoped to retain their hold over the people, Yeshua had to be killed.

As you may already know, Yeshua did not stop there. What else did Yeshua do to provoke the Jewish religious leaders and their powerful supporters? Yeshua went to the temple and overturned the tables and chairs of the money changers, throwing out merchants and customers alike and refusing entrance to any who were carrying goods for sale. He then began to teach the people that the temple was to be a house of prayer for all nations not a den of thieves where the rich and powerful could exploit the poor under the guise of facilitating worship of God.

If you believe Yeshua carried out this public demonstration simply on moral and religious grounds then I ask, could you be wrong? Furthermore, why would Yeshua pick that particular time to do this? Think about it. Money changers and merchants would have used the temple on regular occasions especially during Passover when there would have been a lot of people in the city. This would not have been Yeshua's first visit to Jerusalem and not his first visit during Passover. Therefore, Yeshua would have known that money changers and merchants would occupy the temple selling their wares. Why did

Yeshua not do this before now and why did he choose this particular time to carry out this public demonstration?

By these actions, Yeshua not only directly challenged the local rich and powerful business men but again challenged the Jewish religious leadership who were complicit with, and were most likely benefiting from, this corruption of devotion to God. At the same time, Yeshua was openly adored by the people, not least because he was healing the blind and lame but because the stories that he could raise the dead were spreading.

Yeshua continued to exacerbate the situation by preaching in the temple complex. While preaching, the chief priests approached Yeshua and confronted him regarding his actions the day before; overturning the tables and chairs of the money changers, throwing out merchants and customers alike and refusing entrance to any who were carrying goods for sale. They asked; *'By what authority are you doing these things.'* (Mark 11:28) The chief priests had authority over the temple and its activities and Yeshua had no right to do what he had done. This question and many more were asked of Yeshua in the hope he would give them an answer that would allow the Sanhedrin to have him arrested. But Yeshua was not yet ready to be arrested.

Yeshua rarely answered their many questions directly. In many cases he turned the tables on them by promising to answer their question if they first answered his. Of course, he posed questions that they were incapable of or unprepared to answer, thus further humbling the Jewish leaders in front of large crowds of people. Yeshua followed up his attack by telling a series of parables. There was nothing subtle about these parables and all who were there knew that they were directed against the religious leaders. This was humiliating indeed for the religious elite.

The religious leaders were not deterred by this humiliation but continued trying to figure out a way to have Yeshua arrested. They realized if they seized him then in the temple, the attempted arrest would cause a riot and his followers would not allow it. Therefore, they continued to question Yeshua in the hope he would provide an answer that would incriminate himself.

I won't go into detail regarding all the questions that were asked of Yeshua, but I would like to recount my favorite. This question was fabricated by the combined effort of the Pharisees (a Jewish sect known for its zeal in keeping the law) and the Herodians (those loyal to Herod's Dynasty). This temporary alliance of opposing factions demonstrated that Yeshua was perceived as a major threat to the entire belief based system and all existing power structures contained there within.

'Teacher, they said, we know that you are a man of integrity and that you teach the way of God in accordance with the truth. You aren't swayed by others, because you pay no attention to who they are. Tell us then, what is your opinion? Is it right to pay the imperial tax to Caesar or not?' (Matthew 22:16)

Yeshua, who was quite aware of what they were trying to do, replied; *'You hypocrites, why are you trying to trap me? Show me the coin used for paying the tax. They brought him a denarius and he asked them, Whose image is this? And whose inscription? Caesar's, they replied. Yeshua said to them, So give back to Caesar what is Caesar's, and to God what is God's.'* (Matthew 22:17-22)

When I heard this story as a child, I was overawed by Yeshua's intelligence and his ability to think on his feet. As an adult, not only am I still in admiration of his intelligence but I am humbled by his unwavering commitment to his task in life, to teach us about the Father. Even when these people were posing questions to trap him, he used the question to continue his teaching to all those who could hear him. He could not be deterred from his path, not even for a moment. Truly magnificent I say.

Yeshua persisted in praising his Father whilst at the same time exposing the hypocrisy of the existing power structures. He continued to win the people over by healing the blind and lame and curing all sorts of ailments. The demonstration of his abilities to heal, confirmed for people the rumor that he had indeed raised someone from the dead and that he must therefore be the Messiah that was prophesized. All eyes were now on Yeshua. What would he do?

The Sanhedrin saw the actions of Yeshua as a direct challenge to their authority and his scathing attacks on the current religious authorities made it clear he had no desire to ally himself with the current leadership but rather he was there to overthrow their authority and replace it with his own. They realized their very existence and survival was at stake and thus they could not stand idly by and put up with the challenge to their authority. It was quite clear to them now that Yeshua would assume power if he was not killed. However, they realized they needed the local authority to arrest and kill Yeshua. But how could Yeshua be arrested when he was always surrounded by so many followers? His followers would not allow him to be arrested but would come to his defence. Yeshua by his purposeful actions did not only provide the Jewish Sanhedrin, the local rich and powerful, and the local authority with encouragement to arrest him but he would also provide them with the opportunity they so desperately sought.

During this time it is accepted that the chief priests, scribes and elders were plotting how to have Yeshua arrested and killed. It is believed they met in the house of Caiaphas, the high priest, to discuss the option of how best to dispense with Yeshua; *'The feast of the Unleavened Bread which is called the Passover, was now drawing near, and the chief priests and the teachers of the law were looking for a way to kill Yeshua, because they were afraid of the people.'* (Luke 22:1-2) The desire of the Jewish religious elite to have Yeshua arrested and killed is well documented in the gospels; *'The chief priests and teachers of the law wanted to kill him and the elders of the Jews as well, but they were unable to do anything, for all the people were listening to him and hanging on his words.'* (Luke 19:47-48) The only thing the Jewish leaders lacked was opportunity; *'The teachers of the law and the chief priests would have liked to arrest him that very moment… but they were afraid of the crowd. So they left, looking for another opportunity.'* (Luke 20:19-20)

The general understanding is they had decided to wait until after the weeklong festival of the Feast of Unleavened Bread. They reasoned that once the festival was over, the crowds would disperse from the city and return to their homes. They would then be able to arrest and kill Yeshua without fear of inciting a revolt. Unfortunately for them, Yeshua had plans of his own and would not be deterred from completing them. Yeshua's timetable was also different to those who sought his demise. Yeshua required as many witnesses as possible to bear testimony to his actions. The festival and Yeshua's notoriety had drawn the largest crowds ever seen to Jerusalem. The scene was now set.

The Passover

Yeshua instructed his disciples to secure a large room in a particular house in Jerusalem and to prepare for the Passover meal; *'Go into the city to a certain man and say to him, the teacher says, my time is at hand. I will keep the Passover at your house with my disciples.'* (Matthew 26:17-19) Prior to this day, Yeshua with his disciples had traveled back and forth from Bethany located about one and a half miles to the east of Jerusalem on the south-eastern slope of the Mount of Olives. Why did Yeshua do this, and why did he choose this day to reside in the city?

Some argue that according to the Old Testament regulations (Deut. 16:5-6), the Passover must be eaten within the city of Jerusalem and that Yeshua was simply adhering to the Old Testament. Nonsense! The truth is, Yeshua didn't care about rules and regulations and was often seen openly to flout them. Why would it now be so important to adhere to Old Testament regulations? It wasn't. Yeshua returned to Bethany every night because he was not yet ready to be arrested. He stayed in the city this particular night because he was now ready to be arrested.

But why did he choose this particular day? This particular day was the day before the Sabbath during the biggest festival in the Jewish calendar. Yeshua was about to present the Jewish religious leaders with the opportunity to have him arrested and condemned to death. Yeshua knew the ability of the Sanhedrin to act against him would be limited by the Sabbath. He knew this would force them to act quickly against him, giving them very little time to consider the situation and ponder their actions. Given the fact that their humiliation at the hands of Yeshua was still very raw, he knew they would be in the frame of mind to grab any opportunity to have him arrested and less likely to consider the fortuitous nature and timing of the opportunity itself. Yeshua knew his opponents were highly intelligent and given sufficient time they may have realized he was simply using the situation. Yeshua had prepared the scene with impeccable consideration, intelligence and timing.

Matthew alone records Yeshua telling his disciples on that very morning; *'My time is at hand.'* (Matthew 26:18) Yeshua also thus informed his many followers in the temple where he preached during the festival. This created great excitement both among his followers and disciples alike, with the exception of Judas who was the only one made aware of Yeshua's plans, by Yeshua himself.

Robert Barry

Yeshua's message to his followers was coloured by their beliefs. They understood his claim only in light of their own version of messianic expectations. They believed Yeshua was about to force the ultimate confrontation that would lead to his victory over the Jewish religious leaders and more importantly the occupying Roman forces. They believed Yeshua was about to establish his Father's Kingdom on earth and that his followers would have a place within that kingdom. His disciples of course believed they would have elevated and more senior positions within this kingdom. They were all wrong.

Today we are more enlightened, educated and we have the advantage of hindsight. Today, we believe Yeshua was sacrificed as God's Passover lamb to atone for or make reparations for the sins of the entire world. Again, we are all wrong!

Yeshua knew he was about to set in motion events that would ultimately lead to the destruction of the entire belief based system. He knew that once his actions were understood, and that they eventually would be, people would have the choice and the ability to leave the belief based system and enter the knowledge based system where all things are known including the Source.

Although Judas had hoped that events would not have to unfold as Yeshua had planned, he was still willing to aid Yeshua, as was requested of him by his friend. Judas did not drink at the Passover meal but waited apprehensively for his friend's signal that he was to perform his task of betraying him to the Sanhedrin as planned. Judas did not drink because he knew he would need a clear head for the task he was set.

Judas who sat next to Yeshua, which would have been considered a place of honor, received the agreed upon prompt from Yeshua almost immediately; *'Truly, I say to you, one of you will betray me.'* (Mat. 26:20-29) Whilst the others argued who the betrayer might be, Judas asked Yeshua, "You do not mean me, Master, do you?" By asking the question, Judas demonstrated that he was still somewhat reluctant to betray his friend even by design. Yeshua reminded Judas of his earlier commitment and agreement to perform this act by saying, "You have said so" i.e. "You agreed to it, please now keep your promise to me."

Judas broke bread with Yeshua. Yeshua also did not drink; *'I will not taste the fruit of the vine from now until the day I drink with you, new wine in my Father's kingdom.'* (Matthew 26:29) Yeshua chose not to drink because he, most of all, needed to be clear headed for the night ahead and the completion of the task he had been given by the Source. Yeshua then said to Judas; *'What you are going to do, do quickly.'* (John 13:27) He said these words to Judas because he did not want Judas to deliberate over his actions lest he should reconsider and fail to complete his task. This also shows clear intention on Yeshua's behalf that he had not himself changed his mind and was still willing to complete the task that had been given to him. It is only John who records this interaction between Judas and Yeshua because these instructions were given quietly but John who also sat next to Yeshua overheard this exchange.

Many believe to this day that Judas's demonstration of remorse and return of the money he was given to betray Yeshua was not a demonstration of true contrition because he committed suicide. I beg to differ. I believe that suicide is one of the ultimate signs of remorse, attrition and sacrifice. I understand it is hard not to judge Judas, and it is easier to forgive Peter's denial of Yeshua for example, because the consequences of Judas's betrayal were irreversible. The Jewish religious leaders had used Judas and he had given them exactly what they wanted exactly when they needed it and all his remorse was not going to undo the part he had played in Yeshua's enemy's wicked scheme. I hope you now know that this is not true. The truth is Yeshua and Judas used the Jewish leaders, not the other way around.

The Garden of Gethsemane & The Belief Based System

After some instruction to his disciples Yeshua finished the Passover meal with his friends and departed for the garden at Gethsemane. Yeshua with the aid of his friend Judas was now ready to present to the Sanhedrin their opportunity to have him arrested.

The garden at Gethsemane, a place whose name literally means 'oil press', is located on a slope of the Mount of Olives just across the Kidron Valley from Jerusalem. A garden of ancient olive trees stands there to this day. According to John, Yeshua, when in Jerusalem, often went to Gethsemane to pray. (John 18:2)

Yeshua took with him, Peter and the two sons of Zebedee, John and James. He asked them to wait at the entrance to the garden and remain vigilant. Yeshua knew Judas would bring the arresting crowd through this entrance, as planned. Yeshua proceeded unaccompanied toward the center of the garden, out of sight and earshot. What happened between this time and the time when he was arrested is heavily debated in Christian accounts because no one was there to witness his actions or words.

The Catholic Church provides two possible explanations. The first is that the Holy Spirit inspired Mark and the other gospel writers with the knowledge of what transpired in the Garden of Gethsemane. The second explanation is that, after his resurrection, during the days he spent conversing with and teaching his Apostles and other followers, Yeshua recounted to them many of his otherwise unknowable conversations and actions, some of which were later recorded in the Bible, some of which weren't.

It is my experience that knowledge of events only requires one explanation as there can only be one. Two or more explanations, especially in this case where the explanations are completely divergent, show a complete lack of knowledge. Where two or more explanations exist without knowledge, neither one can be depended on.

In any case, let's consider the details that were directly recorded and those that were later filled in. It's clear from all three accounts that Peter, John and James fell asleep while Yeshua was at the center of the garden. All three accounts agree that Yeshua returned to them, found them sleeping and said, '*So, could you not watch with me one hour?*' (Matthew 26:36-46) However, even where direct testimony can be given, as in the case of their sleep, Luke records this only happening once, where the other two record it happened three times.

Luke's account goes on to defend the three by saying; '*when he rose from prayer, he went to his disciples but found them worn out by their grief and asleep.*' (Luke 22 14:45) They were not asleep through grief. Feelings of acute grief, if this is how they truly felt, are known to create difficulties sleeping. It's chronic grief that wears one down, creating fatigue. The three were asleep because it was late, and they had just eaten and drank wine. It is well known that alcohol is a sedative and can tip you into sleep where you are already fatigued by a long day. This account by Luke strikes me as something written by someone who is somewhat embarrassed by the actions of the disciples and is trying to explain them to the world. The inability to describe events as were witnessed only casts greater doubt on those that were not. Tell the truth. It may feel embarrassing at the time, but this feeling will be short lived. A lie, on the other hand, may live for a very long time.

Luke describes that Yeshua engaged in fervent prayer crying out to God and imploring him to find another way; '*Father, if it is your will, remove this cup from me; yet not my will but yours be done.*' (Luke 22:42) Luke filled in what Yeshua did and said whilst alone by including this sentiment from the prayer Yeshua had given to the people; "Thy will be done on earth as it is in heaven."

It is true Yeshua suffered in the garden, but why? Some say he suffered because he knew what lay ahead for him. It is true that Yeshua knew what lay ahead for him, but this was not the root of his true suffering. Prior to entering the garden, Yeshua lived in the knowledge based system, a system he was born into. In the knowledge based system you are connected to the Source (the Father, God) and thus the power that stems therefrom. Yeshua's true pain only came when he left the knowledge based system and entered the belief based system which he did in the Garden of Gethsemane.

On entering the belief based system, he was overawed by the feeling of being disconnected from the Source. He now would have known true fear which is the root feeling in the belief based system. You cannot know sin until you reside within the belief based system. This is what is meant when it is said that Yeshua took on the sins of mankind. (Isaiah 53:4)

Changing states of existence is very personal. Yeshua would not share this event, not even with his disciples. It's one of the few times Yeshua spent time alone. It is still believed today that Yeshua took on the sins of the world when he suffered on the cross. This is not true. He took on the sins of this world when he suffered in the Garden of Gethsemane.

Yeshua did not beg the Source to be saved from the cross but to be saved from having to enter the belief based system and thus from being separated from the Source. He fervently hoped that there could be another way.

Going from the knowledge based system into the belief based system is very painful, words cannot describe it; the despair and fear is crushing. The pain Yeshua suffered from the scourging and crucifixion which was to follow would have been a picnic in comparison!

Luke describes Yeshua's anguish and torment on entering the belief based system; *'And being in agony, he prayed more earnestly. Then his sweat became like great drops of blood falling down to the ground.'* (Luke 22:44) Matthew and Mark also attest to Yeshua's passion; *'My soul is filled with sorrow even to death.'* (Matthew 26:38, Mark 14:34) After entering the belief based system, Yeshua went to his disciples who were asleep. He was filled entirely with fear which he had never felt before. He then asked them to stay awake and pray. Yeshua returned to the center of the garden, disconnected from the Source for the very first time, to steal himself for the course that lay ahead.

So why did Yeshua leave the knowledge based system and enter the belief based system? And why now, when he so desperately needed the power of the Source for the task that lay ahead. Did he finally succumb to temptation? No. He did this for two reasons. Firstly, the Grail, the gate, the way, had to be fashioned from this side, the belief based system, the world of sin. He was to be the light in this dark realm. He chose to come into this dark realm to show us the way back to the knowledge based system. Secondly, Yeshua had to endure the pain inflicted upon him and forgive as an amalgamation of three energy signatures, otherwise it could be argued that as he was connected to the Source, he didn't experience the pain in the same way we would have.

If you are wondering how Yeshua became the trinity on entering the belief based system when he was born a single energy signature, I remind you of his baptism where he was given the second energy signature, the Helper.

Judas then arrived with a crowd to arrest Yeshua. We are led to believe that Judas was required to show the arresting crowd who Yeshua was. Do you really believe not a single person in the crowd that had come to arrest Yeshua could not themselves identify him? Yeshua was at the time the most popular man in Jerusalem and he had been openly preaching in the temple every day for the last week and many times before. When the arresting crowd came upon Yeshua they instantly recognized him, but they stopped and did nothing. Why? The crowd was afraid of Yeshua and this is why they came in such large numbers for one man. They all knew who he was, his reputation preceded him.

Yeshua took the initiative by asking the crowd, "Whom do you seek?". When they confirmed they were looking for Yeshua of Nazareth, he replied, "I am he." Yeshua's plan is precariously balanced here because the arresting crowd was afraid to act, so Yeshua asked them again, "Who are you looking for?" They replied, "Yeshua, the Nazarene." Yeshua responded, "I told you that I am he. If you are looking for me, let these others go." This response from Yeshua not only verified his identity but also provided encouragement to the arresting crowd because he confirmed for them that they only had to deal with one man, himself. He had basically guaranteed that his disciples would not interfere. Still they were afraid to approach him. Only then did Judas come forward to embrace Yeshua demonstrating to the arresting crowd that he posed no physical threat. Bolstered by this encouragement, the crowd finally mustered the fortitude to physically seize Yeshua.

The arresting crowd were never ordered to beat Yeshua prior to handing him over to the Sanhedrin. Like all bullies who have shown fear they beat him to re-assert their position of dominance and to save face in front of each other. The tension they felt prior to his arrest would also have been broken by the physical act of violence and the relief that realization brings that they themselves were not in any harm and had nothing to fear. This is the typical behavior of a coward, it always has been.

Knowing what was ahead of him, the choice of entering the belief based system was made all the more difficult, but it was the will of the Source and Yeshua was to demonstrate as he did so many times that he was no passive victim but actively and repeatedly took the initiative to ensure his Father's plan was fulfilled. Yeshua here was the master tactician. It never once dawned on his enemies, or even his friends for that matter, what he was doing and why. This was why Yeshua never explained explicitly what he was doing and why, even to his eleven disciples. His enemies had to remain in the dark as to what he was doing.

Chapter Nine

Judgment

Yeshua who so often had to defend himself, and did so expertly, was yet again put to the question. However, this time, he did not defend himself. Instead he allowed those who had congregated in the residence of the high priest Caiaphas to speak for him. This was the first time he did this. Yeshua generally responded to Caiaphas's questions by making it clear he had never concealed his teaching or other activities and had done everything in the public eye. He had nothing to hide and he encouraged witnesses to come forward and speak of what they could attest to; *'I have spoken openly to the world. I have always taught in synagogues and in the temple, where all Jews come together. I have said nothing in secret. Why do you ask me? Ask those who have heard me; they know what I said.'* (John 18:20-21)

Yeshua knew that Caiaphas was not concerned with the truth at this point as he would have known quite well what Yeshua had been preaching because he himself would have witnessed firsthand his teachings. Caiaphas was simply looking for grounds to propose the death sentence. However, before charges could be brought against Yeshua before the Roman governor, the charges had to be formally confirmed by Caiaphas, who was also head of the Jewish High Court.

Yeshua, as a master tactician, could have talked his way out of trouble as he so often did in the past. But this did not suit his purpose here. However, he knew that he must also be careful not to appear to want a rushed judgment against him. Those who sought his death were well educated and highly intelligent men, scribes, elders, priests, council members, and this would have raised suspicion. As the Sabbath was drawing near, Yeshua knew that time was against Caiaphas and that Caiaphas himself would seek swift judgment. Furthermore, Caiaphas wished to expedite the trial and arrive at a sentence of death before the day progressed and news of Yeshua's arrest could spread among the huge number of Passover pilgrims gathered in Jerusalem most of whom supported Yeshua.

Yeshua knew that all who had congregated in the courtyard were supporters of Caiaphas. Among them were included the traders who had their stalls overturned by Yeshua only days earlier and thus had lost a lot of money as a result of Yeshua's behavior. Also, among the gathered crowd were those who had been paid to bear false witness against him. Yeshua knew all this and this is why he now gave power to those who would bear false witness against him, to come forward and speak on his behalf. Again, Yeshua took the initiative by prompting those within the crowd, who had been instructed by Caiaphas to accuse him, to come forward. The Jewish leaders had no real justice or fairness in mind. They wanted Yeshua dead and they were willing to do whatever it took to achieve that.

The accusers came forward and bore false testimony against Yeshua. The testimony was hyperbola and contradictory and made them look and sound ridiculous. This was partly as a result of the rushed nature of the trial. They said such things as, "The accused claimed to be able to destroy the temple and rebuild it in three days. The accused used the power of Satan to heal the sick and he can command evil spirits." Yeshua made no reply. This continued for some time. Caiaphas became impatient and asked Yeshua directly; *'Tell us if you are the Christ, the Son of God.'* (Matthew 26:63)

At this stage, Yeshua realized Caiaphas was having difficulty getting the evidence he required to condemn him to death so again he obliged Caiaphas by responding; *'You have said so. But I tell you, from now on you will see the Son (servant) of Man seated at the right hand of power and coming on the clouds of heaven.'* (Matthew 26:64) Caiaphas then tore his robes which itself was an act of blasphemy and accused Yeshua of blasphemy. *'He has uttered blasphemy. What further witnesses do we need? You have now heard his blasphemy. What is your judgment? The gathered council members replied; He deserves death.'* (Matthew 26:65-66)

When Judas heard the words, "What further witnesses do we need?" he knew that his task had been completed and he departed. He was no longer needed. Yeshua was on his own now and he knew that failure was not an option. The stakes were high indeed.

Although the Romans permitted the Jews a degree of judicial freedom regarding their own cases, being the occupying force, they reserved the final judgment in cases of capital punishment. Therefore, Caiaphas had one last hurdle to jump. He had to bring Yeshua before the local prefect, Pontius Pilate, and convince him to put Yeshua to death. Caiaphas knew this was just a matter of protocol and to maintain the status quo, the existing good relationship with the Jewish High Council, and more importantly, the peace, Pontius Pilate would grant his request.

Caiaphas just needed to make sure of a few things. Firstly, he had to provide the prefect with sufficient reason under Roman law to have Yeshua put to death. Yeshua's blasphemy was only sufficient reason under Jewish law to have him put to death. Caiaphas knew that Pontius Pilate would require sufficient reason under Roman law for such a penalty to be rendered. Secondly, he had to ensure the majority of people that gathered before Pontius Pilate supported his request for the death penalty and thirdly, that as few of Yeshua's supporters were present when this happened. Caiaphas had important preparations to make and very little time to make them.

The formal verdict of the death penalty for Yeshua now only required the advent of sunrise. Caiaphas was adamant the final judgment of death possessed an air of legality in an attempt to at least confuse and stall any reprisals from Yeshua's supporters, if not to win the battle for public opinion entirely. It was important for the Jewish leaders to get this matter taken care of as soon as possible to avoid any civil disturbance at the Passover. Avoiding civil disturbances was also a concern of Pontius Pilate, after all, that was his job. Caiaphas knew this and used it in his negotiations with the prefect.

Whilst time itself was not entirely in Caiaphas's favor, the way forward was now clear. Yeshua was guilty of blasphemy and had been so convicted in accordance with Jewish law and was to be sentence to death. The only hurdle left was to provide reason, and evidence if possible, so that Pontius Pilate could also convict Yeshua to death under Roman law.

Knowledge of Yeshua's trial would have filtered through to his supporters by early morning. Credence of his guilt would most likely have entered the minds of his supporters when they heard that even his closest followers, his twelve disciples, had all abandoned him and one had even betrayed him! Surely if this was true, he must be guilty. This generated great shock and indecision among Yeshua's many followers. This indecision was enough to grant Caiaphas the time he so desperately needed. By the time this information was spreading throughout Jerusalem, Caiaphas had brought Yeshua before the prefect in the hope of a speedy conviction.

Caiaphas knew cases like this were usually held before a private audience with the prefect in his residence. Prior to Yeshua's arrival on the scene, Caiaphas held huge sway over the Jewish people of Jerusalem and was instrumental in helping the prefect maintain law and order in this outpost of the Roman Empire. Therefore, Caiaphas knew the prefect dealt with such cases in a private manner under his very roof.

However, Caiaphas recognized the power of the mob, popular opinion, and that a public display of unrest and the possibility of imminent revolt would be invaluable as a bargaining tool to bring to such a hearing. To pressurize the prefect into condemning Yeshua to death Caiaphas needed a public hearing, not a private one, where the crowd could be controlled by him.

Caiaphas was all too aware of the power of the mob in Jerusalem, he had been at the wrong end of it many times with Yeshua's followers. So how could Caiaphas now manipulate events so that he could present his case publicly to the prefect in front of a sympathetic crowd? The prefect's headquarters were not suitable for this purpose as Caiaphas knew that only a delegate of people, and not the large crowds he needed, would be granted entrance. However, a large open courtyard with a single narrow entrance and exit would be perfect. In this situation, only supporters of Caiaphas, paid or otherwise, would be granted entrance to the courtyard.

Caiaphas, with a delegate from the Jewish High Court and a large mob of his supporters, led Yeshua to the headquarters of the governor. They congregated in the open air courtyard. Caiaphas explained to the centurion on guard duty why they had come and that they sought an audience with Pilate. Caiaphas knew from experience that the prefect was sympathetic to their Jewish laws, rules, regulations and customs. They explained to the centurion that they could not enter the governor's headquarters, as was customary when presenting cases for the death penalty, because it would make them unclean and unable to participate in the ongoing celebrations during the Feast of Unleavened Bread. Under Jewish law, Jews were permitted to enter a Gentile courtyard if there was no roof but were considered defiled if they entered a Gentile building with a roof.

Pilate was both knowledgeable of Jewish law and practices and sensitive to their concerns. He therefore went out to the courtyard to speak with them. Caiaphas, of course, had ordered his temple guards to stand watch at the courtyard entrance and to bar passage to all Yeshua's supporters or any who may have been sympathetic to his cause. Caiaphas's plot was going as planned. He now had the ideal platform to demand the death sentence for Yeshua.

Many, to this day, believe Pilate did not wish to put Yeshua to death and that he did everything he could to keep him alive. This is not true. In all four gospel accounts, Pilate lobbied for Yeshua to be spared his eventual fate of execution and acquiesced only when the crowd refused to relent. What most fail to realize is that the gospels which recorded the trial and death of Yeshua would have been written shortly after the Great Revolt (66-73 AD), the disastrous Jewish rebellion against Rome, in which a large proportion of the Jewish population was annihilated. The gospel writers purposively presented the Roman authorities in a good light and cast the blame squarely on the Jewish hierarchy. It was sensible political policy at the time, if you wanted to survive, not to paint your conquerors in a bad light.

Pilate is often portrayed as an insipid ineffectual governor who was manipulated by the Jewish Sanhedrin into crucifying Yeshua. This couldn't be further from the truth. It is well known that Pilate had no love for the Jews and was consistently hostile toward them throughout his time as governor of Judea. He was known to purposively bait them into reacting and then punish them when they did. A good example of this included the time when he ordered Roman standards brought within the city of Jerusalem which was done under the cover of night, when he knew well that it would infuriate the Jewish people who had strongly held beliefs about the sanctity of the city. When they protested, he threatened to have them killed. On another occasion, he had funds from the temple treasury used to construct a viaduct. When the Jews assembled outside his quarters to protest, he ordered his soldiers to dress like the Jews and mingle among the crowd. On his signal, the soldiers drew their weapons, hidden in their clothes, and slaughtered many of them.

Please be under no illusion, Pilate wanted the Yeshua question resolved. The portrayals that he was only vaguely aware of who Yeshua was are misleading. He was very much aware of the growing unrest among the people that Yeshua's ministry was creating. They were hailing him as a king! He knew if such a movement remained unchecked it may become unstoppable and he was ultimately responsible. He also hated having to come to Jerusalem, which was hot, humid and uncomfortable and preferred residing at his permanent home in Caesarea, Marittima by the sea. A peaceful Jerusalem meant shorter and less regular visits.

The Truth

Pontius Pilate was a consummate and accomplished politician. He recognized the complicated and difficult nature of the situation and like all politicians he was seeking resolution and damage limitation. He had the following considerations:

1. The continued unrest caused by Yeshua's ministry may at some stage trigger an outright revolt against the occupying Roman forces. Judea was always an area of unrest, a boiling pot if you will, with outright conflict permanently on the horizon. Jerusalem in particular was like a perpetual tinder box – a single spark could create disaster. In the space of less than seventy years there were three major rebellions by the Jews of Judea Province against the Roman Empire. The first Jewish–Roman War sometimes called the Great Revolt occurred decades after Yeshua's death, 66–73 AD. The second was the Kitos War in 115–117 AD which took place mainly in the diaspora, and the third was Bar Kokhba's revolt of 132–136 AD.

2. Executing Yeshua may encourage many of his supporters to join the established Jewish militia or freedom fighters, effectively swelling their numbers and thus posing an even greater threat to Roman rule. The greatly enlarged militia encouraged by increased numbers and motivated by the unjust execution of Yeshua would make war inevitable. Yeshua could become a Martyr inciting endless future conflict.

3. One of Pilate's main responsibilities apart from keeping the peace was to overlook and enforce tax collection. Pilate knew that controlling unrest, putting down revolts and fighting wars were expensive endeavors. They also disrupted tax collection. The Great Revolt itself, you will not be surprised to hear, was encouraged by anti-taxation protests. The Jewish elite did not like paying taxes to their Roman conquerors.

4. According to Matthew, Pilate's wife was against any harm coming to Yeshua. She appealed to her husband, saying she had a terrible dream the previous night which frightened and bewildered her so much that she felt impelled to act on it; *'Do not interfere with that holy man. Last night I had a terrible dream because of him.'* (Matthew 27:19) In Roman culture, dreams were given great significance at this time, more so than they are now. Usually they were seen as warnings against some danger, or as prompts sent by God to persuade a person to take a particular course of action. Furthermore, the fact that his wife traveled with him on his journeys throughout Judea demonstrated they were very close, and Pilate would have taken her council seriously.

Many of these considerations could be addressed if Pilate could diminish his, and more importantly the Roman authority's culpability for Yeshua's execution. Let's look briefly at what he did.

The charges directed at Yeshua were that he had encouraged his people not to pay taxes and that he himself had claimed to be the rightful King of the Jews; *'We found this man misleading our nation and forbidding us to give tribute to Caesar, and saying that he himself is Christ, a King.'* (Luke 23:1-2)

We know of course that these charges are false. Yeshua never claimed he was king and his response to the question of whether the Jews should pay taxes to their Roman conquerors is infamous; *'Render unto Caesar the things that are Caesar's, and unto God the things that are God's.'* (Matthew 22:21) Both of these accusations were biting and rendered the death sentence if proven. Incitement not to pay taxes to Caesar was particularly serious as Pilate himself was directly responsible for the collection of taxes in Judea.

Pilate conducted an initial hearing with Yeshua, asking him for his response to the accusations brought against him. All was going as Yeshua had planned so there was no reason to reply to the indictments brought against him. Instead of responding directly to any of the allegations, Yeshua continued his ministry, informing Pilate of his purpose in life; *'I have come into the world to bear witness to the truth.'* (John 18:37) Even then, in the face of an excruciatingly painful death, Yeshua continued to do the will of the Source.

Pilate spoke to the gathered crowd saying; *'I find no guilt in this man.'* (John 18:38) The crowd responded by saying; *'All the country of the Jews is being stirred up with his teaching. He began in Galilee and now he has come all the way here.'* (Luke 23:5) This of course was a veiled threat. They were saying if this unrest was not stopped now it would continue to spread out of control. Blame for any subsequent revolt in Judea would thus be laid squarely at the feet of the prefect. What did Pilate do? He did what all politicians do – he tried to pass the buck.

Herod's entry into Jerusalem just days before would not have gone un-noticed by Pilate. Yeshua was a Galilean and thus there was an argument to say that he was Herod's problem. In any case, to execute a Galilean, famous as Yeshua now was, without consultation with its ruler when he himself was in the city would at the very least be bad politics and at the worst could be interpreted as a grave insult. Good relations had to prevail. Thus, to kill two birds with one stone, Pilate ordered Yeshua should be brought before Herod for sentencing.

To understand Herod's treatment of Yeshua, I feel it's important to give some background on who Herod was. Herod or Herod Antipas was a son of Herod the Great, former king of Judea. Herod the Great was granted the title of 'King of Judea' by Rome and as such he was a vassal of the Roman Empire and was expected to support the interests of his Roman patrons. He was allowed to rule his people as he saw fit and continued support from the Roman Empire was a major factor in enabling him to maintain his authority over Judea. He was a very ambitious man and was willing to go to extreme lengths to protect his interests.

He most famously appears in the gospel according to Matthew (2:1-23), which describes an event known as the 'Massacre of the Innocents'. According to this account, after the birth of Yeshua, magi from the east visited Herod the Great to inquire the whereabouts of the Messiah who had been foretold would be born King of the Jews so that they could pay him homage.

Herod the Great was not a man to entertain a rival so he assembled the chief priests and scribes. He learned from them that the 'anointed one' was to be born in Bethlehem. Herod the Great, therefore, sent the magi to Bethlehem, instructing them to search for the child and after they had found him, to report to him so that he too could worship him. However, after they had found Yeshua, they were warned in a dream not to report back to Herod the Great. Similarly, Joseph (Yeshua's Father) was warned in a dream that Herod the Great intended to kill Yeshua, so he and his family fled to Egypt. When Herod the Great realized he had been outwitted, he gave orders to kill all boys of the age of two and under in Bethlehem and its vicinity. Joseph and his family stayed in Egypt until Herod's death.

Herod's youngest son Antipas had older brothers Antipater, Archelaus, Aristobulus and Alexander. Thus, Antipas as youngest son was not Herod's first choice of heir. Antipas, however, had other ideas. He was not stupid and simply driven by hedonistic pleasures as depicted in many accounts. He was astute, clever and an accomplished negotiator. His reign lasted forty-two years. This did not happen by accident.

Like his father, Herod the Great, Herod Antipas was an extraordinarily ambitious man and he was willing to go to remarkable and sometimes inconceivable lengths to achieve his ambitions. Antipas wanted to be king and he was willing to do anything to get it. He knew his brothers Antipater, Aristobulus, Alexander and to a lesser extent Archelaus stood in the way of realizing his ambitions. Antipas constantly plotted against his two brothers Aristobulus and Alexander, his father's favorites, and deftly incited the aging king's anger with rumors of their disloyalty. His two brothers Aristobulus and Alexander were executed for treason in 7 BC, after which, Antipater, Herod's oldest son became exclusive successor to the throne.

Despite the fact that Antipater was guaranteed the throne, he was convicted of trying to poison his father and was sentenced to death in 5 BC. After the guilty verdict, Antipater's position as exclusive successor was removed and granted to Herod Antipas. Antipas had achieved his goal and his remaining brothers were no longer rivals and thus no longer any threat to his ambition to become king. However, during a fatal illness in 4 BC, Herod had yet another change of heart about the succession. According to the final version of his will, Antipas's elder brother Archelaus was now to become King of Judea, Idumea and Samaria, while Antipas would rule Galilee and Perea with the lesser title of tetrarch. Archelaus had now become a problem.

Herod Antipas's appointment as ruler over Galilee and neighbouring Peraea was endorsed by the Roman emperor Augustus. However, in order for Antipas to rule over Judea he would have to have Archelaus removed. Unlike Antipas's many brothers, Archelaus was his full brother. It's not clear whether this fact softened Antipas's approach to the situation or whether he just never received the right opportunity to have his brother assassinated. Nevertheless, he adopted a campaign against his brother where he surreptitiously interfered with his brother's ruling of Judea, creating an almost constant state of unrest. This of course would not have been hard to do as the Roman occupiers were despised throughout Judea. Antipas hoped that because his brother Archelaus was unable to govern with any degree of success, he would be removed by imperial decree and that he himself, who ruled Galilee and Perea in an exemplary fashion and was after all the next heir in line to rule Judea, would supplant his brother.

In 6 AD Archelaus was deemed incompetent by Augustus and removed from office. Despite Antipas's entreaties to the Roman emperor Augustus, his brother was replaced with a prefect. This minor Roman aristocrat would have been supported by a small Roman army of approximately three thousand men. These soldiers would not have come from Italy but rather would have been conscripts from nearby Gentile cities such as Caesarea which lay about two days march from Jerusalem on the Mediterranean coast where the prefect and his small army lived.

Although the prefect would have been responsible for the areas of Judaea, Samaria, and Idumaea, he would not have governed these areas directly but rather would have relied on local leaders. Regarding the city of Jerusalem, the prefect only came to ensure peace during festivals such as the Passover when large crowds gathered. On a day-to-day basis, however, Jerusalem was governed by the local high priest and his council of elders who had the difficult task of mediating between the remote Roman prefect and the local populace, most of whom wanted to be free of foreign interference. The high priest's political responsibility was to maintain order and to see that tribute was paid to Rome. Caiaphas, the high priest during Yeshua's adulthood, held the office for about eighteen years (18-36 AD), longer than anyone else during this period, indicating that he was a successful diplomat.

Thus, during Yeshua's adulthood, Galilee was governed by the tetrarch Herod Antipas, who was sovereign within his own domain, provided he remained loyal to Rome and maintained peace and stability within his borders. Judaea (including Jerusalem) was nominally governed by the prefect at the time, Pontius Pilate, but the actual daily rule of Jerusalem was in the hands of Caiaphas and his council.

Augustus replaced Archelaus with a prefect because he believed it was important to keep the kingdom of Herod the Great divided and to unite the now divided kingdom under his son Antipas would only increase the chances of a successful revolt against Rome. Uniting the broken kingdom under Antipas would also have given him too much power. Antipas was not happy, and his undying ambition would not let him sit by and do nothing. He wanted to be King of Judea and to unite his father's territorial regions with himself as sovereign ruler.

Although Antipas was close to the Roman imperial family he continued his covert interference with the successful ruling and administration of Judea. In order for any prefect to rule Judea successfully, he needed to maintain good relations with Antipas. Outwardly at least, a good rapport needed to be shown to exist between the two rulers to lend an air of stability to the regions. Therefore, it was necessary for both of them to co-operate in many areas, especially in matters of civil unrest because instability in one region could and would spread quickly to all surrounding regions.

Antipas wanted Judea. He knew that assassinating the prefect would be too risky. If the blame led back to him he would lose everything. He also knew if one prefect was killed a new one would simply take his place. However, Antipas was an accomplished tactician and diplomat. He was also very patient. It had taken years to eliminate his brothers from succession and to become tetrarch and thus he could wait a bit longer to realize his ambition to become king. An opportunity would reveal itself at some stage.

Antipas had been aware of Yeshua's ministry for a while now, which largely took place in his province of Galilee. Antipas was not in Jerusalem by accident. Through his many scouts, he was aware of Yeshua's movements and knew he was in the city for the festival of the Passover, having arrived there a few days before the Sabbath. He was mindful of the general unrest Yeshua's ministry was creating and the large crowds of followers he had. He was also aware of the specific tensions between Yeshua, his followers, and the Jewish elite. Would Yeshua, the man who his father tried to eliminate as a child, create the opportunity he had been waiting for? Could he use Yeshua to destabilise the region of Judea, strengthening his claim and supplanting the prefect as not only the rightful heir but the only man capable of bringing peace to the region?

Yeshua was brought before Herod Antipas. Herod now faced many of the same concerns as Pilate. If he was responsible for Yeshua's death, it could create unrest or more likely outright revolt in the jurisdictions he governed especially Galilee where Yeshua grew up, conducted a lot of his ministry and where the vast majority of the population were Jewish.

The chief priests and scribes relayed to Herod the accusations against Yeshua previously brought before Pilate. Although Herod did question Yeshua at length, he had no intention of convicting him. If Caesar believed a prefect was more suitable to rule Judea than he, then this was a perfect opportunity to test that theory.

Instead of convicting Yeshua, Herod had him dressed in a royal robe and returned to Pilate. He did this to both exacerbate the situation for Pilate and to encourage the death sentence for Yeshua. Dressing Yeshua in a royal robe told Pilate that Herod was now aware of the accusations against Yeshua, that he claimed to be King. Herod knew any open and independent claim to rule Judea, including his own, would be seen as a direct challenge to Caesar's rule. This would not be acceptable and would most definitely incur a death sentence. Dressing Yeshua in a royal robe put more pressure on Pilate to render the death sentence, squarely putting the blame for Yeshua's death at his feet. When Pilate saw Yeshua had been returned in a royal robe, he understood Herod's message.

Pilate then made a vain attempt to punish Yeshua under the law by having him flogged and set free. Caiaphas and his gathered supporters were having none of it and screamed for his crucifixion. They screamed; *'If you release this man, you are not a friend of Caesar. Anyone who makes himself king is defying Caesar.'* (John 19:12) With this statement, the Jewish leaders were effectively threatening Pilate. If he freed Yeshua, word would make its way back to Rome that Pilate was not watching out for Caesar's interests by refusing to dispose of rival kings. Such an accusation would at the very least see him deposed as governor of Judea and ruin any future political ambitions he may have had. In all likelihood, however, failure to dispose of a rival king and quell the subsequent uprising which seemed very much on the cards if he didn't, would have earned Pilate a summary execution. However, Pilate also realized that any uprising caused as a result of Yeshua's crucifixion which required reinforcements from Rome would also be his responsibility and could potentially be his undoing. For him, the stakes of this particular political game were very high indeed!

Pilate had now gone some way to absolve himself of any blame in connection with the death of Yeshua. He gave Herod a chance to save Yeshua and he gave the Jewish leaders a chance to save Yeshua. He had, however, one last trick up his sleeve. He decided to give the Jewish people a chance to save Yeshua. To achieve this, he invoked a custom of releasing a single prisoner during the feast who the crowd wanted. He presented Barabbas to the people. Barabbas was a notorious insurrectionary who had been found guilty of theft and murder and was under the death penalty. When Pilate asked the crowd which of the two he should set free they screamed for the release of Barabbas. When he asked what he should do with Yeshua, they bellowed even louder, "Crucify him!" Pilate addressed the crowd saying, "Shall I crucify your king?" Caiaphas, who we previously witnessed was not beyond committing blasphemy himself, replied sacrilegiously – *'We have no King but Caesar.'* (John 19:15)

Pilate was aware that the crowd was growing increasingly angry and that a riot could ensue at any moment if they were not given what they wanted. Pilate, aware of the Jewish ritual of *Washing of the Hands*, requested a bowl, towel and a jug of water. He washed his hands before the crowd saying; *'I am not responsible for his blood. It is your doing.'* (Matthew 27:24) Caiaphas who was running out of time but now sensing victory shouted; *'Let his blood be upon us and upon our children.'* (Matthew 27:25) The crowd echoed Caiaphas's words. This was what Pilate was waiting for, absolution from all blame. Pilate rendered his final judgment to keep the peace rather than on the basis of truth and justice. Barabbas was set free and Yeshua was sent to be crucified.

Barabbas was used by Pilate. The people chose Barabbas not Yeshua and thus the Jewish people themselves could never blame him for Yeshua's death. Barabbas was immediately followed and arrested shortly thereafter on Pilate's instructions. After all, he was not about to let such a dangerous man on the loose especially given the current unrest.

Pilate absolved himself of all blame for Yeshua's death, to the extent that he could. The Jewish religious leaders could not blame him, Herod and his supporters could not blame him and now the Jewish people themselves could not blame him. He covered his back well, a truly consummate politician and tactician.

However, please be under no illusion, Pilate not only wanted Yeshua dead, he wanted him punished as an example to all those who would dare have themselves named king. Publicly beating Yeshua half to death was not demanded by the Jewish Sanhedrin. This was done on Pilate's instructions. Many people to this day believe Pilate was showing compassion to Yeshua hoping to save his life by attempting to substitute a beating for crucifixion. This is not true. Pilate knew that only the death of Yeshua would assuage the gathered crowd and prevent an outright revolt. He publicly beat Yeshua because he wanted to maximize Yeshua's pain and humiliation.

Crucifixion was regularly performed to terrorize and dissuade its witnesses from perpetrating particularly heinous crimes and the victims were often left on display after death as warnings to others who might attempt dissent. Crucifixion was also intended to provide a death that was particularly slow, painful and publicly humiliating.

Pilate's efforts to maximize Yeshua's pain and humiliation included making him carry his own cross through public streets. It was known in some very serious cases, that the condemned was forced to carry the crossbeam to the place of execution but this was not common practice. Neither was it common practice to carry the whole cross. The crossbeam could weigh around 45kg (100lbs) but the whole cross could weigh over 135kg (300lbs). The Jewish Sanhedrin did not demand Yeshua carry his own cross. In fact, it was quite the contrary. As the Passover was soon approaching, they wanted a swift crucifixion. This public humiliation of Yeshua was done on Pilate's instructions.

Pilate's instructions to maximize Yeshua's pain and humiliation are not the actions of a compassionate man. I'm sure many of our politicians and leaders of today may consider Pilate to be a compassionate figure and in comparison, he may just appear so. However, if Pilate had been a compassionate man, and I assure you that he was not, he would have given Yeshua a swift and painless death, not a public, humiliating and excruciating scourging and crucifixion.

Pilate was willing and well capable of ignoring the Jewish Sanhedrin's demands when it suited his own purpose. In fact it was on the instructions of Pilate himself that above Yeshua's head on the cross they posted the written charge against him – This is Yeshua, the King of the Jews. This was done to give public notice of the legal charge against him for his crucifixion and to serve as a deterrent to all future would be usurpers of Caesars power. John 19:21 states that the Jews asked Pilate, "Do not write King of the Jews", but instead write that Yeshua had merely claimed that title, but Pilate wrote it anyway. Pilate's response to their protests is recorded by John 19:22 – "What I have written, I have written." This not only showed that Pilate was capable of denying demands made by the Jewish Sanhedrin but was also a clear sign from him as governor of Judea that all rivals to Caesar who claimed to be king, whether their claim was legitimate or not, would be dealt with in the most severe way. This was a direct reply to Herod's previous message where Herod had Yeshua dressed in a royal robe and returned to Pilate.

Pilate also knew there were two opposing Jewish factions in play. In order to prevent any possible revolt, he needed to deal with both factions. The first Jewish faction gathered before him wanted Yeshua dead and he needed to deal with them immediately. He dealt with this faction by giving them what they wanted, crucifying Yeshua which suited his purposes anyway. The second faction were Yeshua's supporters and his vain and hollow public histrionics not to crucify Yeshua were all made in an effort to appear innocent of Yeshua's death and to place blame squarely at the feet of the Jewish Sanhedrin. This was done in an attempt to prevent any revolt by the second faction against Roman rule occurring in the future. Pilate had successfully dealt with both factions, offsetting any present or future revolt against Roman rule, whilst at the same time providing a successful and swift solution to the Yeshua question.

Luke's account indicates Herod and Pilate became friends that day despite having previously being enemies. It is believed that, Yeshua, a common enemy to both, rendered them so. This is not exactly true.

After Yeshua was murdered, Pilate requested a meeting with Herod. Pilate knew, despite his successful political maneuverings, that Yeshua's death would create great unrest not only in Judea but also in the surrounding regions including Galilee. He asked for Herod's co-operation in maintaining peace as he knew from prior experience that Herod would try to take advantage of any unrest in Judea to further his claims on the region. Pilate pointed out to an initially unwilling Herod that if the unrest grew out of control he would declare a state of emergency. Legions of soldiers would be sent by Rome and martial law would be imposed, not only in Judea but in the surrounding regions including those now governed by Herod. Herod knew once martial law was imposed, it could remain so for a very long time and indeed that he may never again rule Galilee and Perea. Furthermore, his ambitions to rule Judea would never be realized. Thus, all would be lost.

Pilate, being the consummate politician, after having suggested the worst case, now presented Herod with unequivocal encouragement to join forces with Pilate in maintaining the peace. Pilate, for the first time, openly recognized Herod's rightful claim to rule Judea. He told Herod if peace could be maintained that not only would he not declare martial law, but he would relay to Caesar that Herod was instrumental in preventing unrest and would personally endorse his claim to rule Judea.

Although they could never be described as friends, it was from this day forward that Pilate and Herod became allies. Being an ambitious man, Pilate's endorsement of Herod's right to rule in Judea suited his plans as he saw his governorship of Judea as merely temporary in nature and as a stepping stone to greater things. Herod on the other hand was never to realize his lifelong ambition. He would never govern Judea.

As you can now see, Pilate was not only extremely ambitious, but he was an exceptionally intelligent, cold, calculating and accomplished tactician who would have seen compassion as a weakness. He could not have effectively ruled in Judea for so long if he had not been.

Chapter Ten

The Journey to Crucifixion (Vol.1)

Yeshua, after having been brutally scourged and wounded, was brought by the Roman soldiers into Pilate's headquarters, where, dressed in a scarlet robe, he had a crown of thorns put on his head and a reed in his hand. The soldiers mocked him by kneeling in front of him and saying, "Hail, King of the Jews." Whilst his cross was being prepared, they continued to mock him, strike him and spit on him. Roman soldiers in Jerusalem were known to play cruel games with condemned prisoners, especially Jewish prisoners, so their treatment of Yeshua was not out of character.

Despite the severe physical pain Yeshua was in, and the loneliness he must have felt because he had to walk this path alone, he continued his ministry to all, including those who mocked him. This journey, the way of the cross, brings to life many of Yeshua's earlier teachings. His ministry may have been difficult to understand at the time and still is to this day, but he continued nevertheless in the hope that one day people would finally understand.

There are too many examples of Yeshua's earlier teachings which materialize in the way of the cross to mention them all. Instead, I will select only a few. My favorite is the story of Simon of Cyrene.

Yeshua, weakened and wounded by the severe beaten he had received did not have the strength to carry the weight of his wooden cross and it was reported he fell many times. The last time he fell, he was unable to get up. A man named Simon of Cyrene, a passerby in the crowd, was ordered by the Roman soldiers to take the cross from Yeshua and carry it the rest of the way allowing Yeshua to successfully complete his task. (Matthew 27:32)

Some believe Simon was chosen to carry the cross because he may have shown sympathy for Yeshua. Others point out that religious texts indicate he had no choice, and that there is no basis to consider the carrying of the cross an act of sympathetic compassion. The way of the cross famously depicted in the film, *The Passion of the Christ*, portrays Simon as a Jew being forced by the Romans to carry the cross, who at first is unwilling, but as the journey continues, shows compassion to Yeshua helping him to complete his task. The detail of how or why Simon helped Yeshua is irrelevant. The point here is that, as long as you are willing to do the will of the Source, you will be sent help – not before or after you need it but exactly when you need it. Indeed, if Yeshua had not received the help he so desperately needed, he would not have been able to complete his task.

Yeshua, in his ministry, told us that being prepared to do the will of the Source was paramount, even above completion of the task itself; *'My food is to do the will of Him who sent Me and to finish His work.'* (John 4:34) *'I have come down from heaven, not to do My own will, but to do the will of Him who sent Me.'* (John 6:38) Yeshua repeated this in his ministry continually and habitually.

Yeshua continued to say this so often that only a few of the occasions where he did were recorded.

Doing the will of the Source is paramount. It is even more important than the Grail itself! Using the Grail allows you to open your eyes and witness the truth, the knowledge based system. However, by using the Grail, the only thing that will change is you. Doing the will of the Source will change all things.

Due to its critical nature Yeshua included this instruction in the prayer he gave us, alongside and before the message of how to use the Grail; *'Thy kingdom come, thy will be done, on earth as it is in heaven.'* It is by His will being done that His kingdom will come. This is how important you are. His kingdom, the knowledge based system, will come through you doing His will. Both systems cannot co-exist. When His will is done, His kingdom will come, and the belief based system will perish.

Everyone on the face of this earth is here for a reason. You have been given a specific task by the Source. No two people get the same task. If you do not complete your task, no other person will be sent in your place to complete it. The task will simply not be done. The reason I find this passage of the way of the cross so powerful is that if you consider the task given to you by the Source is too difficult to achieve, remember, as long as you are willing to do the task given to you by the Source, help will arrive when you need it. If you decide to do the will of the Source and things become rough, have courage; a ship is always safe in port, but that's not what it was made for.

Consider Simon. His home town, Cyrene Libya, was located in northern Africa. Cyrene, a Greek colony, also had a Jewish community where approximately 100,000 Judean Jews had been forced to settle during the reign of Ptolemy Soter (323–285 BC). Cyrene is more than 1500km from Jerusalem, quite an arduous migration physically. The journey from Cyrene to Jerusalem would have taken a month or more and would definitely have been perilous, full of wild animals, bandits and Roman soldiers. Simon and the group he traveled with would also have had to forage for water and food which would always have been in short supply. This demonstrates that help will come regardless of the conditions which must be negotiated.

If you do not accept what I say, and you believe that Simon helping Yeshua was an act of mere chance, then I suggest you try it for yourself. Stop whatever you are doing, trust me it's not that important. Figure out what your task is and start walking the path now. This is what Yeshua meant when he said to His disciples; *'If anyone desires to come after Me, let him deny himself, and take up his cross, and follow Me.'* (Matthew 16:24)

I feel the need to explain what Yeshua meant here as it is often misunderstood.

Many will have you believe that to deny oneself means to deny sinful self, ungodliness, and worldly lusts and luxuries. To deny oneself the pleasures and profits of this world and all expectations of an earthly kingdom, worldly grandeur, and think of nothing but reproach, persecution, and death, for the sake of your Lord and

Master. To take up one's cross is to cheerfully receive, and patiently bear, every affliction and evil, however shameful and painful it may be, which is appointed for you, and to which you should quietly submit, and carry, with an entire resignation to the will of God. And to follow Yeshua means to imitate him in the exercise of grace, humility, patience, and self-denial and in the discharge of every duty, moral, or evangelical through suffering and death.

This of course is nonsense. It is propaganda created and spread by the deceiver. Any message by the deceiver is always full of detail, impossible to define and pin down, and is used to both maximize your suffering and confusion, and most importantly to keep you busy from doing the will of the Source.

You do not have to deny yourself the luxuries of this world or other such trivialities. Yeshua never denied himself the luxuries of this world. Consider John 12:3; *'Then Mary took about a pound of expensive perfume, made of pure nard, and anointed Yeshua's feet and wiped them with her hair. And the house was filled with the fragrance of the perfume.'* Although it was recorded that Judas rebuked Yeshua for his indulgence, Yeshua brushed his admonition aside.

Spikenard is a precious and expensive rose-red coloured oil made from the highly aromatic dried roots and oily stems of the spikenard plant. The plant grows in India and was made a very valuable unguent or perfume, used at the ancient baths and feasts. Roughly speaking, a pound of this ointment was equivalent to the average annual wages of a worker of the time. Expensive indeed. I assure you, although Yeshua gave his life willingly to complete his task, he loved life and welcomed all that life had to offer. He only discarded that which could distract him from doing the will of the Source and from completing the task given to him.

Please remember what I said. Only you will be given the task you are responsible for. If you do not complete your task, it will never be done as another will not be sent in your place. Whilst many may consider this to be a scary burden to shoulder, take comfort in knowing that you will not have to repeat Yeshua's task.

The cross is the task you have been given by the Source. Do not patiently bear it but rather rejoice that you have been chosen for this task. Denying yourself is to deny who and what you believe yourself to be in this world (the belief based system) – an engineer, an accountant, an entrepreneur, a judge, a doctor, a priest, an actor, a musician, a parent, a king, or an Olympic athlete. Deny yourself, this is not who and what you truly are, you are greater than this, and above all, do the will of the Source. Only in this way will you truly follow in Yeshua's footsteps. This is what Yeshua meant when he said; *'If anyone desires to come after me, let him deny himself, and take up his cross, and follow Me.'* (Matthew 16:24)

If you do not consider your task to be important, I would draw your attention to Luke's work. In Christian tradition, there are Four Evangelists named Matthew, Mark, Luke, and John. They are the authors attributed with the creation of the four canonical gospels in the New Testament part of the Catholic Bible, all of which give an account of Yeshua's life and ministry. Matthew and John were two of the twelve Apostles chosen by Yeshua and who traveled with him every day during his ministry. They were both direct witnesses to everything Yeshua said and did.

Mark was also a follower of Yeshua but would likely have been in his teens when Yeshua was in Jerusalem. He may have seen and listened to Yeshua on occasion. However, after Yeshua's crucifixion, Mark accompanied the Apostle Peter who traveled spreading the word of Yeshua's ministry to the Gentiles. In his gospel, Mark wrote down the observations and memories of Peter, one of the first Apostles chosen by Yeshua and the founder of the Catholic Church as requested by Yeshua; *'You are Peter (or rock) and on this rock I will build my church.'* (Matthew 16:18)

Not one but three accounts of Yeshua's life and ministry given directly or indirectly by people who ate, slept and traveled with Yeshua and witnessed everything he did. Who did Luke think he was and why did he feel the need to give another account?

Many scholars believe that Luke was a Greek physician who lived in the Greek city of Antioch in Ancient Syria. It is reported that Luke was born a Greek and a Gentile and lived a long life dying in 74 AD in Greece. He is considered the first Christian physician and was venerated by the Catholic Church as the patron saint of physicians and surgeons.

Luke is an interesting writer because he never met Yeshua personally. Luke left the medical profession and became a follower after Yeshua's death when the apostle Paul taught him the gospel. Although not one of the original twelve Apostles directly chosen by Yeshua, Paul, a Jew originally named Saul of Tarsus, claimed a special commission and is considered '*the apostle of the Gentiles*', (Romans 11:13) because his missions spread the gospel message to the Gentiles.

Luke had the opportunity to talk with many of the original twelve Apostles as well as others who were eyewitnesses to special events or moments in Yeshua's life. He evidently had devoted much time to interviewing those who '*from the beginning were eyewitnesses*'. (Luke 1:2) Thus, for example, he was able to give the most thorough account of the events surrounding Yeshua's birth. He alone also reported the beautiful account of the two disciples who met Yeshua as they traveled home to Emmaus (Luke 24:13-35), as well as a number of other events recorded nowhere else.

Though Luke was not present with Yeshua during his ministry, and likely was not a believer until after he met Paul, Luke's attention to detail and abundant eyewitness accounts serve him as a credible historian for the life and death of Yeshua. Luke was the only Gentile to write a gospel and he clearly wrote with a Gentile audience in mind. Furthermore, he was the only scientist among the writers and his gospel is the longest and most detailed of the four canonical gospels.

After what I have said about everyone's task being different you may say that Luke's task was identical and that he was simply re-inventing the wheel by writing yet another gospel. This is not true, although I'm sure that Luke may have harboured such feelings and wondered to himself why he felt the need to give another account. In fact, his introduction to his gospel account seems to suggest that he did indeed have these feelings; *'Many people have already related the events that have taken place among us, writing down what we were told by the first witnesses who became ministers of the word. Yet after I myself had gone carefully over the whole story from the beginning,* **it seemed good to me** *to write an orderly account for you Theophilus, so that your Excellency may know the truth of all you have been taught.'* (Luke 1:1-4)

It seemed good to Luke to write his account. This was the feeling which motivated him to write his gospel. There are a few differences between Luke's gospel account and the other three gospels. The differences between Luke's gospel and the other three have been highlighted and discussed at length in many religious books and works – all but one. The gospel according to Luke is the only account that records Yeshua's words; *'Father, forgive them for they know not what they do.'* (Luke 23:34) Yeshua, through these words, exemplifies how to forgive. He demonstrates that forgiveness must be reasoned. Knowing how to forgive is the key to successfully using the Grail. Although your task may not seem important at the time you are doing it, this is how meaningful and significant your task can be. If Luke had not completed his task, great doubt would have been cast over how to forgive.

If Luke had not completed his task I would not have been able to complete mine. Without Luke's account, my work would have been in doubt, not for me, but for you. There will be those among you who will vociferate, "Who are you to write such a book claiming such things?" I was raised Catholic but like many my age, I only attended church because my parents insisted on it, especially my father who was constantly on my case to go. I stopped going to church when I left home at the age of seventeen. I haven't been to church since nor do I have any intention of returning. Although I am grateful to the Catholic Church for their teachings, doing the same thing repeatedly while expecting something to happen does not interest me.

Look at my task. There is a myriad of people who were and are more qualified than I to write this book, for example, any one of the many priests, bishops, cardinals or popes within the Catholic Church over the last two thousand years. Don't shy away from your task because they ask who you are and what gives you the right to do such things. They asked Yeshua the very same thing! *'By what authority do you do these things?'* And *'Who gave you the authority to do them?'* (Matthew 21:23, Mark 11:28 & Luke 20:2) The words, "you are only the son of a carpenter" were unspoken here. Yeshua's answer to these questions not only demonstrated how remarkably intelligent he was but that he knew exactly to whom he was speaking – "They do not know." Like Yeshua, the authority for you to do your task has been given to you by the Source; *'This mission I received from the Farther.'* (John 10:18) It's for this very reason that you are here.

Doing the will of the Source is paramount and as such I do feel the need to clarify some of what I have just written. You do not have to stop whatever you are doing immediately as Luke did, or indeed maybe at all. Whatever you are doing now you may need to do to give you the skills and prepare you for the completion of your task. Whatever you need to complete your task will be given to you, skills, information, feelings, experience, position and whatever you need to know will be made known to you. You may, for example, have an overriding feeling to continue doing what you are doing. In this case I would suggest that you may want and need to continue. Sometimes you may get a feeling that whatever you are doing is no longer for you, even though you have been doing it for a very long time. Other times, something may happen in your life which changes its direction, radically or otherwise. This is the Helper preparing you to move on and take the next step so that you may complete your task. The list of how you will be helped is endless. Remember, you have been given the *'Helper to be with you forever.'* (John 14:16) Trust in him to guide you. The Helper can see where you cannot.

The Helper is one of the energy signatures which define you as a manifestation of the trinity. Don't worry too much about understanding this. To truly understand yourself as a manifestation of a trinity of energy signatures, you must witness this for yourself. You can only do this by using the Grail. Please understand, however, that you do not need to use the Grail to do the will of the Source. I guess what I am trying to say is that you do not need to 'know' to do the will of the Source. Having said that, I will admit that using the Grail does help focus your efforts by helping you to understand that all things within the belief based system are insubstantial and immaterial and that only through doing the will of the Source can one be what they were truly created to be, an instrument of creation and the guardian and custodian thereof. You are special indeed.

When you invoke the power of the Grail and witness the truth, nothing in this life will matter so much as doing the will of the Source. Furthermore, it's not until you take up your cross and be about your task, that you will truly feel free. It will give you a sense of joy that you will never experience until you do. Until then, you will feel eternally frustrated, unfulfilled and unsatisfied, regardless of how things are going. You will feel like you are missing something, that you don't truly belong, and you won't know why.

Many try to assuage such negative feelings by taking up a new endeavor, whatever that may be. Any relief you get from this will be short lived but your commitment to the endeavor may not. For example, you may decide to raise a family or start a business where this is not your task in life. If this is the case, the negative feelings you experience will not abate until you begin to do the will of the One that created you.

If you do not know what your task in life is, take some time, ask your Helper. I suggest you do this in private as it's not a good look to be seen talking in public to someone who cannot be seen, even by you. Talk to the Helper out loud. Don't hold back. Tell the Helper if you don't complete your task this time round that you are not going to be happy. However, these specific instructions come with a health warning. If, when you directly invoke the Helper's intervention, you are not currently doing your task or at the very least something which is necessary to ensure, or to prepare you for, its completion, your life will change radically. If you are happy with your life as it is, and you don't want to attend to the task you have been given but would rather do your own will, then I would suggest you don't invoke the Helper but rather continue as you were. You have been advised.

Doing your own will in this world is like building sand castles. It can be a lot of fun, but your work will not stand the test of time and all your kingdoms will eventually fall into the sea. It will be like you never even existed. Of course, you will be compensated for your efforts in building your kingdom in the belief based system by something that fundamentally doesn't exist, money. Money is a good example of what can be very powerful in the belief based system without being real in any way. Money does not exist and yet we ignore the will of the Source in pursuit of it. The only reason that money can be successfully used as a means of exchange is that we all collectively believe in it. If we all decided not to believe in it, it would cease to have any power, it would cease to exist. This is not the case with something that is real. That which is real, does exist and does not require our belief in it to continue to exist.

Do you really think that your money and material wealth in general could not be rendered useless overnight? If you want to create something new that time itself will kneel before then do the will of the Source. Scary? Most definitely. However, you will always feel conflicted until you take up your cross and do the will of the Source, after all, this is what you were created to do.

If you continue to be something other than what you are, there will always be conflict. It is only through being what you were truly created to be, the guardian and custodian of creation, and by doing what you were created to do, the will of the Source and not your own, that the conflict between your three energy signatures will ultimately be resolved. Until then, you will suffer conflict and from conflict, and where conflict prevails, unity will not. Satan himself could not stand divided against himself; *'If Satan has risen up against himself and is divided, he cannot stand, but he is finished!'* (Mark 3:26)

If you cannot accept what I say, consider Yeshua's life. Considering this man's great intellect, amazing abilities and his substantial advantage over everyone because he resided in the knowledge based system rather than the belief based system, he could have owned this world and successfully controlled it. Ultimately, however, his life could not be considered a successful life by normal standards. He left no progeny and he possessed no property or worldly wealth. He never received any money or awards for the successful completion of his task. Instead we scorned him, mocked him, spat on him and ultimately killed him. In the end, his material possessions consisted only of the clothes on his back which, before his death, were taken from him and divided out among the witnessing Roman soldiers; *'They divide my garments among them, and for my clothing they cast lots.'* (Psalm

22:18) He died as a tried and convicted criminal in a most humiliating and excruciatingly painful way. Yet despite these 'failures' to amalgamate wealth and power, his true legacy, the Grail, is eternal. He did the will of the Source, the One who sent him, and time itself pays homage to his legacy.

As Yeshua continued his journey to be crucified, he was followed by a great multitude of people. The women mourned and lamented for him. Yeshua continued his instruction to the world when he turned to them and said; *'Daughters of Jerusalem, do not weep for me, weep rather for yourselves and your children. For the days are coming when people will say: Happy are the women without child! Happy are those who have not given birth or nursed a child! And they will say to the mountains; fall on us! And to the hills; cover us! For if this is the lot of the green wood, what will happen with the dry?'* (Luke 23:28-31)

It is widely believed that Yeshua addressed these women out of concern for them. He addressed them compassionately as 'Daughters of Jerusalem,' urging them to stop weeping on his behalf but rather, they should weep for themselves and for their offspring. It is believed he was prophesying and warning them of the heart-breaking event soon to pass – the destruction of Jerusalem in 70 AD and the annihilation of most of its Jewish population which included thousands of crucifixions. This is not true. Yeshua's ministry was not parochial but both universal and timeless. It was intended for all people for all time.

Some believe his admonition was a rebuke. But why would Yeshua be angry? After all, these women were in a way letting him know, through the genuine tears they shed, that they did not agree with the injustices being committed against him. These believers advocate that Yeshua was angry because he was suffering for people who believed he was a victim rather than a willing participant. He was angry because despite the agony he was going through for these people he knew that they did not understand. This also is not true.

Others believe that the 'Daughters of Jerusalem' was a reference to the professional mourners whose responsibility was to accompany the condemned on his way to his cross or at his funeral and lament his grievous end. This is reported as common practice at the time especially among the Jewish faith. In this case, Yeshua's remarks are seen as a rebuff because their tears were not genuine and their behavior disingenuous. This is also not true. Yeshua's ministry was never personal but was always about doing the will of the Source.

There are those who believe that Luke 23:28-31 is a clear statement of the timing of the end of the world. People will seek to hide from the Lord Jesus Christ (And they will say to the mountains, fall on us! And to the hills, cover us!) because he will come to judge all and to take vengeance on those who know not God. I don't know how people got this meaning, it's quite a stretch. I guess people love prophesy and divine forecast because it legitimises their beliefs and thus their existence and importance within the belief based system.

There is also some considerable argument over what Yeshua meant by 'the green wood' and 'the dry.' It is believed by some that Yeshua's use of the term 'dry wood' refers to the Jewish nation. The tree is still spiritually healthy for Yeshua is still present and so are his followers who believe in him. When Yeshua and those who believe in him are taken from the Jewish nation, only a spiritually withered nation will remain, being like a dead tree or dry wood.

It's quite amazing how many different explanations there are regarding Luke 23:28-31 and the above are only an example of some of the ones that exist. In fact, a whole book could be written on Luke 23:28-31 and its possible meanings. People are so interested in the detail and constantly argue over possible meanings that often they can miss the whole point. Don't get caught up in the detail, especially to the exclusion of the message, after all, remember who resides there! It's apparent that we who hold all or any of the above views still do not understand the meaning of this part of the way of the cross.

I would like to address the true significance of Yeshua's words before I attempt to explain their meaning. Up until this time Yeshua has been silent in all his suffering. The effect of prolonged excruciating pain can cause one's mind to seek retreat from the moment to block out the agony. Because of this, it's impossible to get a sensible conversation from anyone who is in extreme pain. Did he not speak until now because his mind had retreated from the moment in an effort to shield himself from the pain or did he not issue a word of protest to ensure that records would reflect his willingness to give his life was never in any doubt?

In truth, he stayed silent to reserve his strength so that he could complete his task. However, where the opportunity arose to continue his ministry and instruction to all, he never failed to deliver. He could not have continued his ministry, and the completion of his task would have been in jeopardy if he had allowed his mind to retreat from the moment to protect himself from the torment. Yeshua used the words 'Daughters of Jerusalem' to make it known that he had not retreated into a delirious state of mind. He knew where he was and to whom he was speaking.

What do the remaining words mean? "Do not weep for me, weep rather for yourselves and your children." This is straightforward. He is saying to them, save your tears for yourselves and your children, "For the days are coming when people (all people not just Jews - his ministry was for all people for all time) will say, Happy are the women without child! Happy are those who have not given birth or nursed a child!" This quote is reflected in his earlier teaching; *How hard it will be for pregnant women and mothers nursing their babies!'* (Matthew 24:19) He is saying the day will come when all women who are without children will be the blessed ones. This is a very dramatic statement, especially in view of the great honor generally attached to the bearing of children in Israel. Barrenness was widely viewed by the Hebrews as a curse from God!

"And they (our progeny) will say to the mountains; fall on us! And to the hills; cover us!" Yeshua is saying the time to come will be so bad that they will seek death and burial as an escape from it, even if it comes in the most brutal fashion possible.

"For if this is the lot of the green wood, what will happen with the dry?" The tree being green and dry is a reference to the passage of time, now and later. If this is our lot now (the green tree) what will happen later (the dry tree) will be worse. It would be better not to have children than to have them experience the suffering that is to come when things will get so bad that even our children will wish they had never been born.

Yeshua's birth heralded the beginning of the end of the belief based system. He was to bring light/knowledge into the world, replacing the belief based system with the knowledge based system. Yeshua is saying that near the end (i.e. when the tree is dry), it will be much worse than it is now (i.e. when the tree is green). Yeshua was right, since his time our ability and willingness to inflict pain on ourselves has grown exponentially. However, don't waste your time looking for an apology for the atrocities of the past. Looking for such apologies would take too much of your time and energies, and if you did receive them, they would ultimately be hollow as we are still today committing such atrocities and worse. Instead, simply stop, take up your cross and be about your work.

Yeshua finally arrived at the place called Golgotha where he was to be crucified. Before he was nailed to the cross he carried, the soldiers *'offered him wine mixed with gall. Yeshua tasted it but would not take it.'* (Matthew 27:33-34) Mark also mentions Yeshua being offered something to drink prior to being fixed to the cross. Mark refers to this drink as wine mixed with myrrh, not gall. (Mark 15:23) There is huge debate over what the drink offered to Yeshua was. Did it include gall or myrrh or both? What is gall? What are the effects of gall and myrrh? Why was he offered the drink and why did he refuse to take it?

Some argue that gall was the poppy from which came the juice call opium. During this time, opium was both eaten and made into a black tea. It was also mixed with wine to be used as a narcotic or medicine. Opium was used as a cure-all, sleep aid, and to relieve pain and suffering. Others believe gall was simply the bitter bile from the gallbladder.

Myrrh is apparently renowned for its use in wound healing preparations though certain varieties may be more efficacious than others. The resin and tincture of myrrh have been used to treat leg ulcers. Many herbalists recommend tincture of myrrh as an astringent for the mucous membranes of the mouth and throat. Myrrh's use as a remedy for mouth ulcers and gargles for sore inflamed throat conditions has been used right up to modern times. Myrrh, pulverised and sprinkled on the inside and the outside of the base of the tooth was supposed to bring immediate relief from tooth ache. Some say it was consumed to treat headache or other types of acute pain.

It is reported that both myrrh and gall were terms often used at this time to denote anything exceedingly bitter and were often used interchangeably. In any case, expired wine, which we refer to today as 'corked wine' was often carried by Roman soldiers for drinking. It was a cheap wine for thirst quenching. It was often considered safer to drink this type of wine than to drink water from local sources which often carried waterborne diseases such as cholera, dysentery and typhoid. Nevertheless, the soured wine tasted like vinegar, and thus it was common practice to infuse myrrh into the wine to give it a more agreeable fragrance and flavour.

Some advocate that it was custom for Roman soldiers to give wine, mixed with myrrh, to the condemned at their place of execution, to intoxicate them and make them less sensible to pain. Others point to the existence of a Jewish custom by which a condemned man was given a stupefying drink to ease his pain. According to this custom however, it was frankincense and not myrrh that was mixed with wine for this purpose.

Were the Roman soldiers and Jewish Sanhedrin now showing mercy and compassion to Yeshua by trying to ease his pain? I don't think so. To say yes would at the very least be incongruous with their previous actions when they brutally scourged him and mocked him and with their subsequent actions when they continued to taunt him on the cross; *'The man who saved others cannot save himself. Let's see the Messiah, the King of Israel, come down from his cross and then we will believe in him.'* (Mark 15:31-32)

So, why was Yeshua offered wine to drink? While it wasn't a custom per se for Roman soldiers to offer wine to the man to be crucified, it was common practice. Why? The first time Yeshua is offered wine is just prior to nailing him to the cross. It was common practice by Roman soldiers to do this, not to ease the pain and suffering of the condemned man but to make him more compliant, easier to handle. It is more difficult to nail someone to a cross if they resist, which was often the case. Plying the condemned man with alcohol facilitated the soldier's job, making the condemned man docile and thus more submissive to his fate. It is also well documented that surgeons of old who needed to render stitches to close a wound, for example, would often give the patient alcohol when available, to relax him, making the surgeons task easier. Without the stupefying effect of the alcohol, the patient would move and make the process more difficult.

So why did Yeshua refuse to consume this drink? Maybe Yeshua was accustomed to a better standard of wine and didn't drink what he was offered simple because he didn't like the taste. Possible but improbable. Real thirst does not discern, and his thirst could not be in any dispute. If you were dehydrated to the extent that Yeshua must have been you would drink filth.

Some conceive the drink offered to Yeshua was poisonous and when he tasted it he recognized it as such and thus refused to drink it. Again this is unlikely, as poisoning the condemned on the cross was never done and thus to have poison readily available at this particular crucifixion would have been extremely doubtful. Furthermore, to kill someone who is in a lot of pain and destined for death anyway would be an act of compassion. Thus, I believe this supposition is somewhat weak at best.

Some posit that the offering of the wine to Yeshua and his refusal to drink it was in fulfillment of a prophecy given by King David who according to the Hebrew Bible was the second King of Israel and Judah, reigning in 1010-970 BC. If you wish to believe in prophesies, then you have every right to do so. You have earned that right by entering the belief based system. I guess you know by now, however, how I feel about such predictions.

Believers advocate that Yeshua understood he had to die in excruciating pain for him to become the supreme sacrifice for the sins of all man and thus he refused to drink the wine as he did not want to lessen his pain. They promote the belief that the Lord Jesus Christ refused both sour wine and gall desiring to remain conscious throughout his crucifixion without any pain relieving agent, such was the strength of his humanity.

These believers maintain that the pain he suffered was necessary for the atonement of our sins. They like to play with words saying, "rather than drinking the wine that was offered to him to blunt his pain he chose to drink from the cup which his Father had given him." They encourage us to emulate Yeshua, to be courageous servants who would hold steadfast to our faith no matter what, just as Yeshua did, who was now willing to bear the pain of crucifixion to ensure God's saving grace to all. Fine words. Although this scenario is possible it's dubious. Taking a mouthful of the bitter alcoholic drink would have eased his thirst slightly and made his mind a bit wooly maybe. However, it would not have detracted from his pain to any significant degree. If you don't believe me, imagine a nail being driven through your hand and consider the pain you would be in. Do you really believe a mouthful of wine would diminish your pain to any perceptible extent?

Yeshua did not take the alcohol-based drink for the very same reason he did not drink at the Last Supper. His task was not yet completed and to drink an intoxicant could impede and impair his ability to do so. Furthermore, if he drank now or at any time before the completion of his task, it could cast doubt over his actions and words. Did he do and say such things because his mind was intoxicated with alcohol? The simple and only answer is no because Yeshua had not taken any intoxicant. Even now, though exceptionally dehydrated and extremely thirsty, he refused to drink the alcoholic libation that was offered to him in case it would interfere with the completion of his work. Furthermore, Yeshua's ability to recognize the drink offered him was not water further proves that Yeshua's mind, even after being nailed to the cross, was still present and had not retreated from the moment into a delirious state to shield himself from the pain. Even now, Yeshua showed a self-discipline second to none and an unparalleled determination to do the will of the Source. This man was truly great.

Chapter Eleven

The Journey to Crucifixion (Vol.2)

Yeshua hung of the cross in acute and agonizing pain with gaping wounds in the midday sun. He was mocked by everyone. The soldiers continued to deride him saying; *'So you are the King of the Jews? Free yourself!'* (Luke 23:37) The Jewish chief priests, scribes and elders also did not pass up the chance to publicly taunt the one who had so often in the past ridiculed them for their hypocrisy. They jeered him saying; *'The man who saved others cannot save himself. Let the King of Israel now come down from his cross and we will believe in him. He trusted in God; if God loves him, then he will save him, since he himself said; I am the Son of God.'* (Matthew 27:42-43)

The Jewish leaders must have felt vindicated in their judgment of Yeshua, his intense suffering and imminent death was God's punishment for his blasphemy. Passers-by also laughed at him and jeered him. They said; *'So you will destroy the temple and build it up again in three days. Now save yourself and come down from the cross, if you are the Son of God.'* (Matthew 27:40) He was mocked and derided to the very end.

Today we have no idea of the physical torture and public shame that crucifixion involved. The condemned usually died either from physical trauma, loss of blood, or suffocation when they no longer had the strength to lift themselves up to breathe. It truly was a long, painfully drawn out and publicly humiliating execution, and it was a very effective deterrent to discourage dissention and rebellion against Roman rule of law.

Only Luke records Yeshua's response to his crucifixion and the mockery. Yeshua looked down on all before him and presented mankind with a gift which would be his legacy for all time. Yeshua spoke the words; '***FORGIVE THEM FATHER FOR THEY KNOW NOT WHAT THEY DO.***' (Luke 23:34)

These words created the Grail, a gate through which we can now return to the knowledge based system, the system into which we were originally born, the Garden of Eden, our home. This is why Yeshua referred to himself as the 'gate'; '*I am the gate. Whoever enters through me will be saved.*' (John 10:9) It was his mission to show us the way back to the knowledge based system; '*I am the way, the truth, and the life. No one comes to the Father except through me.*' (John 14:6)

When Yeshua said "Forgive them", he was not just referring to those who had crucified him. He was referring to all of us. Anyone who resides in the belief based system does not know what they are doing because they have their eyes closed to the truth and thus reside in darkness. As I have previously written, the act of forgiving has a dual nature. To successfully unlock the Grail and pass through the gate, you must forgive and allow yourself to be forgiven, "forgive us our trespasses as(because) we forgive those who trespass against us." This is what Yeshua meant when he said; *'And when you stand to pray, forgive whatever you may hold against anyone, so that your divine Father may also forgive your sins.'* (Mark 11:25)

It is imperative that you must truly accept your reason or reasoning to forgive and to be forgiven. If you cannot accept or believe your own reasoning then you will not be able to complete the acts of forgiveness and your eyes will remain closed, leaving you in darkness, the belief based system. As you can now understand, whilst Yeshua may have been the broken one, we were the ones that needed saving.

One could be forgiven for believing that Yeshua's work must surely now be completed. It wasn't.

Yeshua acknowledged both his mother and his disciple John who were standing nearby. He said; *'Woman, this is your son. Then to the disciple, there is your mother.'* (John 19:26-27) This passage of the way of the cross has been interpreted by many as Yeshua tenderly considering his mother at his moment of death. Many believe it is probable that Joseph, her husband, was long since dead, and that her son Yeshua had supported her. Now that he was dying what would become of his mother? He saw her standing nearby and was worried for her. He saw John standing beside her. Then Yeshua said, "Woman, behold, your son!" Then he said to John, "Behold, your mother!" From that hour Yeshua established a new relationship between his beloved mother and his beloved disciple and John took her into his own household.

Those who choose to reside within the belief based system like to draw attention to the care Yeshua took of his dear mother. Yeshua knew, as he hung on the cross in severe pain, his death was near. Despite the agony, Yeshua was concerned about his mother and her care after he was gone. Since Yeshua was the oldest son, it was his responsibility to insure the care of his mother. This was Jewish custom and part of honoring one's parents in accordance with the commandment. He made provision for his mother by charging one of his disciples to take care of her as if she was his mother.

Within the belief based system, argument arises (as it always will) as to why Yeshua used the word 'woman' instead of 'mother'. One argument is that using the word 'woman' at the time to refer to a female was a term of respect and endearment. Some argue he did so not out of disrespect to her but partly that he might not raise, or add strength to her passions by speaking tenderly, and partly to conceal her from the mob lest she should be exposed to their insults and possible persecution. The later argument was always my favorite as it demonstrated that Yeshua was, despite his agony, still very much aware of what was happening around him. The established Christian religious dogma created around Yeshua argues that this act by Yeshua toward the 'woman' who was his mother shows us that we are to love our parents and to provide for them as much as we are physically able. By so doing, we show our love for Yeshua and for God, Our Father.

All this reasoning and argumentation are founded and deeply rooted within the belief based system and bear no reflection to the truth, the knowledge based system. As I previously stated, you may hold certain things in this life very dearly and compassionately, but these will need to be relinquished if you wish to enter and reside within the knowledge based system. What Yeshua held most dear in this life was his mother. He was now letting go.

I guess the argument I would present to you within this belief based system is that, if we are all created equal, how could this woman be his mother; *'Whoever does the will of my Father in heaven is my brother, my sister, and my mother.'* (Matthew 12:50) We all have only one mother or creator which is the Source. Furthermore, if Yeshua knew God, he would also know his mother would be cared for. Remember his sermon about 'worrying'. (Matthew 6:25-34) It goes like this:

'This is why I tell you, not to be worried about food and drink for yourself, or about clothes for your body. Is not life more important than food and is not the body more important than clothes? Look at the birds in the sky; they do not sow, they do not harvest and do not store food in barns, and yet your Heavenly Father feeds them. Are you not worth much more than the birds?

Which of you can add a day to his life by worrying about it? Why are you so worried about your clothes? Look at the flowers in the fields how they grow. They do not toil or spin. But I tell you that not even Solomon in all his wealth was clothed like one of these. If God gives such clothes to the grass in the field – which blooms today and is burned tomorrow in an oven, how much more will he clothe you?

Do not worry and say: What are we going to eat? What are we going to drink? Or what shall we wear? The pagans keep themselves busy with such things; but your Heavenly Father knows that you need them all. Set your heart first on the kingdom and the justice of God and all these things will be given to you. Do not worry about tomorrow for tomorrow will worry about itself. Each day has enough trouble of its own.'

If Yeshua was now 'worried' about his mother after such a speech, it could be argued he was now being a hypocrite. This of course, I know, will deeply offend some people, in particular those with strong and deeply held beliefs but I did warn you that one of the greatest barriers to entering the knowledge based system will be your current belief based system, whatever that may be.

Yeshua, in his ministry on earth, tried to teach us that the more difficult we find to let go of all we hold dear in this world, the more difficult will be our passage from the belief based system to the knowledge based system. Yeshua explained this in many ways but the teaching I like best is when he said; *'…it is easier for a camel to pass through the eye of a needle than for a rich man to enter the kingdom of heaven.'* (Matthew 19:24, Mark 10:25, Luke 18:25) For those of you who may not know, the eye of a needle is the section of a sewing needle formed into a loop for pulling thread, located at the end opposite the point. These loops are often shaped like an oval or an eye, hence the metaphor.

There have been several different and equally inaccurate schools of thought on what Yeshua was referring to in saying it was easier for a camel to go through the eye of a needle than for a rich man to gain eternal life. The saying was a response to a young rich man who had asked Yeshua what he needed to do in order to inherit eternal life. Yeshua replied, sell your possessions and give your wealth to the poor. The young man was saddened by this response as he was unwilling to do this. Yeshua then spoke this response, leaving his disciples astonished; *'Again I tell you, it is easier for a camel to go through the eye of a needle than for a rich man to enter the kingdom of God.'* (Matthew 19:24)

When the disciples heard this, they were greatly astonished because it was widely accepted at the time that wealth was proof of God's approval and it was commonly taught by the Rabbis that rich people were blessed by God and thus were the most likely candidates for heaven. The disciples utterly amazed by Yeshua's teaching (and not for the first time I may add) asked; *'Who then can be saved?'* (Matthew 19:25) If the wealthy among them, which included the super-spiritual Pharisees and scribes, were unworthy of heaven, what hope was there for a poor man?

I would like to point out here, that nobody asked the question, "Why is it easier for a camel to pass through the eye of a needle than for a rich man to enter heaven?" This to me seems the pertinent question. Therefore, one could rightly argue that we will never know what Yeshua actually meant by these words. However, unfortunately or otherwise, the question that was asked was "Who then can be saved?" The nature of the question seems to suggest that the person who asked the question is simply worried about himself rather than understanding the meaning of such a statement.

The established and accepted school of thought regarding the meaning is that it is those who recognize their spiritual poverty and their utter inability to do anything to justify themselves to a holy God, who will inherit the Kingdom of God. (Matthew 5:3) In short, it is the poor and humble who will be ushered through the 'pearly gates' of heaven. The rich man's life, however, is consumed by making money. His primary interests are to maintain his wealthy lifestyle and status, often giving little or no thought to those in need around him. In short, the rich man is seen as selfish, arrogant, proud and with little or no regard to the wellbeing of others, traits not acceptable in heaven. The rich man is thus often blind to his spiritual nature and its impoverished state because he is too proud of his accomplishments. It is believed because of this, the rich man is no more likely to humble himself before God as a camel is to crawl through the eye of a needle.

This is complete and utter nonsense. I'm sure this may offend some of you, especially those of you who believe you are financially poor and/or rich in spirit, whatever that means. The reason why Yeshua said, "It is easier for a camel to go through the eye of a needle than for a rich man to enter the Kingdom of God", is because a rich man will find it difficult to let go of his wealth.

What a person holds dear in the belief based system is irrelevant. It could be your money, property, achievements, charity work, wife, husband, father, mother, child, intellect or even your spirituality! It could even be something as seemingly insignificant as a coat or other item or idea you hold dear for whatever reason. What Yeshua held dear was his mother whom he loved very much. This is why he referred to his mother as 'woman'. He was relinquishing all ties with this world, the belief based system. If you do not completely relinquish the belief based system and all that you hold dear within that system, whatever or whomever that may be, you cannot permanently reside within the knowledge based system. Remember, it's not what you hold dear that will anchor you within the belief based system but rather it is your relationship with it. This may sound very cold to some of you, but it is exactly that compassion that blinds you from the truth.

While I am on the point of who will and will not inherit the kingdom of heaven let me say that you cannot enter the knowledge based system through good deeds effected in the belief based system; *'Not everyone who says to Me, Lord, Lord, will enter the kingdom of heaven, but only he who does the will of My Father in heaven.'* (Matthew 7:2) The corollary is also true. You cannot be prevented from entering the knowledge based system through any bad deeds you may have perpetrated. Do you remember what I wrote in chapter six about good and bad simply being opposite sides of the same coin in the belief based system?

I understand there are many sources which touch on this subject so let us consider what they say. For those of you unfamiliar with this topic, the million-dollar question is – "Are we saved by grace or works?" Believe it or not there are quotes which support both sides. I hope by now you are not too surprised by this as I did inform you that everything in the belief system is subject to opinion and everyone has one. Every event or topic in the belief based system can be viewed in an infinite number of ways. Each view or opinion is equally valid, but no singular view could ever hope to reflect the truth.

Before we look at the quotes and consider them, I would like to draw your attention to the fact that nobody explains what 'saved' means nor do they ever consider what we are being 'saved' from. For the sake of brevity, let's agree to say the position we are in is in some way precarious and if we are not saved from it, it can only get worse. I guess most religions would say we need to be saved from a sinful life otherwise we will go to hell and hell is not a nice place.

Here are some references that support being saved by grace.

1. *'For by grace you have been saved through faith; and that not of yourselves, it is the gift of God; not as a result of works, that no one should boast.'* (Ephesians 2:8-9)

2. *'No one will be declared righteous in [God's] sight by observing the law; rather, through the law we become conscious of sin!'* (Rom. 3:20)

Here are some references that support being saved by works.

3. *'You see that a man is justified by works, and not by faith alone.'* (James 2:24)

4. *'And behold, one came to Him and said, Teacher, what good thing shall I do that I may obtain eternal life? And He said to him, Why are you asking Me about what is good? There is only One who is good; but if you wish to enter into life, keep the commandments.'* (Matthew 19:16-17)

There are other sources which also discuss this topic but I don't want to get bogged down with too much detail. Let us first see how the above quotes are justified.

It's my understanding, from what I have read on this topic, that according to points 1 and 2, it is by grace through faith that we are saved. It is grace on God's part and faith on man's part that provides for our salvation. Our salvation is not affected by human effort but rather is a gift from God without price. No man will ever be able to boast of himself – "I have earned salvation." Therefore, trying to keep God's laws for the sole purpose of salvation will not work.

Thus, there will be no room for boasting by any man of gaining entrance to the heavenly kingdom through being a good and righteous person that never sinned and kept the law perfectly. It's my understanding that this is the case because we have all sinned and fallen short of the glory of God. Therefore, we can all only gain entrance into the kingdom in the same way, which is by grace through faith in the sacrifice of Christ. It is not through our own righteousness that we are saved and gain entrance to the kingdom but through the righteousness of Christ who is the only one who kept the law perfectly.

The above understanding begs the question that if we are saved by grace and faith alone, does this mean we do not have to obey the Ten Commandments? From quotes 3 and 4, it appears that grace and faith is not enough and we must indeed obey the commandments.

It would be appropriate to point out here that Yeshua himself did not keep the Ten Commandments in the strictest sense and he was often accused of breaking the Sabbath. For example, one Sabbath, when Yeshua went to eat in the house of a prominent Pharisee, he was being carefully watched. There in front of him was a man suffering from abnormal swelling of his body. Yeshua asked the Pharisees and experts in the law, "Is it lawful to heal on the Sabbath or not?" But they remained silent. Taking hold of the man, he healed him and sent him on his way. Then he asked them, "If one of you has a child or an ox that falls into a well on the Sabbath day, will you not immediately pull it out?" The Pharisees again remained silent. (Luke 14:5) This is a single example of many where Yeshua broke Jewish religious law.

James argues that faith which does not produce mercy, compassion and acts of charity is dead and in vain; *'Even so faith, if it has not works, is dead, being alone. Yes, a man may say, You have faith, and I have works: show me your faith without your works, and I will show you my faith by my works. You believest that there is one God; you doest well: the devils also believe, and tremble. But will you know, O vain man, that faith without works is dead? You see then how that by works a man is justified, and not by faith only.'* (James 2:17-24)

In short, we are told we should not be deceived or confused, as just believing in God by faith alone and doing nothing else will not save you. Evil men also believe in God and thus God does not want a faith that is empty and hypocritical.

Wow, what I must do now to enter heaven is as clear as mud! The deceiver has done his job well. Let me see if I can untangle this mess for you. Firstly, let me repeat what I said at the beginning of this topic as it is very important to have this clear in your mind. You cannot enter the knowledge based system through good deeds effected in the belief based system. The corollary is also true. You cannot be prevented from entering the knowledge based system through any bad deeds you may have perpetrated.

We have been brought up to believe that if we do good things in this life we will reap the reward in the next life. This is not the truth. As I already said, good and bad in the belief based system are simply opposite sides of the same coin. What is right or wrong in the belief based system is simply a matter of opinion of which there is an infinite number. This is why bad things can often occur from a good act and vice versa. Let's consider an extreme example of this.

Imagine you are an obstetrician and you have helped an expectant mother to deliver her baby. Without you the baby would have died. Have you done a good thing? I think we can all agree you have done a good thing, right? I would imagine such an act would also have made you feel good about yourself. Again, I think we would all agree that failure to act to try and save the child would be considered a bad thing. Not only would this be a bad thing but as an obstetrician, failure to act would probably result in disciplinary action being taken against you which could ultimately result in you being struck from the medical register. Thus failure to act would be bad for the child, mother and you.

Now imagine you are an obstetrician living in Germany around 1889 and the mother's name is Klara Hitler. Have you now done a bad thing? Alternatively, imagine you are an obstetrician living in India around 1869 and the mother's name is Putlibai Gandhi. Have you now done a good thing? You may consider this to be hyperbole but this I find is sometimes a good way to get a point across. You may also say it's impossible to predict all the possible outcomes of one's actions and I say that's exactly right! So don't worry about doing the right thing or be in fear of doing the wrong thing. Do not be paralysed by societies laws or expectations or by religious law, words in old books.

So where does that leave us regarding what we should and shouldn't do here in the belief based system. Again, Yeshua helped us out here. According to Yeshua we should not do what we think is right or wrong, nor what we think is the righteous thing to do, nor should we do what we believe is expected of us by society. You don't need to work hard, get married, have children, recite prayers, go to mass, or even help your neighbour just because you think it's the right thing to do. Whilst these things may be admirable they do not provide for passage into the knowledge based system. Only the Grail provides for passage into the knowledge based system.

So what should one do within the belief based system? – One should do the will of the Source.

Everybody has a task to do and if you do not do it, it will not be done. Why? Because only you have been asked by the Source to complete your particular task. Of course, in the belief based system if you wanted a particular task completed, you may ask more than one person to do it. After all, the more people you ask to complete the task the greater the probability the task will be completed. So why does the Source only ask one? I hope at this stage you understand this is a rhetorical question. But just in case you've missed the point, let me explain. Some will say only one person is asked to do a particular task because by doing so the Source shows complete faith in you that you will complete the task. This is not entirely true. If you are attending to the task you were given, you are doing the will of the Source. This is what is important. Why? Because it is by His will being done that His kingdom will come. Yeshua told us this in his prayer, The Our Father – thy kingdom (will) come (by) thy will be (being) done.

I feel I must conclude this topic by saying you should not let anyone tell you what you must and must not do. Nobody else knows what your task in life is. Therefore, if you follow the instructions of another, you are not doing the will of the Source, and you will find your journey very onerous indeed. As I said before, everybody in the belief based system has an opinion and most sell theirs very cheaply. Why? Because most opinions are just not worth paying for.

Let me explain by way of parable what I mean. A young boy and his grandfather set out on a long journey. They have planned well and have all the provisions they need which are carried by their donkey. As they journey the boy becomes tired, and the grandfather puts him up on the donkey's back. When they pass through the first town, the grandfather and grandson hear the people comment that the boy should be ashamed of himself. He is young and strong and up on the donkey's back while the poor old man has to walk. The boy feeling embarrassed by the people's comments, dismounts the donkey and asks his grandfather to rest on the back of the donkey. The grandfather mounts the donkey. They continue their journey. As they enter the next town they hear the people comment that the man on the donkey should be ashamed of himself. Here is a strong grown man on the back of a donkey while the poor young boy must walk. The grandfather feeling humiliated by these comments dismounts the donkey and both grandfather and grandson continue their journey on foot towing the donkey behind them.

Arriving at the next town the inhabitants snigger at them and say look at the strong donkey they have which could easily carry both of them and they choose to walk. Feeling shamed and mortified, both grandfather and grandson mount the donkey and continue their journey. As they pass through the next town, both mounted on the back of their donkey, they hear the people of the town say, look at those two lazy and selfish people riding together on the back of that poor donkey. Both grandfather and grandson dismount the donkey feeling contrite, distraught and abashed. How can we now continue our journey they ask, should we carry the donkey?!

I'm not saying advice cannot help you on your journey. Good advice can be considered the good provisions you carry on the back of your donkey. Be assiduous in what you carry and trust the Helper. The Helper will prepare you and provide you with all you need to know in order to complete your task. As a rule of thumb, ask yourself what you would do with the information you seek if you got it. If you can't answer that question, then you don't need the information you seek.

Chapter Twelve

The Journey to Crucifixion (Vol.3)

Most of those who had gathered to mock Yeshua had by this time departed, and all that could be heard was the muted weeping of women. With his head bowed, there was a lull in the atmosphere surrounding Yeshua, as though nature itself was holding its breath.

It is well known that Yeshua was crucified along with two thieves, one on either side of him. Both thieves witnessed Yeshua's time on the cross. One of the thieves, the 'bad criminal', decided then to speak to Yeshua. Knowing now who Yeshua was, he spoke to Yeshua saying; *'So you are the Messiah? Save yourself and us as well.'* (Luke 23:39) Yeshua makes no reply but remains still, with head bowed, waiting. His task is not yet finished.

We are educated to believe that the bad criminal could not be saved because he did not believe in Yeshua, whatever that means. It is also recorded that the bad criminal's statement of fact "So you are the Messiah?" was spoken as a question. A question mark indicates he didn't truly believe whereas a statement of fact would have demonstrated he did. The latter of course would not support the Catholic Church's understanding that you can only be saved if you truly believe.

Who was Luke to decide whether the bad criminal truly believed or not. Who was Luke to decide whether the bad criminal spoke the words, "So you are the Messiah?" as a question and not as a statement of fact. Who is the Catholic Church to propagate this myth? In truth, even a direct witness could not discern this. To truly know one way or the other you would have to know the heart and mind of the bad criminal. This is not possible. However, if we consider who the bad criminal was and his particular situation, we can make a more educated and balanced decision rather than simply twisting the facts to suit religious dogma.

Given the location of the crucifixion, the bad criminal would most likely have been Jewish. As such, the bad criminal would most probably have been brought up to believe in the Messiah as their savior just as Christians are brought up to believe Yeshua is theirs. Given the fact the bad criminal was indoctrinated from such an early age to believe in the Messiah, it's most likely then that this was in fact the case. The only unknown to be considered, therefore, is whether the bad criminal spoke the words "So you are the Messiah" as a question or a statement of fact.

I understand the Catholic religion would have us believe these words were spoken as a question as this fits in with their view that you can only be saved if you believe in Yeshua as Lord and Savior. However, given the bad criminal's background and current situation I believe he meant it as a statement of fact. If you don't trust what I say, imagine a time you are in a situation where your life is forfeit, as his was, and there is nothing you can do to save yourself. In this case it would be natural to truly believe and call on God, Yeshua, the Messiah or any other deity you were brought up to believe in to save your life. This is a very normal course of action, we all cling to life. What is not a normal course of action, given his circumstances and the pain he was in, is to ask a question. The bad criminal truly did believe, he would not have asked Yeshua to save him if he did not. However, his belief didn't save him, and it will not save you.

It is recorded that the second thief (the 'good criminal') rebuked the first, saying; *'Have you no fear of God. You received the same sentence as he did. We deserve the punishment; this is payment for what we have done. But this man has done no evil.'* (Luke 23:40-41) He then turned to Yeshua and said; *'Remember me when you come into your kingdom.'* (Luke 23:42) Yeshua then raised his head and looked directly at the second thief and declared to him; *'Truly I tell you, today you will be with me in paradise.'* (Luke 23:43)

I have read, although not exhaustively, the discussions and general consensus about what people believe Yeshua meant when he spoke these words. What I first noted was that many argue over the translation and in particular, the punctuation of the sentence – should the comma be put before or after the word 'today'. In short, it is argued whether Yeshua was saying, "Truly I tell you, today you will be with me in paradise", meaning that very day is when the thief would be in paradise, or was he saying, "Truly I tell you today, you will be with me in paradise", meaning that 'today' is when Yeshua was speaking and thus the timing of when the thief would enter paradise is indeterminate. Most major Bible translations, however, insert the comma before the word 'today' and if I was to involve myself in such an argument, I would say that this seems the most probable choice to me.

However, I'm sure it will now come as no surprise to you that we have yet again missed entirely the significance of this part of the way of the cross. One of the reasons why this happens so often is not because we reside in the belief based system and thus are blind to the truth, although this does not help, but because our focus is entirely on Yeshua and what he does and says. We argue over the detail of his words and actions and miss or fail to consider in any depth what is said by others or what has occurred around him.

It is still believed to this day by many that the good criminal confessed his sin on the cross and asked Yeshua for forgiveness. It is believed Yeshua forgave the criminal and offered him eternal life right there on the spot. The bad criminal made no such confession and his only plea was not for forgiveness but for Yeshua to save all three of them from death on the cross, a not entirely useless request under the circumstances! This part of the way of the cross has often perplexed Christians who believe salvation comes only by explicitly confessing Yeshua as Savior and Lord. In general, I find it disturbing the range of unexplored beliefs so let us explore briefly.

First of all, as we do not know exactly what the good criminal was guilty of, he could not have confessed his sin.

Secondly, he did not show any clear signs of contrition. Contrition requires feelings, or an expression, of sincere regret or remorse about one's wrongdoing or sin. There is no evidence of this. Furthermore, penitence oftentimes requires the sinner to do good deeds to make up for the wrong they have done which is clearly impossible now for the good criminal who is out of time. Apart from the belief he deserved his punishment for what he had done, there is no clear statement of remorse or shame. Maybe his lack of contrition is because he is guilty of killing a high ranking Roman soldier. Maybe this Roman soldier was responsible for the slaughter of his family, including children. I doubt the good criminal would ever have felt truly sorry for killing such a man.

So why did Yeshua say to the good criminal; *'Truly I tell you, today you will be with me in paradise.'* (Luke 23:43) This is a statement of fact by Yeshua and not a promise to intercede on behalf of the good criminal with God so that he could enter paradise. Let me be clear. Yeshua did not save the good criminal, the good criminal saved himself. How did he do this? The good criminal saved himself by using the Grail. Yes, the good criminal was the first person to ever use the Grail. Is this not truly amazing?

As I explained, the act of forgiveness requires choice, pain, reason and belief. It's quite clear the good criminal chose to say the words he did and he was in pain, physically, mentally and emotionally, when he did. This completed the first two steps. The next step is to provide a reason why you should forgive. The good criminal did this. What was his reason to forgive? He forgave those who crucified him because he believed he deserved to be crucified for what he did – "(We) I deserve the punishment; this is payment for what (we) I have done." Did he in fact deserve to be crucified for what he did? Does anyone deserve to be crucified no matter how heinous the crime? The reasoning does not have to be right, after all, what is right and what is wrong? However, you must truly believe your reason to forgive is correct, right and true. The good criminal did this and in doing so he completed the first act of forgiveness.

The second part to successfully using the Grail is a mirror image of the first part; *And when you stand to pray, forgive whatever you may hold against anyone, so that your divine Father may also forgive your sins.'* (Mark 11:25) You must now ask for forgiveness and this act of forgiveness also requires choice, pain, reason and belief. It's quite clear the good criminal chose to say the words he spoke, "Remember me when you come into your kingdom" and that he was in pain when he did. This completed the first two steps. The next step is to provide a reason why you should be forgiven. Saying you're sorry and truly feeling it will not work. The Grail requires a reason you truly believe. It's quite apparent from the words of the good criminal that he wanted to be forgiven for his sins. Which sin or sins he wished to be forgiven for is not clear to us, but it would have been to him. Given the circumstances it might have been the action which led to his crucifixion. It's not clear and it's not important for you to know. What is important is that you provide reason to receive forgiveness and that you believe your reason or reasoning.

What was the good criminal's reason to be forgiven? It's not clear. However, there must have been a "reason" to ask Yeshua to "Remember me when you come into your kingdom". Maybe he had reasoned God could never forgive him for the sin he had committed. If this was the case then it would seem logical, especially if he believed Yeshua was the Messiah as did the bad criminal, that he may have believed God would forgive him if Yeshua intervened on his behalf. Although the specific reason or reasoning of the good criminal to be forgiven is not clear, a reasoning process is, otherwise he would not have spoken such words.

So why didn't the good criminal automatically enter the knowledge based system upon successfully using the Grail? Yeshua's life was necessary for completion of the Grail; '...to give his life to redeem many.' (Matthew 20:28) Yeshua had to go first and only then could we follow. This is what Yeshua meant when he said to Peter; 'Where I am going you cannot follow me now, but afterwards you will.' (John 13:36) Until Yeshua completed his task, there would be no gate back to the knowledge based system. The gate had to be created first, then all those who finally understood what the Grail was and how to use it could follow later.

Are there other ways to enter the knowledge based system? No. This is what Yeshua meant when he said; 'I am the way and the truth and the life. No one comes to the Father except through me.' (John 14:6) He didn't say I am 'a way,' but 'the way'. You can only enter the knowledge based system by using the gate (the Grail) Yeshua created for us. This is what he meant when he said; *'I am the gate. Whoever enters through me will be saved.'* (John 10:9)

I would like to highlight that we do not know what the crime or crimes of the good and bad criminals were. Were they guilty of the same or different crimes? It appears the criminals may have known each other at the very least as the good criminal says, "We deserve the punishment, this is payment for what we have done." However, this is not conclusive evidence that they were both guilty of the same crime. What if the good criminal was guilty of a viler crime than the bad criminal? What if the good criminal is guilty of indiscriminately raping and murdering innocent women and children? What if the bad criminal is only guilty of protecting his family against an unprovoked Roman attack? What if the bad criminal begged Yeshua to save him because he had a wife and children whom he loved very much and to whom he so desperately wished to return? Who now is the good criminal and who is the bad criminal? Which one of them deserves heaven? The truth is, we do not know. The truth is, we will never know. The truth is, it makes absolutely no difference! It is only through using the Grail that we can enter the knowledge based system.

I would also like to add that the process of looking for someone to blame, which is a very natural thing to do, has an equal and opposite effect to that of looking for a reason to forgive. It is counterproductive and will assert a block between you and the power of the Grail. You are the only one who will suffer for this. Your failure to forgive the person who wronged you will not inhibit that person from successfully using the Grail no matter what they have done. In this way, you are only held responsible for yourself. (Q 4.84) This may seem unfair, but I say to you, the Source created us all equal and loves us all equally.

Yeshua had now been on the cross for a number of hours, his open wounds exposed to the midday sun. However, his task was not yet completed. He cried out; *'My God, my God, why have you forsaken me?'* (Matthew 27:46) These words that Yeshua cried out as he hung on the cross have been a source of much confusion and debate among Christians, even today, almost two thousand years later. His followers find it difficult to understand in what sense Yeshua was 'forsaken' by God. Most say this cry was simply in fulfillment of Psalm 22:1, one of many parallels between that psalm and the specific events of the crucifixion. Some argue he was forsaken so that God might never leave nor forsake us. Nice sentiment, but God never disowned us, and he never will. Others argue the mystery surrounding those words is far too deep even for the most mature believer to fathom.

Many Bible commentators and teachers have promoted the idea that at some moment on the cross Yeshua became sin on our behalf, whatever that means. He died in our place and on our account so that our sins would be forgiven. It was through this suffering endured by him that was due to us, that we are reconciled with God. Yeshua died as a substitute sacrifice for the sins of the world and the righteous Heavenly Father had to judge him fully according to that sin. It is believed when this judgment was passed he cried out, "My God, my God, why have you forsaken me?" You who love judgment, I promise you, Judgment you shall have.

The more agnostic among us argue that Yeshua was suffering excruciating physical pain, severe emotional distress and dehydration and thus these words he spoke were the product of a delirious mind. This I accept is a fair argument. Yeshua was most definitely suffering both physical and emotional pain and had not drunk anything since the Last Supper so of course he was suffering from dehydration and had been for some time. However, if you believe he was suffering from delirium, I ask you, at what point do you believe he started raving?

Was he delirious throughout the way of the cross? It's quite clear that, prior to this moment, Yeshua acted and spoke purposively and clearly. It's also clear that Yeshua knows his task is not yet finished as he has not yet committed his spirit back to the Source. Just because you cannot explain why he said this, it does not mean he was now confused. Trust me when I say, Yeshua at no point suffered from delirium, but demonstrated a single-minded dedication to a task I have never witnessed. He proved this throughout the way of the cross and indeed throughout his life. Why would you doubt him now and how much more proof do you need?

Some people believe Yeshua despaired in his final moments and that's why he uttered these words. In truth, this is a similar argument to whether he suffered from delirium or any other state of physical or psychological decline. What else might we claim he suffered from? I only include this argument because it is a belief held by some and quite frankly it is more reasonable than most. Reasonable although it may be, it could not be further from the truth. Such believers simply do not understand the measure of this man and never will until they enter the knowledge based system and witness it for themselves.

Some believe that although Yeshua knew he would have to bear our sins, to suffer and die in his human form, he probably did not know how long his suffering would take and thus this was a plea to God for his suffering to end. This is also untrue. Yeshua knew exactly how long his suffering would take and when his task would be finished. He goes on to prove this. How? By saying it – *'It is accomplished.'* (John 19:30)

Some believers assert that it was an appeal for divine help and such a plea would be expected under the circumstances. This view doesn't make sense. If Yeshua had decided not to complete the task he was given but rather to call for divine intervention to save him, I think he would have done it long before now, maybe even in the Garden of Gethsemane; *'Father, if it is your will, remove this cup from me; yet not my will but yours be done.'* (Luke 22:42), but not now when his task was practically completed.

Yeshua did not want anyone, divine or otherwise, to come to his aid which would interfere with the completion of his task. A good example of this is when Yeshua was arrested in the Garden of Gethsemane and would have been at his most vulnerable after having just entered the belief based system. Peter pulled out his knife to fight the arresting soldiers, but Yeshua stopped him by saying; *'Do you think I cannot call on my Father, and he will at once put at my disposal more than twelve legions of angels?'* (Matthew 26:53) However, if Yeshua did this, how could he complete his task? In other words; *'How would the scriptures be fulfilled? This is what has to be.'* (Matthew 26:54)

Others, the true believers among us, contend that Yeshua was God incarnate and that he came to earth in Yeshua to experience life as a human and the suffering was so great, he cried out, "My God, my God, why have you forsaken me?" Because of this belief, the question has been asked, "How can God forsake God?" Fair question I think. By way of explanation, these believers advocate a trinity of equal gods – God the Father, God the Son, and I assume God the Holy Spirit. Yeshua was God in human flesh. They claim this to be a miracle event they call sovereign departure, as somehow God was separated from God.

These true believers proceed to use scripture to support their hypothesis. They use, for example, John 10:30, where Yeshua said; *'I and the Father are one. Whoever sees me sees the Father.'* (John 14:9) *'I am in the Father and the Father in me.'* (John 14:11) They argue that God in his human nature knew he would have to bear our sins, to suffer and die. But, in his human consciousness, he probably did not know how long this suffering would take. This is a very complicated explanation indeed.

These believers go on to support their argument for a trinity of gods by pointing out that after his resurrection, just before he went to heaven, Yeshua commanded his disciples to baptize people *'in the name of the Father and of the Son and of the Holy Spirit.'* (Matthew 28:19) Again, we conveniently see the trinity of gods here in the words of Yeshua. They believe they have proven that the Father, Son, and the Holy Spirit are equal and are equally God. The logic here is truly twisted and misshaped around the seed of truth.

Let's put an end to this two-thousand-year deception. Yeshua was not and is not God, the Source, nor an incarnation thereof. (Q 4.171 & 5.75) Yeshua is a son of God. He is the first among us, sent by the Source to create for us a way back to the knowledge based system, a system he chose not to leave when we did; *'Now, Father, give me in your presence the same glory I had with you before the world began.'* (John 17:5)

The best way I can explain the relationship between Yeshua and the Source is to say, if he is a drop in the ocean then the Source is the ocean; *'...for the Father is greater than I.'* (John 14:28) Thus when you see the drop, you see the ocean and vice versa. They are inseparable. This is what Yeshua meant when he said; *'I and the Father are one.'* (John 10:30) He did not mean he was the Father, otherwise he would have said so. Yeshua was not trying to be obscure. As I said at the beginning, it is difficult to describe the knowledge based system with a language that's deeply rooted in the belief based system. Yeshua was a prophet and this is how he saw himself when he said; *'No prophet is honored in his own country.'* (Luke 5:24) The Quran also acknowledges Yeshua as a prophet. (Q 4.171)

Despite what the true believers advocate, Yeshua did not command his disciples to baptize people *'in the name of the Father and of the Son and of the Holy Spirit.'* (Matthew 28:19) This translation was based on the understanding that there was a trinity of gods. However, what Yeshua actually told his disciples was to baptize, "in the name of the Father, the Son and the Holy Spirit." In other words, or to put it more plainly, he instructed his disciples to baptize each person, being the Son and the Holy Spirit, in the name of the Father. The Holy Spirit is the Helper, your Helper. It is part of your trinity of energy signatures.

I would like to add, although not recorded in any of the new testaments, Caiaphas asked Yeshua this very question when he was being tried before the Sanhedrin, "Are you God?" Caiaphas asked Yeshua many questions which don't appear in any of the new testaments. Yeshua was thoroughly interrogated by the Sanhedrin for many hours. I trust you didn't believe that in all this time Caiaphas only asked Yeshua a single pertinent question? Yeshua did not answer in the affirmative to any of the questions put to him until Caiaphas asked him, "Are you the Christ, the Son of God?"

None of this, of course, answers our question why Yeshua cried out; *'My God, my God, why have you forsaken me?'* (Matthew 27:46) As you now know, Yeshua entered the belief based system in the Garden of Gethsemane. This is where his true suffering occurred. Though he uttered these words whilst on the cross, he was not in truth forsaken and neither are we. This was a feeling that Yeshua experienced, which is a feeling we all experience. This feeling did not come because he was forsaken but because he was disconnected from the Source after having entered the belief based system.

In this statement, Yeshua not only confirms for us that he is not God but more importantly that he never left the belief based system since entering it in the Garden of Gethsemane. The way of the cross was done entirely from the belief based system, cut off from the Source. Yeshua felt the physical pain just like you or I would but it was worse for him because it was the first time he was ever disconnected from the Source. More important than all this is the fact that by uttering these words, Yeshua demonstrated he died whilst residing in the belief based system. He was teaching us, yes even now, that death itself would not prevent you from using the Grail and entering the knowledge based system. Is this not truly amazing!!

Though we may feel forsaken, we are not forsaken any more than Yeshua was forsaken. Many claim God has abandoned them, and they blame God for all the misfortunes they experience in life and for all the bad things that happen. They ask, why would God let this happen? If you believe you are abandoned because you experience hardships in your life, or for any other reason, let me share with you the parable of the prodigal son given to us by Yeshua himself, the first son. The parable can be found in Luke 15:11-32 and generally reads as follows:

There was a man who had two sons. The younger one said to his father, 'Father, give me my share of the estate.' So he divided his property between them.

Not long after that, the younger son got together all he had, set off for a distant country and there squandered his wealth in wild living. After he had spent everything, there was a severe famine in that whole country, and he began to be in need. So he went and hired himself out to a citizen of that country, who sent him to his fields to feed pigs. He longed to fill his stomach with the pods that the pigs were eating, but no one gave him anything.

When he came to his senses, he said, 'How many of my Father's hired servants have food to spare, and here I am starving to death! I will set out and go back to my Father and say to him: Father, I have sinned against heaven and against you. I am no longer worthy to be called your son; make me like one of your hired servants.' So he got up and went to his father.

But while he was still a long way off, his father saw him and was filled with compassion for him; he ran to his son, threw his arms around him and kissed him.

The son said to him, 'Father, I have sinned against heaven and against you. I am no longer worthy to be called your son.'

But the father said to his servants, 'Quick! Bring the best robe and put it on him. Put a ring on his finger and sandals on his feet. Bring the fattened calf and kill it. Let's have a feast and celebrate. For this son of mine was dead and is alive again; he was lost and is found.' So they began to celebrate.

Meanwhile, the older son was in the field. When he came near the house, he heard music and dancing. So he called one of the servants and asked him what was going on. 'Your brother has come,' he replied, 'and your father has killed the fattened calf because he has him back safe and sound.'

The older brother became angry and refused to go in. So his father went out and pleaded with him. But he answered his father, 'Look! All these years I've been slaving for you and never disobeyed your orders. Yet you never gave me even a young goat so I could celebrate with my friends. But when this son of yours who has squandered your property with prostitutes comes home, you kill the fattened calf for him!'

'My son', the father said, 'you are always with me, and everything I have is yours. But we had to celebrate and be glad, because this brother of yours was dead and is alive again; he was lost and is found.'

It's okay for us to feel abandoned by the Source even though it was us who abandoned him by closing our eyes to the truth and entering the belief based system (the distant country). All who reside in the belief based system feel isolated and abandoned. However, would you blame the Father for the hardships which befell the prodigal son? Of course not, it was the prodigal son's decision to leave that resulted in his own hardships.

On entering the belief based system, we became the prodigal son. However, the Source is watching, waiting for you to return, for you to open your eyes and once again reside with Him in the knowledge based system. The love the Source has for you is constant, it was from the beginning, it still is and will ever be. It's the only constant, everything else is subject to change. He showed his love for us by asking his son, the first among us, to enter the darkness and show us how to return to the knowledge based system into which we were created. However, His gift of free will to us means He will not make us return home. We have to want this for ourselves.

Up until the very end, Yeshua continued to teach us from the cross. Yeshua now said he was thirsty. A sponge soaked in bitter wine was raised to his lips and he consumed the wine; '*I am thirsty. A jar full of bitter wine stood there; so putting a sponge soaked in the wine on a hyssop stalk, they raised it to his lips. Yeshua took the wine.*' (John 19:30)

Again, surprisingly, this is the subject of much debate. It is not understood why Yeshua would now drink the wine offered to him when he refused the prior offer. It is maintained the wine that was first offered to him was laced with bitter narcotics, which he would not drink, and the second type was simply wine and free of drugs. I tell you, there was not two different types of wine on hand nor was there an à la carte menu.

The more spiritual among us hold that Yeshua assumed our human weaknesses including thirst in order for us to partake of eternal salvation and thirst no more. Nice sentiment, but it is given by those who do not understand the significance of this action. Simply put, Yeshua's task of creating the Grail was complete. He knew this, so he decided then to drink. This shows quite clearly that Yeshua knew exactly how long his suffering would take and what exactly needed to be done in order to create (complete) the Grail. Yeshua then raised his face skyward and uttered the cry; *'Father, into your hands, I commit my spirit.'* (Luke 23:46)

I would like to bring to your attention that Yeshua was not born with the spirit or as I prefer to call the Helper. Yeshua, unlike us, was not born into the belief based system but into the knowledge based system as a single or pure energy signature. (Q 19.19) He did not live in darkness and without knowledge of the Source like we do and thus he had no need of a Helper. So why would he have a Helper now and when was it given to him?

As Yeshua lived in the knowledge based system, he knew his Father's plan. He knew that in order to complete his Father's plan (the creation of the Grail) he would need to leave the knowledge based system and enter the belief based system. He left the knowledge based system and entered the belief based system in the Garden of Gethsemane. In the belief based system he would be blind like the rest of mankind and he would need the Helper's guidance and support. The Helper was given to Yeshua during his baptism by John the Baptist.

For two thousand years many Christians and non-Christians alike have been confused by Yeshua's baptism at the hands of John. Many believe John baptized for the remission of sins (Luke 3:3) but as Yeshua was without sin his baptism made no sense. Many also see Yeshua's baptism as a source of embarrassment as they believe it positioned John above Yeshua. This is not the truth.

From the moment of Yeshua's baptism, he not only resided within the knowledge based system, but he now had the Helper with him at all times. Although John the Baptist initially tried to stop Yeshua being baptized saying; *'I need to be baptized by you, and yet you come to me! Yeshua answered him; Let it be so for now. We must do justice to God's plan.'* (Matthew 4:15) As you can now appreciate, the baptism of Yeshua was not a symbolic gesture, nor was it done for the remission of sins, but was a necessary step in the completion of the Grail, the task given to him by the Source.

This is why Yeshua went to the desert after his baptism; *'Then the Spirit led Yeshua into the desert.'* (Matthew 4:1) He went to convene with the Helper which the Source had given him. This was a very personal time. During this time, he would have discussed with the Helper what he needed to do. They would have discussed this together and planed for the time ahead. He also met with the deceiver who tried to dissuade him from his course of action. The deceiver crafted very astute, intelligent, subtle and insidious arguments. Yeshua did not listen to any of his reasoning, suggestions or promises. Instead, Yeshua used this opportunity to understand and feel the difference between the deceiver and the Helper so that when he eventually entered the belief based system he would recognize the difference between the Helper and the taint of the third energy signature which would become a part of him, separating him from the Source and plunging him into darkness, bringing him blinding pain.

We, however, do not need to be baptized to receive the Helper. Unlike Yeshua, we were born into the belief based system. As a result, we received the Helper at birth. All those who are born into the belief based system do. Nevertheless, performing the act of baptism truly is a special ritual of remembrance and acknowledgement. This act, done consciously, acknowledges the Helper in our lives. It also instructs the Helper to lead on, that we are ready to do the will of the Source.

Yeshua's cry of "Father, into your hands, I commit my spirit." also resonates with two of his earlier teachings. Firstly, that Yeshua's life was not taken from him but he gave it up willingly so the Grail could be created for us; *'No one takes it from Me, but I lay it down of My own accord. I have authority to lay it down and authority to take it up again. This charge I have received from My Father.'* (John 10:18) Secondly, when his task was complete he rendered back to the Father that which was given to him by the Father; *'Give back to Caesar what belongs to Caesar, and to God what belongs to God.'* (Matthew 22:21, Mark 12:17, Luke 20:25)

Yeshua confirmed to the world that his task was now complete by saying; *'It is accomplished.'* (John 19:30) He then gave up his spirit and bowed his head.

Epilogue

John alone records the final moments after Yeshua's death. The crucifixion of the first son occurred on the day of preparation for the Sabbath of Passover week. This is a huge event in the Jewish calendar and according to Jewish custom, the bodies of crucified criminals defiled the land by remaining on the cross overnight and the Jewish leaders did not want any such defilement in Jerusalem. They requested the Roman soldiers to speed up the death of those crucified. The common practice to end the life of the crucified was to break their legs. This encouraged the death of the condemned by asphyxiation because the crucified were no longer able to use their legs to push themselves up to breathe.

Instead of breaking Yeshua's legs, they ruptured his heart. His heart was not pierced because it was prophesized he would not have any broken bones but because it was known at the time for criminals, when they had their legs broken and later thrown into an open pit for the dead, to still be alive and oftentimes could be heard moaning for some time. For obvious reasons, the chief Pharisee watching the crucifixion wanted to make sure Yeshua died so he ordered the centurion to perforate his heart not to simply pierce his side as it is sometimes reported.

It is believed the Roman soldiers not breaking Yeshua's legs fulfilled Psalm 34:20, which claims – *'He keeps all his bones; not one of them is broken.'* The chances that none of his bones were broken would be minimal. The scourging of Yeshua would have both fractured and broken some of his bones. When he was nailed to the cross, the nails would have shattered and broken bones at the point of entry. Removing the nails would also have caused further damage and breakage. Piercing his side to rupture his heart would have been done with a spear head that was not small enough to fit between two ribs even if the perpetrator had been trying not to break a rib when trying to rupture his heart!

It is also believed the spear piercing Yeshua's side fulfilled the prophecy in Zechariah 12:10; *'They will look on me, the one they have pierced, and they will mourn for him as one mourns for an only child and grieve bitterly for him as one grieves for a firstborn son.'*

The one who twists details to fit prophecy is distracted from the truth and is also distracting those who read and believe such contortions. Yeshua's task was not to fulfill prophesy but to create the Grail. He completed his task. The time will come when you will have to choose a side. You will have to choose between residing within the belief based system or the knowledge based system. This is your choice and now you know how to make it.

PART 3

The Grail and the Promised Kingdom

Chapter Thirteen

Yeshua & Judas

Despite his notorious role in the gospel narratives, Judas remains a controversial figure in Christian history. Although Judas betrays Yeshua, his betrayal is seen as setting in motion the events that led to the crucifixion and resurrection of Yeshua, which, according to traditional Christian theology, brought salvation to all humanity. Some Gnostic texts including the 'Gospel of Judas', rejected by the mainstream Catholic Church as heretical, praise Judas for his role in triggering humanity's salvation, and view Judas as the best of the Apostles.

Many people have considered the question of Judas's betrayal and have speculated concerning his motives. There exist several opinions as to why Judas betrayed Yeshua and I will consider some of them in turn using both Occam's razor and the Socratic Method.

For those of you who may never have heard of Occam's razor or the Socratic Method, Occam's razor is a problem-solving principle attributed to William of Ockham (c.1287–1347), who was an English Franciscan friar and scholastic philosopher and theologian. The principle can be interpreted as stating, the solution with the fewest assumptions should be selected. In short, the simplest explanation is usually the right one. The Socratic Method is named after the classical Greek philosopher

Socrates. The Socratic Method is a method of hypothesis elimination, in that better hypotheses are found by steadily identifying and eliminating those that lead to contradictions. In other words, the Socratic Method is a means of arriving at a solution by asking questions.

Among the many reasons postulated why Judas betrayed Yeshua, the following are the most popular:

1. **Greed**

The most widely held and accepted reason for Judas's betrayal is avarice.

In the earliest gospel account, the Gospel of Mark, Judas goes to the chief priests to betray Yeshua to them. They were excited by what he had to say and promised him money as a reward. (Mark 14:11-12) In the Gospel of Matthew, on the other hand, Judas is recorded as having asked the chief priests what they will pay him for handing Yeshua over to them; *'What are you willing to give me to deliver him up to you?'* (Matthew 26:15) It is therefore believed by some that Judas betrayed Yeshua out of pure Greed.

Was Judas simply greedy and opportunistic? John notes that Judas was a thief and often stole from the common purse; *'Judas, indeed, had no concern for the poor; he was a thief and as he held the common purse, he used to help himself to the funds.'* (John 12:6)

If Judas's main interest in life was the acquisition of money and wealth, why was he following Yeshua, a poor carpenter? Why did he follow a man of such limited financial means for almost three years? Furthermore, based on Judas's actions subsequent to his betrayal, it is clear that money was not his motivation. He handed the money back almost immediately after his betrayal of Yeshua and then committed suicide. These are not the actions of a greedy man.

2. **Political**

Experts often suggest Judas's actions were politically motivated. Ever since the first Roman legionnaires marched into Judea, a heightened tension permeated Jewish society. Jews prayed, and not for the first time in their history, for God's deliverance from the harsh Roman oppression. They prayed God would send the promised Messiah during their lifetime. Judas believed Yeshua was the prophesized Messiah and thus he expected Yeshua to establish his kingdom by overthrowing Roman rule in Israel.

It is claimed that Judas desired position and power within Yeshua's new kingdom as one of the twelve. If Yeshua was now reluctant to establish his kingdom by force and thus deprive him of a prestigious position, then he would have to force the issue. What better means of doing this than by bringing Yeshua before the Sanhedrin to precipitate a popular uprising that would crown Yeshua King? Would Yeshua's many followers not riot against his captors and hail him as their king? Had not the Sanhedrin delayed dealing with Yeshua for this very reason?

It is considered that Judas may have thought the arrest of Yeshua would have goaded both Yeshua and his many followers into action against the occupying Roman forces, ultimately delivering the nation Israel from Roman authority as prophesized. If this was indeed the case, why didn't Judas organise the Jewish resistance forces and have as many of Yeshua's followers present at the time when he was arrested or the many opportunities thereafter? By doing this Judas may have gained an elevated position within the ranks of the rebels ensuring his rise to prominence in a successfully established Jewish kingdom. In the absence of doing this, there was nothing to be gained by having Yeshua arrested. There was also nothing to be gained by Judas through Yeshua's death.

Furthermore, Judas would have known that betrayal of one's militaristic leader, would mean he would never have received a position of power within the new kingdom established under Yeshua's rule. Indeed, he would have been lucky to have been spared his life by Yeshua's followers. In addition, and on the face of it, his plot was going to plan. Yeshua was successfully arrested. Had Judas simply forgotten to organise and arrange for Yeshua's followers and the many Jewish freedom fighters to be there at his arrest, at any of his three trials or indeed at his conviction and subsequent crucifixion? Instead, it appears that once Judas sees Yeshua has been arrested and has incurred the death penalty at the hands of Caiaphas, he commits suicide. These are not the actions of the politically motivated.

3. **Revenge**

Due to the obvious lack of preparation on Judas's part and the fact he had nothing material to gain (apart from thirty pieces of silver which he readily returned) some believe he betrayed Yeshua on impulse, through anger, and thus without thinking.

Judas may have truly believed that the Messiah, which was foretold, would overthrow the occupying Roman forces and establish his new kingdom on earth, Israel. Judas would have known, after three years of following this Messiah, that he was most likely not the one foretold as he preached love and reconciliation, not war and conflict. According to this view, Judas is a disillusioned disciple betraying Yeshua not for love of money, but because he loved his country and thought Yeshua had failed it. Judas was angry and wanted revenge.

This view does not make sense. Did it really take Judas this long to figure out that Yeshua had no intention of starting a war against the Roman forces, when from the very outset he preached love and forgiveness? Furthermore, why perpetrate such an elaborate and public plot to have him killed which carried with it a good chance of failure? If Judas sought revenge, why not kill or arrange to have Yeshua killed in a more expedient, efficient and sure way?

4. **Hate**

Some argue Judas hated Yeshua so much that he wanted to have him publicly humiliated but he never intended for him to be killed. If this was the case, wouldn't Judas want to be there to witness Yeshua's humiliation? After all, considering the part he played in the arrest of Yeshua, the Sanhedrin would have given him a ring side seat. Instead of watching the spectacle he desired and helped to orchestrate, Judas instead commits suicide.

Furthermore, Judas knew the Sanhedrin wanted to have Yeshua killed and that delivering him to them would not simply result in his chastisement but would most definitely condemn him to death, irrespective of whether he was there to bear false witness against Yeshua or not.

5. **Possession**

In the Gospel of Luke and the Gospel of John, the devil enters into Judas, causing him to offer to betray Yeshua. I think Luke and John would have made good script writers for Hollywood. In any case, both Luke and John are overestimating the powers of the deceiver. The deceiver has no power over you, over and above what you give him. After the deceiver showed us how to close our eyes to the truth, all he has done since then is watched the show.

Free will was a gift given to us by the Source, it cannot be taken from us. Therefore, neither the Source nor the deceiver can interfere. Hence, it is you and I who dictate the outcome of events on earth. Even if the deceiver could do anything other than tempt us to affect our free will, he probably wouldn't because he doesn't need to. We, the pinnacle of creation, are running around like headless chickens bumping into each other, afraid of our own shadow and causing mayhem. Because of this, the deceiver feels vindicated (and very amused I'm sure) because he can say that all he did was show us how to close our eyes, we have done the rest.

In any case, if Satan could enter anyone at any time to do his bidding, then what is the point? Would we not be mere puppets? Maybe Satan can only enter bad people to do bad things? Does that mean only good people have free will? Some argue Satan didn't enter Judas but that he did successfully tempt Judas into betraying Yeshua. How did he tempt Judas?

If either of these two suppositions were true, then it is Satan's timely intervention which helps Yeshua complete his work. How fortuitously timely was Satan's intervention?! Certain people will argue the answer to this dilemma is that God used Satan. I would respond by asking another question, why? Why not simply use Judas? Why use an intermediary? Is God bound by rules and regulations, a certain code maybe? Maybe God can or will only influence bad people to do bad things and good people to do good things. In this case, God used Satan, Satan used Judas, God used Yeshua, Yeshua used Judas and thus indirectly Satan.

It is a widely held view that Judas was destined for damnation. Judas's betrayal, although was inspired by Satan, does not remove Judas's guilt or responsibility in the matter but highlights the spiritual warfare that was playing itself out on that night. People always need someone to blame, a villain, as much if not more than they need a hero. But surely, if the Source willed Yeshua be delivered up to death then Judas was doing the will of the Source rather than that of the deceiver. Should we ascribe guilt of the crime to Judas and credit to the Source for our redemption through Yeshua's death... or the other way around? Should the deceiver receive some credit for inspiring Judas?

Ultimately, was Judas's betrayal of Yeshua not a good thing? It helped Yeshua complete his work which I guess most of us would consider a good thing, right? Can a good deed lead to a bad outcome and vice versa? When do we decide the outcome of a good or bad deed has completely manifested itself, maybe there are more repercussions, good and bad, to come from the original deed? As you can see, both scenarios are becoming very complicated indeed suggesting that neither is the right one (Occam's razor). As if you couldn't have come to this conclusion on your own!

6. **Prophesy**

It is told Judas Iscariot fulfilled the prophecy of Psalm 41:9; *'Even my close friend, someone I trusted, one who shared my bread, has turned against me.'*

The Catholic Church created and foster the belief that Yeshua's death was pre-ordained as part of a divine plan in which he had to suffer and die as a sacrifice to pay for everyone's sins. The gospels suggest Yeshua foresaw (John 6:64, Matthew 26:25) and allowed Judas to betray him (John 13:27–28) because it would allow God's plan to be fulfilled. It is said that regardless of the betrayal, Yeshua was ultimately destined for crucifixion. It is believed if Judas had never existed or if he had never offered his cooperation to the Sanhedrin, Yeshua would have been crucified on that particular Passover regardless. It is widely believed that Yeshua's foreknowledge of Judas's betrayal in fulfillment of scripture highlights God's sovereignty and control over all that was about to take place.

Do we really believe, if Judas and Yeshua had refused to complete their tasks, that Yeshua would have been crucified anyway? Or do we simply believe if Judas had refused to complete his task that Yeshua would have been crucified anyway?

It is believed, until Judas entered their chambers, the Sanhedrin had decided to delay their move against Yeshua for more than a week, allowing the largest crowds ever assembled for a Passover to return to their homes after the Feast of Unleavened Bread. It is believed the actions of Judas simply ensured Yeshua died at three o'clock on the day of the Passover, as prophesized. I assume this is three o'clock local time and the time keepers of the day exercised a rigorous, decisive and precise approach to their profession and had the technology to tell time to at least the nearest minute! It is thus widely acknowledged among Christians that Judas had unwittingly altered the equation, and unknown to all but Yeshua, had maintained the God-ordained schedule for his crucifixion.

Believers are so hung up on prophecy and its fulfillment, they will accept the most incredulous, convoluted, complicated, nonsensical and conflicting explanations and end up missing the important thing – what Yeshua did and why he did it. This is the kind of material that is written by people in retrospect of an event they never truly understood.

The four canonical gospel writers do not shed light on Judas's possible motives because the truth is, they did not know, and they did not understand. How could they? Even today, almost two thousand years later, we still do not know and do not understand. How could we? We have not used the gift of the Grail given to us by Yeshua as his final act. In fact, until now, we did not even know this was his purpose. Instead, the four canonical gospel writers depend on God, Satan and prophesy to explain what happened.

The Cover Up

The Catholic Church conveniently has no view on Judas's damnation. The Vatican only proclaims individuals' eternal salvation through the Canon of Saints. There is no 'Canon of the Damned', nor any official proclamation of the damnation of Judas. The church holds the view that God in his wisdom was able, as always, to manipulate Satan's rebellion for the benefit of mankind. In truth, they specifically avoid this topic because of the many paradoxes it raises.

How would the canonical gospels, retrospectively, fix this problem? It is speculated that Judas's damnation, may not stem from his betrayal of Yeshua, but from the despair which caused him to subsequently commit suicide. This position is not without its problems since Judas, according to John (17:12), was apparently already damned by Yeshua even before he contemplated and committed suicide; *'When I was with them (the apostles), I kept them safe in your Name, and not one was lost except the one who was already lost…'.* It does, however, conveniently avoid the paradox of Judas's predestined act setting in motion both the salvation of all mankind and his own damnation.

The canonical gospels would have us believe Yeshua knew from the very beginning what Judas would do. According to John, Yeshua told his disciples; *'Have I not chosen you, the Twelve? Yet one of you is a devil! Yeshua spoke of Judas Iscariot, the son of Simon. He, one of the twelve, was to betray him.'* (John 6:70-71) John would also have us believe that at the Last Supper, Yeshua not only predicted his betrayal but also identified the betrayer. John (13:21-27) describes the situation like this;

'...*Yeshua was distressed in spirit and said plainly, Truly, one of you will betray me. The disciples then looked at one another, wondering who he meant. One of the disciples, the one Yeshua loved, was reclining near Yeshua; so Simon Peter signalled him to ask Yeshua whom he meant. And the disciple who was reclining near Yeshua asked him, Lord, who is it? Yeshua answered, I shall dip a piece of bread in the dish, and he to whom I give it, is the one. So Yeshua dipped the bread and gave it to Judas Iscariot the son of Simon. And as Judas took the piece of bread, Satan entered into him.*'

John would have us believe Yeshua specifically identified his betrayer as Judas and the other disciples did nothing. The truth of the matter is, if the other disciples had known Judas would cause Yeshua's death they would have killed him or at the very least stopped him, which of course would have damned us all.

A lot of the details in the gospels were misrepresented because the Apostles wanted the actions of the Christ to reflect theology and prophesy. This was a mistake. They missed the whole thing. Although the canonical gospels were written in retrospect and by those with a clear lack of understanding of what Yeshua wanted to achieve, John often indulges in artistic licence rather than sticking to the facts and he oftentimes comes undone as in this case.

The Truth

Judas had always been unpopular with the other eleven disciples because he and Yeshua were very close and were often to be seen talking alone together. Yeshua was able to explain things to Judas that he knew the other eleven, would not only fail to understand, but would be unable to accept. His close relationship with Yeshua spread jealousy among the others. These feelings of jealousy harboured among the eleven intensified their feelings of hatred toward Judas after his apparent betrayal of Yeshua.

So why did Judas betray Yeshua?

Although many people have considered, over the centuries, the question of Judas's betrayal and have speculated concerning his motives, many of which I have considered and discussed above, not a single person postulated the obvious. Judas betrayed Yeshua because Yeshua asked Judas to deliver him up to the Jewish religious leaders who hated him. This had to be done so that Yeshua could complete his task, to create the Grail and show us how to use it.

Why Judas? Why not one of the other eleven disciples?

Judas never believed Yeshua to be God incarnate. Unlike the other disciples who called Yeshua 'Lord', Judas never used this title for Yeshua and instead called him 'Rabbi', which simply acknowledged Yeshua as a teacher, nothing more. While the other disciples at times made great professions of faith and loyalty, Judas never did so. Why? Because Judas knew the truth. He knew what Yeshua's task here on earth was. How did he know this? Because Yeshua told him. He knew Yeshua was here to show us how to open our eyes, to leave the belief based system and enter the knowledge based system. Therefore, Judas had to be the one to betray Yeshua as he knew what was at stake.

Judas was the only apostle who knew who Yeshua really was. He understood Yeshua's task and what he needed to do, and he was prepared to help him in any way that he could. Judas was reluctantly willing to betray Yeshua so that his task here on earth could be completed. None of the other disciples would have been able to help in this way. Indeed, most of them would have tried to stop Yeshua or at the very least would have tried to persuade him not to go ahead with such a plan. For example, when Yeshua told his disciples he was going to die, Peter spoke up vehemently saying; *'Never Lord! No, this can never happen to you. Yeshua replied; Get behind me Satan! You would have me stumble. Your thoughts are not from God but from man.'* (Matthew 16:22-23)

Remember, your thinking will always be illogical, unintelligible, discordant and twisted until you leave the belief based system where everything is shrouded in darkness and enter the knowledge based system where all things will be made known to you.

Knowing of Judas's close friendship with Yeshua during his three years of ministry, it was always hard for mankind to reconcile how Judas could commit such a dastardly act of betrayal. This is why Judas's betrayal has been the focus of debate for so many years. I hope this now puts an end to the debate. Yeshua and Judas colluded together without telling the other disciples. Why? – The less people who knew about Yeshua's plan, the less that could go wrong.

Although Yeshua and Judas colluded together, Yeshua kept many of the details of his plan to himself. For example, Judas was unaware of the timing of his betrayal. Yeshua told Judas he would let him know when the time had arrived by raising the subject which he did at the Last Supper; *'Truly I say to you; one of you will betray me.'* (Matthew 26:21) Each of the disciples asked in turn; *'You do not mean me, do you, Lord?'* (Matthew 26:22) When Judas asked the question; *'You do not mean me, Master, do you?' Yeshua replied, 'You have said it.'* (Matthew 26:25), meaning, "You have promised me you would do it". This is why Yeshua said to Judas; *'What you are about to do, do quickly.'* (John 13:27) Yeshua wanted Judas to do what he had promised to do and to do it quickly. Why? For the same reason Yeshua kept the timing of the event to himself – because if Judas had been given enough time to think about what he was asked to do, he may have changed his mind. Yeshua did not want this to happen.

Yeshua prompted Judas as he knew Judas was hoping he would change his mind, or circumstances would change so that the betrayal would not be necessary. Why else would Judas wait for Yeshua's prompt to betray him before setting off to betray him? Surely the act of a true betrayer should be more definite and independent of the injured party? Furthermore and subsequent to his betrayal, Judas lingered until Yeshua was condemned to death by Caiaphas. Only then, did Judas know his task was complete. He then handed the money back to the Sanhedrin and committed suicide. Judas didn't want to die but he was willing to give his life so that Yeshua could complete his task. By doing this, Judas demonstrated ultimate faith in Yeshua.

The Apostle John suggests that when Yeshua uttered the words, "What you are going to do, do quickly", none of the other disciples knew why he said this. He also suggests the others may have thought, because Judas controlled the money purse, Yeshua was telling him to go buy provisions or give alms to the poor. The fact is, night was falling. They had all the provisions they needed for the night and further provisions would have been very difficult to procure at this time. Furthermore, the temple where the poor congregated during the day would have been emptied. The truth of the matter is Yeshua gave these instructions to Judas quietly and it's most likely, apart from John who sat next to Yeshua, the other disciples simply did not hear. In any case, as Yeshua and Judas had a special relationship, Yeshua often gave Judas instructions he did not explain to the rest. Therefore, Yeshua's instructions to Judas at this time, whether audible to the other disciples or not, was not seen as something out of the ordinary.

Many sources report that Judas, after his betrayal of Yeshua, was like a man possessed and this gives credence to the belief that Satan had entered him. The simple truth is Judas and Yeshua were very close. Now that Judas had time to think about his actions in betraying his friend, the world caved in on him. Judas was grief stricken that his friend had to be sacrificed and because of the role he had played. He also felt lost and alone as he knew nobody else was aware of Yeshua's plans and that not even the most reasonable among us would ever believe his story, least of all an angry mob of believers.

The Catholic Church would have us believe Judas's lack of faith in Yeshua is the foundation for his betrayal. They would have us believe the same holds true for us. If we fail to recognize Yeshua as God incarnate, and therefore the only one who can provide forgiveness for our sins, and the eternal salvation that comes with it, we will be condemned to eternal damnation. A story to frighten kids, but unfortunately it gave the church a strong hold over most adults for almost two thousand years.

The Catholic Church postulate that Judas, who felt such guilt and remorse because of his betrayal of Yeshua, but instead of turning to God to ask for forgiveness in humility and repentance as Yeshua had taught us, took his own life. Of course, the truth of the matter is Judas took his own life not because he thought God would not forgive him, but he knew people would not. After all, if people were capable of physically punishing and crucifying Yeshua who was innocent, either directly or indirectly by doing nothing to stop it, imagine what they would have done to Judas who would have been seen as betraying the

Messiah! He knew that he and any offspring he may have had would be persecuted for all time; *'..alas for that man who betrays the Son of Man; better for him if he had never been born.'* (Matthew 26:24)

If Judas had refused Yeshua's request for help, who among the other disciples could he have asked? Could St Peter, the Catholic Church's favorite, have fulfilled Judas's role? Well let's consider the question. Peter was very strong physically but often lacked the mental capacity to understand the teachings of Yeshua. He was a very simple man, a product of his upbringing, and his outlook on life was simple. He believed Yeshua to be God or the Son of God, the Messiah that was foretold. He believed this so strongly that he was willing to lay down his life for Yeshua; *'Lord, I am ready to go with you both to prison and to death.'* (Luke 22:31-34) He did this as he privately hoped his loyalty would be rewarded by receiving a senior position in God's Kingdom that was to come, after all, Peter was the first among his disciples.

Peter was to demonstrate his loyalty in the Garden of Gethsemane (where he slept) when a crowd appeared to seize and arrest Yeshua. Peter drew his sword to defend his master and struck one in the crowd and cut off his ear. (Matthew 26:47-56) But when Yeshua was arrested and brought before the Sanhedrin for questioning and the crowd against Yeshua had grown, Peter's loyalty and recent claims of fealty were really tested and found wanting. He was challenged by the crowd to be one of Yeshua's disciples and he denied knowing Yeshua; *'I do not know that man.'* (Matthew 26:72)

The gospels describing Peter's denial of Yeshua stand out as one of the most poignant and memorable events that transpired during Yeshua's judgment. The juxtaposition of Peter's earlier declaration of loyalty, a mere few hours before where he had sworn to stand by Yeshua no matter what, with his abandonment of his friend in his time of need just hours later where he denies even knowing him is very plaintive indeed.

It is often recounted that Peter, upon remembering that Yeshua had foretold his denial, leaves the courtyard and weeps bitterly. He is full of self-recrimination, everything he may have thought he knew about himself, all his self-confidence and belief in his strength and undying loyalty to his friend had been shattered. This story is heartrending indeed. However, please do not place too much importance on, or read too much into, the actions of Peter to the extent that you are distracted by the main event – the actions and words of Yeshua.

I am not in any way judging Peter and nor should you. Although Peter could sometimes be brash, over confident and prone to audacious and pretentious acts and verbal declarations of loyalty, which I'm sure irked the other eleven at times, he was at heart a good man and the situation he was in was terrifying in the extreme.

The simple truth is that it was neither Peter's task to betray Yeshua nor to defend him. Peter had to complete his own task and allowing himself to be taken and killed by the crowd that night would have prevented him from doing so. Although at a superficial conscious level he may not have realized this, his denial of his friend kept him alive and allowed him to do the will of the Source. In technical speak, although the motive force for his denial of Yeshua was fear, the reason why Peter denied knowing Yeshua was because he had to stay alive to complete the task he was given.

This example, I hope, clearly shows that you should not judge someone's actions in this life because you do not understand the task they have been given and, in most cases, neither do they understand until they are ready and willing to do it. Until that moment, one of the three energy signatures (the Helper) will keep you alive and prepare you for the task ahead.

If you had been Judas would you have refused to accept your task? Would you have refused to do the will of the Source? Would you have refused to help Yeshua? No one ever said it would be easy. Judas wanted us to know he completed his task, payment wasn't necessary, and that's why he returned the money.

Would you have preferred Yeshua's task? If you had been given Yeshua's task, would you have refused to do the will of the Source? Would you have preferred Peter's task? If you had been given Peter's task, would you have refused to do the will of the Source? Don't judge. You have your task, so be about your work. If you fail, it will not be done.

Many people believe Yeshua had to die for our sins to be forgiven but at the same time we judge and hate Judas for the role he played in it. This type of reasoning is incongruous at best and downright insane at worst. This is the type of thinking that could only exist in the belief based system. If you agree Yeshua had to die for our sins, then how do you think it was going to happen? Maybe angels should have appeared and put him on the cross. Would we then have hated the angels? Furthermore, and in this case, how then could Yeshua demonstrate to us the act of forgiveness?

Judas knew human nature. He knew Yeshua's followers would show him no understanding or forgiveness for his betrayal of Yeshua, but rather they would pull him limb from limb. Yeshua also knew this; '...*alas for that man who betrays the Son of Man; better for him if he had never been born.*' (Matthew 26:24) Judas knew we would never understand during his lifetime what he did and why. Even now, almost two thousand years later, there are many who will refuse to believe it. Judas did not kill himself out of remorse but because he knew we would not understand and would seek revenge both on him and his kin. A person who even contemplates suicide is in a very dark place indeed and does not think about such details as returning money. Judas returned the money, not in the vain hope that such an act would convince the Jewish leaders to reverse their decision to condemn Yeshua nor did he do it out of guilt, but as a sign for future generations that one day the action of returning the money would help people understand what he did for mankind and why.

Chapter Fourteen

The Promised Kingdom

What and where is the Kingdom of God?

The perception and understanding of the Kingdom of God is perhaps one of the most important concepts in the New Testament. Many Christians and non-Christians alike who study the New Testament are confused about what the Kingdom of God really means. The translations from Hebrew into Greek and then into English are often used as a scapegoat and labeled inaccurate. Be that as it may, language has been, and invariably must be, used as a central tool in understanding the New Testament.

In the belief based system, language and understanding, unfortunately, often go hand in hand. What I mean by this is, oftentimes a word or sentence is translated from one language into another only after consideration of what message the primary or original language is trying to convey. However, if the understanding of the message in the original language is misunderstood, which is generally the case here, then the translation will be misleading at best. Further translations will only exacerbate our misunderstanding.

The reality we are therefore faced with is that a lot of the New Testament failed to recount the teachings of Yeshua, word for word, not because they couldn't remember the exact words at the time of writing, but because they could not at the time understand the words that were spoken. Each author of the New Testament, understandably, tried to comprehend the teachings first and then to write them, where what they should have done was to write the teachings first, word for word, and then and only then try to understand them. If they failed to understand in their lifetime, so be it, following generations might succeed. Nevertheless, as the New Testament is all we have, let us have a look at what Yeshua taught us about his Father's Kingdom.

As you now know, the knowledge based system of which I speak is the Kingdom of God and within this kingdom is the eternal life of which Yeshua spoke; *'For this is eternal life; to* **know** *you the only true God.'* (John 17:3) God in the belief based system is a God created by the belief based system, it's not the true God. So, where is this knowledge based system? As the knowledge based system is not a place but rather a state of existence, the kingdom is all around you!

If the kingdom is all around me, why can I not see it?

Yeshua said; *'Verily, verily, I say unto thee, except a man be born again, he cannot see the kingdom of God.'* (John 3:3) This is a passage from the New Testament of John (John 3:1-13) and reads as follows;

'There was a man of the Pharisees named Nicodemus, a ruler of the Jews. This man came to Yeshua by night and said to Him, Rabbi, we know that You are a teacher come from God; for no one can do these signs that You do unless

*God is with him. Yeshua answered and said to him, Most assuredly, I say to you, **unless one is born again, he cannot see the kingdom of God**. Nicodemus said to Him, How can a man be born when he is old? Can he enter a second time into his mother's womb and be born? Yeshua answered, Most assuredly, I say to you, **unless one is born of water and the Spirit**, he cannot enter the kingdom of God.'*

Nicodemus was Jew, a Pharisee, a member of the Sanhedrin and a highly respected teacher of the Old Testament Scriptures. Like many, he thought that his birth as a Jew and work in keeping the traditions of the Talmud assured him a place in the coming promised kingdom. He prided himself on keeping the Old Testament Law and being morally upright, righteous and religious. However, Yeshua told him that all of this was not enough to get into the Kingdom of God. Nicodemus was told that his natural birth, as a Jew, would not save him, and that he must be born again. If a man like Nicodemus is not good enough for the Kingdom of God, then who is?

There is some debate over what Yeshua meant by **water and spirit**. Some believe **water** refers to a natural or physical birth and **spirit** refers to a spiritual rebirth. In this case, one must first be born physically and then reborn spiritually. Others believe **water and spirit** should be taken as a single expression which together refers to a spiritual rebirth. In any case a spiritual rebirth seems to be essential as prior to this we are spiritually dead, whatever that means.

Some Christians today, assert that **water** refers to baptism. They say a life of faith, righteousness, obeying the gospels and fulfillment of the Catholic sacraments especially that of baptism will allow them to be reborn spiritually and thus see the kingdom. Sounds very like a repeat of Nicodemus's situation and belief, doesn't it?

Those who claim to have experienced this type of **rebirth** are always in a hurry to tell people they have been reborn and maybe they have, but not in the sense that Yeshua meant. Why not? Because, being reborn is not a vision or an event in one's life but a fundamental change in existence. Faith, allegiance to a religion and living a righteous life did not work for Nicodemus and it will not work for you.

Nicodemus believed Yeshua must have been referring to some kind of physical rebirth and asked him, "How can a man be born when he is old? He cannot enter his mother's womb and be born a second time, can he?" People today sneer Nicodemus's lack of understanding and childlike questioning of Yeshua's teaching accusing him of being blinded to the truth by his carnal understanding and self-righteousness. Nicodemus was a very well educated, learned, moral and intelligent individual and his questioning of Yeshua was instrumental in understanding. The truth, however, is we still do not understand what's involved in being born again. Does our rebirth happen immediately after baptism or only after a lifetime of doing good deeds and a dedication to the Catholic Church, or is it different for everyone?

Many will tell you the new birth is more than an initial reformation of life. It is the long-term commitment after baptism. It is the maintenance of life with God through Christ. The new birth is only the start. After being born of water and Spirit, there is an ongoing future life of righteousness to be maintained and grown. They say a person is spiritually dead before he is born again and that being reborn begins a convert's progress toward his transformation into Christ's image and living in the Kingdom of God for all eternity.

I have always found the words of the fanatical to be both supernatural and vague. Of course, there will be those among us who say that it is beyond the capacity of even the born-again believer to explain or fully understand. That's very convenient. Others say it is not necessary for us to understand all the particulars of the born-again doctrine to be saved. They advocate that anyone who believes in Yeshua will not perish but have everlasting life.

I say to you, salvation is not received by belief in Yeshua, but by understanding him. Furthermore, if we are honest, being baptized does not miraculously render us reborn and allow us to see the Kingdom of God. Living a life of righteousness, and a dedication to both religion and mankind will also not provide for our rebirth. Many a canonised saint I'm sure would attest to this if they could.

So, how can one truly be born again?

Yeshua's ministry included detailed instruction about how to be born again and see the Kingdom of God. Yeshua told us to *'Repent, for the kingdom of God is at hand.'* (Matthew 3:2) Some bibles use the word **near** instead of **at hand**.

This quote has been repeated so many times over the last two thousand years, but do we actually understand its meaning? If we are honest we will confess that we simply do not understand what Yeshua meant by these words. Here, however, confusion and misunderstanding arise because this teaching was mistranslated. Let me explain.

Some people believe **at hand** simply means near, but does this refer to a location or a time? I am told if we use the Greek translation of the word **near**, the implication is the Kingdom of God is not here yet but will be at some time in the future. Therefore, **near** refers to a time in the future. But surely this can't be true as these words were spoken almost two thousand years ago. If Yeshua had meant near in this way then surely the kingdom would have arrived by now, right?

Some believe, when Yeshua said the Kingdom of God was **at hand**, he meant near or proximal. It is believed you can approach, or indeed enter the kingdom through faith in Yeshua, following him in his footsteps, good deeds, prayer and completing religious rituals such as baptism. If you believe this to be true, then I say it's your prerogative to do so. You have earned that right by entering the belief based system. However, just because you believe it to be true does not make it so. I do accept that the opposite also holds. However, if you believe this to be true, it raises the obvious question of when has this approach ever worked? There has been no evidence of this working in the last two thousand years!

As you may remember, I did try to explain in chapter six what the chances were of your beliefs (any one of them) being an accurate reflection of the truth – impossible. Belief and anything that requires belief can only be sustained in the belief based system. It has no place in the knowledge based system. This is true of all things belief based such as, for example, religion or science, yes even science. In the knowledge based system where all is made known to you, such things have no place. Only in the belief based system, where we are blind to the truth, are such crutches required. This is a source of some amusement for me because science and religion have fought each other for thousands of years for place of power and prominence in people's lives, and not one but both of these can only exist in the darkness, the belief based system. Neither one of these, nor both together, will allow you to be reborn and to see the truth, the kingdom.

Please do not be confused here. I am not saying that belief in all or any of its forms, both positive and negative, cannot be powerful in the belief based system. It can be very powerful and the more of us who believe or buy into something the more powerful it can become. The corollary is also true. The more of us who choose not to believe in something, the less powerful it becomes. The best example of this, outside of religion and science, is money. We spend so much of our time trying to acquire it. We are often judged by how much of it we have. We cheat, steel and kill for it. But the only reason money exists is because we believe in it. If the whole world stopped believing in money at the same time, it would cease to have any power in this domain, the belief based system.

In short, what I am saying is belief only has power in the belief based system. Belief, both negative and positive, no matter how assiduously held will not bring you nearer to or render you further from the kingdom, the knowledge based system. Therefore, in the belief based system, any one person cannot be closer to the Kingdom of God than any other person residing in the same system. Why? Because there are only two states of existence in which you can permanently reside, the belief based system, or the knowledge based system, and these two systems are mutually exclusive. You cannot reside in the belief based system and the knowledge based system at the same time. You must make a choice.

Let me be clear, the only way to be born again is to use the Grail created for us by Yeshua. The Grail or gate can only be opened through the act of repentance, the dual act of forgiveness, to forgive and to be forgiven.

Some ask, "What kind of repentance must we do?" Those who ask this question are either trying to mislead others or simply don't understand the act of repentance. They say we need to repent from anything that leads us away from God. What does that mean? It does not make the action of repentance any clearer. People never give you details of how to repent but rather in a similar way to sin, they give endless examples. They say repentance means to turn away from a life of sin. This of course makes it even more confusing because now instead of one undefined term we have two, sin and repent. By those who do not understand, both are defined by examples. They say to repent means to say you are sorry for your sins and to mean it. This may be a nice thing to do but it will not provide your rebirth. If you don't believe me, try it. To further distract you, they say repentance must include reparation, such as performing a good deed, which of course we now know is veritably untrue. This is evidenced by the good criminal who had no time to make amends with those he injured and yet he entered the kingdom.

The amount of good deeds you could do are endless, infinite, and even if it was possible to do them all in a lifetime, not one of them individually or all of them collectively will allow you to be reborn and grant you access to the knowledge based system. You could be canonised a saint in this life for your selfless acts and dedication to mankind. None of these actions will gain you entry into the knowledge based system, but rather, this teaching enslaves you to doing a life time of good deeds, trapping you within the belief based system. Seems unfair, right? Trust me when I say, this is the deceiver at work and he is very good at what he does.

Some believe if you do not repent you will perish. This is true and Yeshua told us so; *'unless you repent, you too will all perish.'* (Luke 13:3) However, many believe they will perish because the judgment of God will fall on those who don't repent. Let me say again that God has not, does not and will not judge you. He simply hopes for your return.

So what did Yeshua mean by **perish**? For those of you who may not yet have figured this out for yourselves, let me briefly explain. It is only when you reside within the knowledge based system that you are connected to the Source. In the belief based system, you are disconnected from the Source and become like a leaf that has fallen from or being disconnected from the tree. The leaf can only last for so long after it has been disconnected from the tree. If it fails to become reconnected, it will eventually perish. There is no judgment here, just a failure on behalf of the leaf to save itself by returning to the tree, to the source which gives it life. This is why Yeshua's message for repentance was central to his ministry.

So how does one repent? Repent is the umbrella term for the two acts of forgiveness – to render forgiveness onto others and then to ask for forgiveness. This is critical. If you cannot complete both steps of forgiveness, you will remain in the belief based system, disconnected from the Source where you will ultimately perish. As you may now have surmised, the true translation of Matthew 3:2 should not have been translated; *'Repent, for the kingdom of God is at hand'* but rather it should have read; *'Repent, for the kingdom of God is in your hands.'* The means for your rebirth and thus entrance into the kingdom is in your hands. Even as I further explain to you that the Kingdom of God is the knowledge based system of which I speak and to see it you must effectively use the Grail, you will never truly understand how it works until you invoke its power for yourself. However, let me try to explain.

We were all born into the belief based system as an amalgamation of three individual energy signatures, the trinity. To see the kingdom, we must enter or be born again into the knowledge based system. However, only two of the three energy signatures can enter the knowledge based system (water and spirit). Do you recall when I wrote that sunlight is made up of seven individual and independent energy signatures that are visible to the naked eye? The seven visible energy signatures as you may recall are red, orange, yellow, green, blue, indigo and violet. When they appear together in nature we call the display a rainbow. However, to reproduce this rainbow effect in a laboratory, one simply passes a white light through a glass prism. The prism splits the white light up into the seven individual energy signatures which are visible to the naked eye. If you have never seen this, try it. The effect is very pretty. It produces your very own rainbow.

Our trinity of energy signatures operate in a similar fashion and when you use the Grail, it acts in a comparable way to the prism – it splits up your three individual energy signatures. However, unlike the prism, the Grail also acts as a filter or sieve. It filters out the second energy signature as this signature can only reside in the belief based system. The second energy is blocked from entering the knowledge based system. The Grail removes the second energy signature like a sieve removes the dirt from spoiled water, making the water pure again. It is this second energy signature which blinds us to the truth. It is the blindfold of which I have written, and which prevents us from knowing who and what we are – the custodians and guardians of all creation.

When you pass through the Grail, you are fundamentally changed, recreated and born again as two energy signatures – water and spirit. This is what Yeshua meant when he said; *'Truly, truly, I say to you, unless one is born of water and the spirit he cannot enter into the kingdom of God.'* (John 3:5) When you do use the Grail and your trinity of energy signatures is split up into its component parts, be not confused for *'that which is born of the flesh is flesh; and that which is born of the spirit is spirit.'* (John 3:6)

When can we expect God's Kingdom to arrive?

Many Christians ask, when will the waiting end? Fair question, after all, we have now been waiting almost two thousand years. Have we not been patient?

The New Testament teaches us that Yeshua was indeed asked by the Pharisees when the Kingdom of God would come. He answered; *'The kingdom of God does not come with observation; nor will they say, See here! or See there! For indeed, the kingdom of God is within you.'* (Luke 17:20-21)

From this passage some have concluded the Kingdom of God only exists in people's hearts or minds. I hope you realize now that this is not the case. Others argue that the word 'within' should have been translated as 'in the midst of' and as such Yeshua was talking about himself, that the Kingdom of God had already arrived in him and thus was in the midst of those he was preaching to. Others believe the Kingdom of Heaven is Yeshua's name for his followers, his disciples and believers; *'When they welcome you in any town, eat what they offer you. Heal the sick who are there and tell these people; the kingdom of God has drawn near to you.'* (Luke 10:8-9)

The misunderstanding and vagary of the New Testament can give rise to much deception. It allows 'Holy People' to preach about the Kingdom of God and its coming in ambiguous terms. They use this as a means of control, deception always has. They build religion in their image and tell you that you must adhere to the religious laws and customs if you wish to save your soul and enter the Kingdom of God. This pursuit to subjugate and control people is not new nor is it the sole proprietorship of a single religion or indeed is it restricted to any particular domain within the belief based system.

The need to control and indeed to be controlled is born out of fear which is the core and primary feeling within the belief based system. In order for those who have control to maintain control there must always exist those who can be controlled. However, you can only control and be controlled within the belief based system. As soon as you leave the belief based system and enter the knowledge based system, you can no longer dictate or be dictated to. Not even God Himself can dictate to you! Why? Because he gave you free will. Imagine that. God Himself cannot and will not force you to do His will but we submit to others allowing them control over us. This is how deep the hypocrisy can run in the belief based system. It's the ultimate betrayal of who and what you are.

Many believe they are living their faith correctly and that they have a proper sense of what sin is. Because of this, they believe they are destined for heaven. Can all these different ideas of how to express faith be correct and ultimately effect entry into the knowledge based system? If so, there is not only one way to enter the knowledge based system as Yeshua said, but there are billions as everybody's faith is ultimately different. However, when you ask such believers and self-proclaimed experts what sin is, all they can give are examples, endless examples.

Sin is not an action or inaction in this world. Sin is a state of existence. To reside in the belief based system is to reside in sin regardless of what you do. This is the definition and only definition of sin. Those who say certain actions or inactions are sinful and others are not are trying to distract you from the truth, creating confusion which they use as another means of control. However, this definition of sin makes it clear who in this world is sinful (all of us) and who is not (none of us). To go from the knowledge based system into the belief based system was the original or first sin. The Garden of Eden, from whence we left, was also not a place but a state of existence. The Garden of Eden is the Kingdom of God, the knowledge based system of which I write.

Most Christians believe that while the Kingdom of God currently exists in heaven, it is destined one day to encompass all peoples and all nations here on earth. Yeshua will return someday and establish the Kingdom of God here on earth. They believe those who have kept the faith (whatever that means) will enter this kingdom on Yeshua's return. Those who have not kept the faith will perish. It is advocated that the Kingdom of God being at hand indicates that a major change is coming, and people have a choice. Those who choose to accept Yeshua as their lord and savior will be saved and those who refuse will end up in the fires of hell for all eternity. Apocalyptic literature was always very fashionable and still is today.

When Yeshua came to earth, the Jews were looking for the Messiah to come and elevate the Jewish nation to prominence. They anticipated a deliverer who would lead them in a successful liberation of their nation. Some of the Jewish religious authorities believed they, through careful investigations, would be the ones to first discover the promised savior's coming. Although Yeshua told them not to look for such signs as they were misleading, we as Christians still do it to this day. We created 'Revelation' and look for signs of a second coming. (Rev 1:7) Matthew and Luke also indicate Yeshua's return will be heralded by dramatic signs that all will be able to discern. (Matthew 24:27-40 & Luke 21:25-27) This prophesy of a second coming justifies us doing nothing and thus in two thousand years nothing has really changed. We are still waiting for a Messiah to do something for us. First it was only the Jews who waited for their Messiah. Instead of Christians bringing their faith to the Jews, it was the Jews who instilled their belief to Christians. Not only are the Jews still waiting for their Messiah to come but now so are Christians.

Yeshua told us; *'For indeed,* **the kingdom of God is within you.***'* (Luke 17:20-21) What he meant by this is that the evidence of God's Kingdom is within you. He wasn't referring to your heart or mind but to the Helper which was sent to you by the Source. The Helper, the third energy signature, resides in the knowledge based system. He can see where you cannot. Therefore, it's about choice. Do you wish to perpetuate this belief based system or do you wish to establish the knowledge based system here on earth, through you? When we follow the lead of the Helper we are doing the will of the Source. Yeshua referred to himself as the Son of God. Those who allow or instruct the spirit to lead them, truly are children of God (Romans 8:14), for it is through you the spirit does the will of the Source and it is by His will being done that His kingdom will come. Yeshua told us so in the prayer he gave to all of us; *'thy kingdom (will) come, (by) thy will be(ing) done on earth as it is in heaven.'* Therefore, the arrival of *'the kingdom of God is in your hands.'* It always was.

Chapter Fifteen

Miracles

Miracles are considered a critical aspect of most religions. The occurrence of miracles strengthens people's belief. Oftentimes, it's miracles which make people believe in the first place. If people are honest, most of Yeshua's followers believed in him because of the miracles he performed. As such, I guess I better address this subject.

In the belief based system, we are always waiting for something to happen, for a miracle. When you enter the knowledge based system all will be made known to you. You will need to know all things if you are to take up the mantle of being the guardian and custodian of all creation.

You cannot cherry pick what you want to know in the knowledge based system as nothing will be hidden from you. Most importantly, when you enter the knowledge based system, you will know who and what you are. You will become aware of your connection to all things. It is through your connection to all things that you will know all things and be able to communicate with all things. You will be able to ask the waters to support you as you walk across them. You can ask boulders that have entombed you to move allowing you passage from your tomb. Because people didn't understand, they considered these things to be miracles. They are not. They saw Yeshua do so many things that couldn't be explained to one who resides in the belief based system. They catagorised all such things as miracles and missed the true miracles.

Yeshua's main ministry here on earth was to teach us how to return to the knowledge based system, his Father's Kingdom. However, he knew it may take time for some to be prepared for such a step. How right he was. Therefore, he supplemented his ministry with instruction on how to live and how we should treat our neighbour while we resided within the belief based system.

Yeshua understood that a person needed instruction on how to navigate this life if they resided in darkness, the belief based system. Personally, I thought this teaching was a waste of time because if a person could be shown how to enter the knowledge based system successfully, then teaching that person how to live in the belief based system would be made redundant. Furthermore, I thought it was impossible to change the hearts of men, after all it's difficult enough to change a person's mind! Yeshua was to prove me wrong. He did this through the miracle of the loaves and fishes, the greatest miracle of his ministry.

For those of you who have never heard of the miracle of the loaves and fishes, this is generally how Christian dogma recounts it.

When Yeshua heard John the Baptist had been killed, he withdrew by boat privately to a solitary place near Bethsaida. Crowds of people followed Yeshua on foot. When Yeshua landed and saw the large crowd, he had compassion for them and healed their sick. As evening approached, the disciples came to him and said; *'This is a remote place, and it's already getting late. Send the crowds away, so they can go to the villages and buy themselves some food.'* (Matthew 14:15, Mark 6:35)

'When Yeshua looked up and saw the great crowds coming towards him, he said to Philip, Where shall we buy bread so that these people may eat? He asked this to test Philip, for he himself knew what he was to do. Philip answered him, Two hundred silver coins would not buy enough bread for each of them to have a piece. Then one of the disciples spoke to Yeshua. Andrew, Peter's brother, said, There is a boy here who has five barley loaves and two small fish; but what good are these for so many?' (John 6:5-9)

'Yeshua said; Make the people sit down. There was plenty of grass there so the people, about five thousand men, sat down to rest. Yeshua then took the loaves, gave thanks, and distributed them to those who were seated. He did the same with the fish and gave them as much as they wanted. And when they had eaten enough, he told his disciples, Gather up the pieces left over, that nothing may be lost. So they gathered them and filled twelve baskets with bread, that is with pieces of the five barley loaves left by those who had eaten. When the people saw this sign that Yeshua had just given, they said, This is really the Prophet, he who is to come into the world.' (John 6:10-14)

Nice story for children who like magic tricks, but here is the truth about the miracle of the loaves and fishes.

It is true that Yeshua directed the people to sit down in groups on the grass. (Mark 6:39-40) However, please don't get bogged down by too much pointless detail, after all, remember who resides there! I only mention this particular detail because he did it for a specific reason. He did this, not only because there were so many people present and thus he wished to prevent congestion by all gathering upon the food at the same time, but also because he was preparing the scene for a true miracle to occur.

When Yeshua saw the limited amount of food that was available, he told one of his disciples to take all the food gathered and give it to the nearest group with instructions. He told his disciple to "tell the group that the food they are being given is all the food that is in it. Tell the group to take only what they need and to think of their neighbours' needs, many of whom may have traveled further than they did. Tell the group that when they have finished, to have one in the group pass the remaining food with those same instructions onto the next group." The food went around to each and every group present with the same instructions.

When the food had passed through each group, leftovers came back. Why, what had happened? His disciples did not understand. Was Yeshua a magician? Had he created food from thin air? Surely this was proof that Yeshua was the Prophet that had been foretold would come into the world and set his people free. Nonsense. It was not the purpose of the One to perform such magic tricks, hollow acts to improve his popularity.

The truth is, each group of people having heard Yeshua's instructions were so worried and concerned for the next group of people to receive the food that they took little or none of the food that was offered to them so that their neighbour would not have to go without. Others who had food of their own, also shared what they had with their neighbours and thus the number of food baskets available to the crowds grew in number. When Yeshua saw there were leftovers he knew his teachings on how to live were finding root and bearing fruit. His teachings were not only changing minds but were changing the very hearts of men and this is the true miracle of the loaves and fishes.

Truly blessed are those, who without knowledge of the Source, treat their fellow man in this way.

Chapter Sixteen

Summary

In the beginning we knew the truth. We knew who and what we are, the guardians and custodians of all creation. We knew we were made equal and in the image of the Source, the creator, our Father. Later, we were offered a choice. We could accept the truth we were given, or we could believe whatever we wanted to believe. We were told that choosing to believe whatever we wanted to believe would set us free. It would open our eyes and allow us to create the world in our image. We were deceived.

Instead of opening our eyes, it closed them, plunging us into darkness. After all, one cannot truly choose to believe what they want to believe unless they are in complete darkness. Because our eyes were closed we could no longer see the truth; *'we have eyes but we cannot see.'* (Mark 8:18) We no longer knew the Father.

Choosing the belief based system over the knowledge based system was our first sin. The original sin. To live in the belief based system is to live without knowledge of the Source, the Source from which all life springs. This is the definition of sin. Do not give ear to those who claim to know what sin is and then when they are asked, they give endless examples rather than a clear definition. These examples are not sins but rather are simply actions perpetrated by one who is leading a sinful life, i.e. one who has closed their eyes to the truth, the Source. Sin is not an action or inaction, it is a state of being. To live in the belief based system is the definition of sin. According to this definition of sin we now know who among us are living sinfully (all of us) and who among us are living without sin (none of us). I guess we can all stop pointing fingers now.

The day will come when we will be given an opportunity to atone for this sin, reversing its affect by opening our eyes and allowing us to make the choice of accepting the truth and returning to the Source. We will not be expected to make this choice until we again see the truth.

How does one open their eyes to the truth? Our eyes can only be opened by invoking the power of the most sought-after artefact in human history, the Grail, often referred to as the Holy Grail. The Grail was created and given to us by Yeshua almost two thousand years ago. The Grail is a gate through which you can go from the belief based system to the knowledge based system.

So how is the power of the Grail invoked? What do we have to do to earn passage through the gate? Yeshua put the instructions of how to invoke the Grail's power in a prayer. For those of you who don't know the prayer, here it is;

Our Father, who art in heaven,

Hallowed be Thy Name;

Thy kingdom come,

The Truth

Thy will be done,

on earth as it is in heaven.

Give us this day our daily bread,

and **forgive us our trespasses,**

as(because) we forgive those who trespass against us;

and lead us not into temptation,

but deliver us from evil. Amen.

I have put the message of how to invoke the power of the Grail in bold. This is where the message has been hidden, in clear view, unmoved and unused for the last two thousand years! Surprised? So was I.

Please understand, invoking the power of the Grail requires two steps which must be undertaken in order, step-by-step. First you must forgive and then you must be forgiven. The first step is a mirror image of the second step; *And when you stand to pray, forgive whatever you may hold against anyone, so that your divine Father may also forgive your sins.'* (Mark 11:25) When you have completed both steps in order, your eyes will be opened, allowing you to pass through the gate and enter the knowledge based system.

As this point is of paramount importance, let me re-state it. You must complete the steps in this order. *'For if you forgive men their trespasses, your Heavenly Father will also forgive you. But if you do not forgive men their trespasses, neither will your Father forgive yours.'* (Matthew 6:15)

Due to the gravity of these instructions, Yeshua put them in a prayer for us, which we call the **Our Father**. Yes, Yeshua put the message of how to unlock the Grail's power in a prayer. This prayer is probably the most widely and repetitively spoken prayer in the world over the last two thousand years. Yeshua put the instructions of the Grail in plain view of the world and we missed them!

Due to their critical nature, showing us how to forgive and to be forgiven in turn was at the very heart of Yeshua's ministry. Please don't think you know how to forgive because you have heard the word spoken a thousand times. If you have not witnessed the truth, then you have not yet completed the dual act of forgiveness. This may be through a lack of understanding how to complete the dual act of forgiveness or maybe you are not yet ready. In any case, here are the steps required to complete the first act of forgiveness which is to forgive.

Step 1: Choice

Step 2: Pain

Step 3: Reason

Step 4: Belief

The first step may seem somewhat redundant, but it is in fact the most important, not because it expresses a desire to forgive but because it is an expression of the freewill we have been given. Freewill is the greatest gift that has been bestowed upon us. Therefore, you cannot be prevented from or indeed coerced into making this decision. This is your choice.

In order to take the second step, one must have been wronged and experience pain due to this wrong. Pain can come in many forms and I use it as an umbrella term to include all forms of disturbing physical and emotional experiences such as hurt, hate, anger, rage, humiliation, fear, anguish, sorrow, grief, shame, guilt and remorse. This list is not conclusive or exhaustive in any way but is given by way of example only.

Pain acts as a motive force for movement from the belief based system to the knowledge based system. If you have no pain, you will not be able to forgive. Having said that, if you do not feel pain, you probably have not been wronged and thus have nothing to forgive. Nevertheless, I think you will agree when I say that it's impossible to pass through this life without having wronged and being wronged in return. Furthermore, the pain you felt at the time of the wrong being perpetrated, if not expressed at the time, will reside inside you waiting for its release. The body will remind you from time to time that the pain still resides inside you waiting for its release. It may do this through the manifestation of an illness, for example.

You must recognize that you are in pain. You must feel this pain. When you recall the injustice, which you will do in the first step, the pain associated with it should return to you. This pain is the motive force which will fuel the process of the first act of forgiveness. This may be the hardest step for some. For example, it is not uncommon for people in their eighties to live with anger over injustices they endured as children. Whilst they are still suffering from the emotional pain, they have over time coped with it by dissociating themselves from the pain. As a result, they no longer feel the pain and thus don't recognize that they are angry. While this pain resides within, waiting for its release, it may change form and become less and less familiar. The pain may also disassociate itself from the reason of its own creation. This is not good because the act of forgiveness must be reasoned. Therefore, it is best if you can forgive earlier rather than later. However, having said that, it is never too late to forgive.

The third step in the first act of forgiveness is reason. Forgiveness must be reasoned. As a child I had always wondered why Yeshua used the words; *'Father, forgive them for (because) they know not what they do.'* (Luke 23:24) Why not just say, "Father, forgive them" or "I forgive you"? Please don't believe that Yeshua's words here were superfluous. Throughout his teachings, he chose his words very carefully. This was no exception. This is how the Grail was created. You will not be able to invoke the power of the Grail unless you reason your forgiveness. Let me be clear, the third step must be conducted as follows, "I forgive you because…"

The fourth and final step of the first act of forgiveness is belief. It is imperative that you must truly accept your reason or reasoning for forgiving. The reason or reasoning you apply here does not have to be factually correct or accurate, but you must believe it completely. If you cannot accept or believe your own reasoning, then you will not be able to complete the first act of forgiveness.

There is a certain justice here. In the beginning we resided in the knowledge based system and thus we knew the truth. However, we chose to close our eyes to the truth so that we could reside within a belief based system allowing us to believe whatever we wanted to believe. Now we have been given the opportunity to open our eyes again to the truth allowing us to reside within the knowledge based system. However, to take advantage of this opportunity, given to us by Yeshua, we must truly **believe** our reasoning. In the beginning we knew but we wanted to believe. Now to know again, we must truly believe!

The second act of forgiveness is to be forgiven. Here are the steps required to complete the second act of forgiveness.

Step 1:   Choice

Step 2:   Pain

Step 3:   Reason

Step 4:   Belief

There is not much to explain here as the second act of forgiveness is a mirror image of the first act. When you take the first step of seeking forgiveness for yourself you will automatically recall the injustice you committed. With this recollection, the second step will immediately follow with the return of the pain associated with that injustice, which in this case could be sorrow, grief, shame, guilt or remorse, or a combination of these and other feelings.

Following this, you can then take the third step which is to provide a reason why you should be forgiven. As with the first act of forgiveness, it is crucial that you must truly accept your reason or reasoning. Again, the reason or reasoning you apply here does not have to be factually correct or accurate, but you must believe it completely. If you cannot accept or believe your own reasoning, then you will not be able to complete the second act of forgiveness.

This bears repeating as it is most important. To unlock the power of the Grail requires two acts of forgiveness which must be undertaken in order, step-by-step. First you must forgive and then you must be forgiven. The second act is a mirror image of the first act. *And when you stand to pray, forgive whatever you may hold against anyone, so that your divine Father may also forgive your sins.'* (Mark 11:25)

You may wonder why seeking forgiveness is the second act and not the first act of forgiveness. Apart from the fact that free will dictates that you must make the first move, I will say that some negative feelings are stronger than others and must be dealt with first. Forgiving clears the emotional anger you were feeling toward the offender because of what they did to you, allowing you to feel lesser forms of pain such as guilt or shame which you may then realize you feel because of how you reacted to the injustice, for example, the hate you held in your heart toward the offender for so many years or indeed the part you played in the whole situation.

When you have completed both acts of forgiveness in order, you will have invoked the power of the Grail.

This will open your eyes to the truth allowing you to pass through the gate and enter the knowledge based system. You may, however, wish to close your eyes again to the truth and re-enter the belief based system allowing you to believe whatever you want to believe. This is your choice.

One of the greatest barriers to entering the knowledge based system will be your current belief based system, whatever that may be. If you choose the truth you must accept it completely. This means you must accept that this life, the belief based system, is a mirage. You may hold certain things in this life very dearly, but these will need to be relinquished if you wish to enter the knowledge based system. Please let me be clear. You cannot choose to believe and know at the same time – this is impossible. One's eyes cannot be open and closed at the same time.

There are only two permanent states of existence. One where we have our eyes open to the truth (the knowledge based system) and one where we have our eyes closed to the truth (the belief based system). Which you want to reside in, is now your choice.

Chapter Seventeen

Final Thoughts

It has been said that unless Yeshua had risen from the dead he would have been just another failed messianic pretender, of which there were many, who had a brush with the Roman Empire and the established Jewish leaders of the time and paid the ultimate price for his foolishness. Some say his resurrection was a hoax perpetrated by his followers to give credence to his life and teachings and to create a legacy which would live forever. Non-believers extol that the accounts of the resurrection are contradictory at best and lend credence to a conspiracy. Believers defend the accounts by saying if Yeshua's followers had stolen his body to create a conspiracy to deceive people, then surely they would have created more uniform and concurrent accounts. They most certainly would not have posited women as among the first eyewitnesses as at that time the testimony of women carried very little weight. Ultimately, believers argue that none of the differences in the accounts of his resurrection represent an irreconcilable contradiction.

A veritable library of books could be dedicated to the topic of whether Yeshua did or did not rise from the dead, but the reality is, as important a topic as it may be to some and to others it is the whole foundation of their belief system, it's a distraction from the truth.

The Truth

How Yeshua died is more important than how he was resurrected. If you do not believe me, consider this. Yeshua made a public display of his death so that all could understand how to use the gift he created for mankind. If his resurrection was as important as his death, why did he not also make a public display of his resurrection? Do not be distracted. Yeshua's true legacy is not that he rose from the dead but rather it is his gift to us of the Grail which provides for our way home and more importantly his teaching that doing the will of the Source takes precedence above all things…even death.

Is it ever too late to begin doing the will of the Source? No. As long as you draw breath in your lungs it is never too late. How do I know this? Yeshua told me so. This is the meaning of the parable of *'The workers in the vineyard.'* (Matthew 20:1-16) Yeshua told this parable in response to Peter's question in Matthew 19:27; *'We have left everything to follow you! What then will there be for us?'* Peter wanted to know what reward would be given to those who give up everything to do the will of the Source. In response, Yeshua explains this truth about the kingdom of heaven. This is generally how it is written;

'For the kingdom of heaven is like a landowner who went out early in the morning to hire workers for his vineyard. He agreed to pay them a denarius for the day and sent them into his vineyard. About nine in the morning he went out and saw others standing in the marketplace doing nothing. He told them, you also go and work in my vineyard, and I will pay you whatever is right. So they went. He went out

again about noon and about three in the afternoon and did the same thing. About five in the afternoon he went out and found still others standing around. He asked them, why have you been standing here all day long doing nothing? Because no one has hired us, they answered. He said to them, you also go and work in my vineyard.

When evening came, the owner of the vineyard said to his foreman, call the workers and pay them their wages, beginning with the last ones hired and going on to the first. The workers who were hired about five in the afternoon came and each received a denarius, so when those came who were hired first, they expected to receive more. But each one of them also received a denarius. When they received it, they began to grumble against the landowner. These who were hired last worked only one hour, they said, and you have made them equal to us who have borne the burden of the work and the heat of the day. But he answered one of them, I am not being unfair to you, friend. Didn't you agree to work for a denarius? Take your pay and go. I want to give the one who was hired last the same as I gave you. Don't I have the right to do what I want with my own money? Or are you envious because I am generous? So the last will be first, and the first will be last.'

Don't be confused by the last line; 'So the last will be first, and the first will be last.' (Matthew 20:16) This is not a rebuke of those who came first to work in the vineyard nor is it an elevation of those who came last over those who came first. It is a promise that all who do the will of the Source will receive what the knowledge based system has to offer. Yeshua uses the denarius to symbolize eternal life.

The reward of eternal life is the same for all who do the will of the Source.

Who then will be the greatest among us? The greatest among us will be the one who serves all. Yeshua did this by creating the Grail, a gift for all, a way back home for us. He continued to serve all mankind even when we mocked him, struck him, spat on him... even when we killed him. Yeshua explained to us who would be the greatest among us in his actions recounted in (John 13:1–17) which generally reads as follows;

'Then he poured water into a basin and began to wash his disciples' feet, drying them with the towel that was wrapped around him... When he had finished washing their feet, he...returned to his place at the table and said to them, Do you understand what I have done for you? You call me Teacher... and rightly so, for that is what I am. Now that I, your... Teacher, have washed your feet, you also should wash one another's feet. I have set you an example that you should do as I have done for you. Very truly I tell you, no servant is greater than his master, nor is a messenger greater than the one who sent him. Now that you know these things, you will be blessed if you do them.'

Yeshua further explains who will be the greatest among us in his words recounted; *'...whoever wants to be more important...shall make himself your servant. And whoever wants to be first must make himself the slave to all. Be like the Son of Man who has come, not to be served but to serve and to give his life to redeem many.'* (Matthew 20:26-28)

It's human nature to need a sense of purpose, to feel important and wanted. This feeling is intrinsic in every human being. Feeling important is often closely associated with what you do. Doing something we feel is important gives us that sense of purpose we seek and often restores our feelings of significance. Do you want to do something important? Do you want to remember how important you are? If so, then do the will of the Source.

Did the Grail exist before Yeshua? No. This was Yeshua's task, to create the Grail so that we could return to the knowledge based system. *'I have come… to make lawful to you that which was before forbidden to you…'* (Q 3.50) We were banned from the knowledge based system (the Garden of Eden) and forever forbidden entry. However, Yeshua's creation of the Grail provided a means for our redemption, a gate allowing our return home to the knowledge based system.

Like the stories, however, the Grail will remain dormant within you until you have the courage to wield it. Wielding this weapon is achieved through expression of the message of the Grail, i.e. completing the acts of forgiveness. Once you have done this the door will be opened for you through which you can enter the knowledge based system. Remember, repentance is a weapon. Once used, it will destroy your belief based system and all claims and control that the belief based system has on you. You will be free.

As much as I have tried, I cannot describe the knowledge based system with any greater degree of clarity than I already have – you must see it for yourself. To know the truth, you must engage the power of the Grail and this is done through repentance, i.e. by completing the acts of forgiveness. Repentance allows us to witness firsthand, the truth, the knowledge based system, the Kingdom of God, heaven, our home. You now know the choice you are presented with. Choose to repent or choose not to. There are no small and large acts of forgiveness – there is forgiveness or there is no forgiveness. Remember, where there is no forgiveness there will always be death; *'unless you repent, you too will all perish.'* (Luke 13:3) If you can't forgive, you will perish and all heaven will mourn.

Anyone who has witnessed the truth will recognize anyone else who has witnessed the truth. Yeshua explained this nicely when he said; *'Everyone who is on the side of (or has witnessed) the truth hears (or recognizes) my voice (or more simply, recognizes me).'* (John 18:37) It's an experience that can't be explained or shared with those who have not yet borne witness to the truth. Between those who have witnessed the truth, there is nothing further to discuss as all was made known to them. Nothing is hidden in the knowledge based system. This is what Yeshua meant when he said; *'If you really know me, you will know my Father as well.'* (John 14:6) You cannot cherry pick knowledge when you enter the knowledge based system as all will be made known to you.

Movement from the knowledge based system to the belief based system is like putting on a virtual reality helmet. Unfortunately, when you have the helmet on, you don't know how to take it off, so you are stuck in the belief based system. How to go from the knowledge based system to the belief based system is more apparent than the other way around simply because in the knowledge based system, one knows all things. Therefore, the path of how to go from the knowledge based system to the belief based system is readily apparent. The opposite of course is not true.

When you invoke the power of the Grail you will feel things that you have never felt before. This may cause some distraction. Don't worry, there is a guardian at the gate and there is no reason to fear. Although the guardian may be very powerful, you will know an incredible depth of compassion emanating from his signature. You will know this because you will know all things.

Passing through this gate and entering the knowledge based system does not preclude you from re-entering the belief based system should you so choose. One of the side effects of passing through this gate, however, is that on your return, people may not recognize you immediately or at all. Would this be such a bad thing? In any case, change is inevitable once you have witnessed the truth. On entering the knowledge based system, you will find that you can come and go between both systems as you wish, but I guarantee that you will not return to the belief based system unless you have something you need or wish to accomplish.

You now know what the Grail is and how to use it. When the time comes, those of you who refuse to use the Grail will do so by conscious decision. You will do so to remain within the belief based system, you will do so to keep your eyes closed to the truth, you will do so to remain in darkness, you will do so to reject the will of the Source and in the hope of establishing your own will, here, within the belief based system. I am not judging whatever decision you make. I am simply describing the options available to you.

I clarify the options available to you because the end of the believer here on earth is near. Believers have been given free rein for the last two thousand years and look at what we have produced. The atomic bomb, the Spanish Inquisition, World War I, World War II, genocide, famine, ethnic cleansing, rape, Hitler, Harry S. Truman and Stalin. We have waged war over race, creed, rubble and words in old books. I think quite a number of books could be written solely on the subject of the atrocities we have committed over the last two thousand years. I limit the list of our atrocities to the last two thousand years because it wasn't until the advent of Yeshua that we were made aware of our sin and shown how to enter the knowledge based system.

If Yeshua's teachings were so important, why did he not write them? Why leave something so important to mere mortals who would follow later? I often wondered this as a child as I am sure many other people have done. Yeshua promised us that; *'From now on the Helper, the Holy Spirit whom the Father will send in my name, will teach you all things and remind you of all that I have told you.'* (John 14:26) It had to be this way, because one can never understand the truth by reading it, one will only understand the truth by living it.

If you do not believe what I tell you, I am glad because I am not here to spread belief but rather I am here to instigate its destruction. This is my task. I am here to clarify Yeshua's message of how to leave the belief based system and enter the knowledge based system. When the belief based system is destroyed all that resides there will also meet its end.

Some of you may wonder who I am. To those I say, if you consider Yeshua to be the first, then I am the last. No one will follow me. *'This gospel of the kingdom will be proclaimed throughout the world for all the nations to know; then the end will come.'* (Matthew 24:14) Please let this not be a source of worry for you. This simply marks an end to a beginning, after all, you didn't think this would go on forever, did you? If it is a source of worry for you, remember these words in the prayer Yeshua gave to you - 'world without end'.

In truth, I am not the important one, nor is this end of which I speak. What is important is what Yeshua did, and what he did was very personal. His creation of the Grail was for you. His guidance and instructions of how to use the Grail were for you. His teachings regarding the importance of doing the will of the Source, were for you. Now you know that his true suffering occurred, not on the cross, but in the Garden of Gethsemane where he entered the belief based system and became disconnected from the Source for the very first time. This also was done for you.

Many of you may ask what I believe. To those I would say, as belief has no bearing on the truth, I believe what I need to believe when I need to believe it. If you adopt ridged beliefs it will impinge on your ability to do the will of the Source. Are you going to let your beliefs get in the way of what you must do? Remember, what I believe is as equally valid as what you believe. Why? Because our beliefs are both equally wrong. What I mean by this is that our beliefs bear no reflection to the truth. Therefore, make your beliefs work for you, not the other way around.

Belief during life, at times, is like an illness. It's like a drug that has addled your brain. Belief when it comes time to shed it will be your biggest hurdle to entering the knowledge based system. Belief will become like a rock hanging around your neck whilst you are trying to tread water. If you don't remove the rock from around your neck you will drown. The deception here is very subtle. Your faith which you may have turned to many times in your life to keep you afloat, will ultimately drown you!

Many of you may hate me for this and accuse me of abandoning my faith when it suits me but if you understood what I went through to bear witness to the truth and what I gave up to return to the belief based system so that I could clarify the work of the one who went before me, you would not hold such anger for me in your hearts. Nevertheless, in this case, I am comforted by my friend who said; *'If the world hates you, remember that it hated me first.'* (John 15:18)

Some may say that this book promotes hedonistic values as it advocates the importance of the one while appearing to neglect the wellbeing of others. The message here is analogous to the policy that airlines adopt – attend to your own oxygen mask first and before attending to others. If you cannot save yourself, how can you ever hope to save others?

Judgment. What's in it for me? Is there anything to be gained by judging others? Yes, there is. If you wish to stay in the belief based system, this is the best way to do it. Passing judgment on others will anchor you here in the belief based system preventing your passage to the knowledge based system. The more you judge, the larger and heavier the anchor will become. Ultimately it will drown you.

Many believe that when you die you simply cease to exist. To those I would say the following – where there is a beginning there will be an end, but where there is consciousness there will always be consciousness.

To those who wish to know whether they have a soul, I say this. The word "soul" is a corruption of the word "sole" meaning "one". Therefore, you do not have a soul, you are the sole. You are the one. You are a single pure energy signature created by the Source. You became corrupted by a second energy signature from the deceiver when you closed your eyes to the truth and were plunged into darkness. You became a trinity of energy signatures when the Source sent you your Helper or Spirit to guide you. This is when you became human, a trinity of energy signatures.

Will the grail, the gate, remain open in perpetuity? No. When the spirit of truth, the Helper, leaves the belief based system, the gate will close. The closure of the gate will represent a Darwinian event in man's development; an evolutionary opportunity on a scale never witnessed since our creation as a single pure energy signature. This event will occur soon. When the gate closes, those who remain in the belief based system will become less, reverting back to that which more closely resembles our animal relatives. This will be a difficult transition for all those who reside in the belief based system. Those who choose to enter the knowledge based system will exist as a single pure energy signature, as they did in the beginning, and their evolution will proceed unhindered as it was intended when we were first created.

I am sure there are those among you who have many more questions. Let me answer all your questions by saying this. After experiencing the truth, I had three options. I could have stayed quiet and said nothing. I could have endeavored to explain to you what the knowledge based system is like in more detail or, I could show you how to enter the knowledge based system for yourself. I chose the third option. Therefore, I wrote this book, not to provide you with answers but to show you how to get them for yourselves.

If you do not believe anything I've written, then I am glad as it was not my intention to strengthen your beliefs or to create new ones. For those of you who do not believe me, I say good, I don't want you to believe any longer,

I want you to know! It's my hope to help progress what Yeshua started – the end of the belief based system and the establishment of the knowledge based system here on earth. It's time now.

To all Grail hunters, I hope this book puts an end to your quest for the Grail. Why continue to search for something you have already found? If you now feel a bit silly you ever thought the Grail was a magic cup or other such artefact, I'm glad. I'd hate to think that after what you have read, you still believe it's a cup! I am not saying the cup from the Last Supper does not exist or indeed hasn't already been found or will not be found at some time in the future if we keep looking. Furthermore, I am not saying Yeshua did not have progeny which may have survived to the present day. What I am saying is that neither have the power you are looking for – the gate, the Grail of which I speak does.

Reign in hell or serve in heaven? We are the guardians and custodians of all creation. The knowledge based system into which we were created is our home. Belief is a sickness. It's a slumber from which we must wake. You now know how to do this. The choice is yours. The belief based system has produced nothing but war, famine, pestilence and death. It does not work. I say this to all within the belief based system, both to you who believe you are in control and to those who believe they are controlled. As we reside in the belief based system, we can choose to believe whatever we wish to believe. This is not so in the knowledge based system. In the knowledge based system, you must accept the truth. If you cannot do this, you can again close your eyes to the truth and re-enter the belief based system. Some may say that doing the will of the Source makes us slaves. We are not slaves. We were given free will.

What will you do with your free will?

References

1. Spiritual Enlightenment – The Damnedest Thing - Jed McKenna

2. Der Jüngere Titurel - a late-13th-century Grail romance - Albrecht

3. Parzival - Wolfram von Eschenbach

4. Diu Krône - Heinrich von dem Türlin

5. War in Heaven - Charles Williams

6. That Hideous Strength - C.S. Lewis

7. A Glastonbury Romance - John Cowper Powys

8. Queste del Saint Graal – Authorship Unknown

9. The Kings of the Grail - Margarita Torres and José Ortega del Rio

10. Spirit of Vatican II: Buddhism – Buddhism and Forgiveness

11. Abhayagiri Buddhist Monastery - Preparing for Death

12. Manusamhita,11.55, Mahabharata Vol II, 1022:8

13. Abdu'l-Bahá, The Promulgation of Universal Peace, p. 92

14. American Psychological Association. Forgiveness: A Sampling of Research Results. 2006

15. What Is Forgiveness? The Greater Good Science Center, University of California, Berkeley

16. Forgiveness is a choice - Dr. Robert D. Enright.

17. Forgive for Good: A Proven Prescription for Health and Happiness – Dr. Fred Luskin

18. Can I Give Him My Eyes? - Richard Moore

19. The Book of Forgiving - Archbishop Desmond Tutu & Revd Mpho Tutu.

20. Forgiveness: Theory, Research, and Practice. New York: Guilford Press, 2000 -McCullough, Michael E., Kenneth I. Pargament, and Carl E. Thoresen.

21. Cornish, M. A.; Wade, N. G. (2015). "A therapeutic model of self-forgiveness with intervention strategies for counselors". Journal of Counseling & Development. 93 (1): 96–104.)